# MAIL STEAMER *BRITANNIC*

## CK PLANS A, B, C & BOAT DECKS

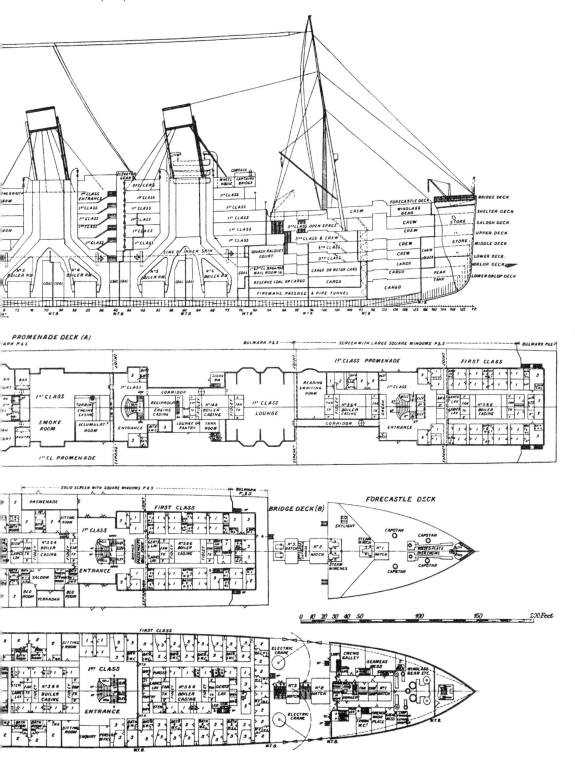

# Hostage
# To
# Fortune

*The dramatic story of the last Olympian*

*HMHS Britannic*

**Wordsmith**

Published in the United Kingdom by
Wordsmith Publications
Chiltern House,
120, Eskdale Avenue,
Chesham,
Buckinghamshire HP5 3BD.

First Published September 2002

Joint Copyright
© Simon Mills and Wordsmith Publications

ISBN 1-899493-03-4

**British Library Cataloguing in Publication Data**
A CIP catalogue record for this book is available
from the British Library.

While every care has been taken in compiling the
information contained in this book, neither the
publisher nor the author accept responsibility for
errors or omissions.

© Illustrations.
Exhaustive searches have been made, where
relevant, to locate all possible copyright holders of
photographs and illustrations in this publication.
Any omissions will be honoured where proof of
copyright can be established.

Designed and typeset by
Communications Management International.

Printed in Great Britain by
Bookcraft (Bath) Ltd, Midsommer Norton,
Bath, Somerset.

Front cover design
Ian Garner

Dedication

*For Rosemary Elanor....*
*Without whose help, friendship, support and constant*
*encouragement, this book would have been completed in half*
*the time.*

# CONTENTS

# TEXT ILLUSTRATIONS

# FOREWORD

It is ironic that Britannic, the lesser known of the White Star Line's great liners of the early 1900s, will more than likely survive the longest, thanks to the careful steps being taken to insure her longevity. Unlike Titanic, which continues to be exploited by the salvagers that followed our 1985 discovery, those associated with Britannic - including the Greek and British Governments as well as Governcheck Limited which holds the UK rights to her - are making sure she does not suffer a similar fate.

When I first saw Britannic in 1995, I will never forget how amazed I was by her high state of preservation considering her shallow depth and sun-drenched superstructure. After exploring Titanic in her deeper watery grave, torn apart by her tragic sinking and head on plunge to the bottom, I was so pleased to see Britannic in one piece. What caught my eye the most was the stern section of the ship. Titanic's stern has been so badly damaged, it is now almost unrecognizable. With Britannic, it was as if I were finally completing my tour of this magnificent class of ship.

After our dives on *Britannic,* I became convinced that the best way to appreciate underwater wrecks such as hers was through the newly emerging technology of "telepresence". I imagine a future quite different than the present. Instead of a few daring divers descending to *Britannic* and exploring her on the Greek sea floor, I see millions of people visiting her interior and "walking" her decks. They will be aided by fiber-optic wire-guided vehicles controlled from anywhere in the world via the Internet.

In fact, we are implementing this very concept as you read this book. For the moment, however, technology is restricting our access to the underwater world off North America where access to *Internet II* is already available. But I am confident such access will spread until the *Britannic* becomes an underwater museum easily reached by all. Until that day comes, however, we must resist the temptations of the past and work hard to protect and eventually restore this important link to history so that future generations can visit her just as I did.

**Dr. Robert D. Ballard**
*Director, Institute for Archaeological Oceanography*
*University of Rhode Island*

*President, Institute for Exploration*
*Mystic, Connecticut*

# INTRODUCTION

The spring of 1912 was a supremely confident time for the industrialised nations of Europe, and especially Great Britain. In an age where people were becoming accustomed to one scientific marvel after another, an arrogance prevailed as leading industrialists and countries competed with each other to go one better in the pursuit of a 'technological utopia'.

For the British mercantile marine, especially, it was a golden age. The Cunard sisters *Lusitania* and *Mauretania* had long secured their reputations as the fastest ships in the world, while Cunard's chief British rival, the White Star Line, was also poised on the verge of renewed greatness. With its recently launched flagship, the *Olympic*, already proving to be a popular commercial attraction as the largest and most luxurious ship afloat, the *Titanic* due to enter service shortly after Easter that year and the construction of a third ship of the same class already under preparation, White Star's prospects appeared to be virtually limitless.

And then, in the space of 160 unforgettable minutes on the night of 14th and 15th April 1912, the unthinkable happened. The *Titanic*, reputed to be the safest ship afloat, struck an iceberg in the North Atlantic and sank on her maiden voyage, taking with her fifteen hundred souls and leaving behind only 705 dazed survivors to tell the story to an equally bewildered world. In one night the western industrial world had received a shattering blow to its technological confidence. But for the White Star Line and the Belfast shipbuilder, Harland and Wolff, the disaster would have far greater repercussions. The following weeks would see them both subjected to unprecedented public scrutiny and censure, as they attempted to salvage their reputations and ensure that such a catastrophe could never happen again.

As *Titanic's* younger sister, *Britannic*, perhaps more than any other ship became the focus of attention as its designers set about extensive and costly design modifications to eliminate the technical deficiencies that had been so publicly demonstrated by *Titanic's* tragic demise; and on paper at least, it really did look as if Harland and Wolff had at last designed a ship that was "practically unsinkable." With a double skin running for almost sixty percent of the ship's length and sixteen internal transverse bulkheads, of which five had been especially strengthened and raised, *Britannic* was theoretically capable of remaining afloat with any six compartments completely flooded, thereby preserving her from the calamity which had overwhelmed *Titanic*.

However, as events in Europe unfurled, instead of a glittering career on the North Atlantic, *Britannic* would never quite escape from the shadow of her more notorious sibling and the destiny of Great Britain's largest ship prior to the advent of the *Queen Mary* would be played out in an altogether different arena. Even so, *Britannic's* eleven-month life was not totally without drama of its own and it is only now that hitherto forgotten personal papers and diaries are beginning to emerge from hidden, dusty corners to shed new light on the human story of the Last Titan. Now, using the official records held at the British Public Records Office together with fresh information discovered from recent expeditions to the wreck, it is finally possible to paint a more complete picture, as new revelations help the *Britannic* to grasp an identity of her own.

Eclipsed at birth, in life and at her passing by events beyond her control, the *Britannic* was very much a hostage to the events of her time and will never attain the status or notoriety of her older sister, but as the mist which surrounded her existence begins to clear and the chronicle of her short life is carefully pieced together, it has become increasingly apparent that many of the sensational elements which make the tale of the *Titanic* so compelling, can also to be found in the no less dramatic story of His Majesty's Hospital Ship *Britannic*.

This is that story.

# CHAPTER ONE

# BETTER THAN TITANIC

On the morning of Tuesday 16th April 1912 the activity on slip No. 2 at the Belfast shipyard of Harland and Wolff was eerily muted. Instead of the usual smell of oil mingled with sweat, the amber glow of the riveters' braziers and the cacophony of steel against steel that underscores the toil of heavy industry, there was now only silence.

Two weeks earlier it had all been so different. Shortly after 6.00 a.m. on the morning of 2nd April, the White Star Line's latest creation, the RMS *Titanic*, had proudly steamed into Belfast Lough to undergo a day of trials, before leaving that very same evening for her new home terminal at Southampton, where she would join her sister, *Olympic*, on the White Star Line's Southampton to New York service. Between them, *Olympic* and *Titanic* represented the last word in shipboard luxury, and at over 45,000 gross tons, also attracted the proud title of being the largest ships in the world, and this was no idle boast. Since 1907 the North Atlantic had been dominated by the Cunard sisters, *Lusitania* and *Mauretania*, in both size and speed, but with *Olympic*'s entry into service in June 1911 the White Star Line clearly thought that it had regained the competitive edge. *Titanic*'s arrival somehow never quite captured the headlines in the way that *Olympic* had done, but with the new ship due to depart on her maiden voyage on 10th April, the fortunes of the White Star Line appeared to be very much in the ascendant.

History shows, however, that it was not to be. At 11.40 p.m. on the evening of Sunday 14th April 1912, *Titanic*'s fate was sealed when the ship steamed into an ice field and was mortally wounded when she scraped past a massive iceberg which gouged a 250 ft tear in her hull. In spite of the claims that the ship was a masterpiece of marine construction, all that proud technology could do nothing to save her, and at 2.20 in the early morning of 15th April, the "practically unsinkable" ship foundered in the icy waters of the North Atlantic, taking with her over 1,500 passengers and crew.

For Harland and Wolff, the tragedy was a major blow. *Olympic* and *Titanic* had come to symbolise the technological prowess of the Belfast shipyard, and the loss of the largest ship in the world on her maiden voyage would become a corporate nightmare. It was also a very personal tragedy, for not one of the nine shipyard personnel who had been on board to oversee the maiden voyage would ever return to Belfast. To make matters worse, one of those men was senior designer Thomas Andrews, who was not only a company general manager but was also the nephew and heir apparent to the shipyard's owner, Lord William Pirrie. While Belfast mourned, the task of picking up the pieces began. During the next few weeks the work rate on slip No. 2 appeared to be at a virtual standstill, but the frantic turmoil in the drawing offices and design departments probably told a very different story.

*Left: **By February 1913, Britannic's fully framed hull dominated slipway number 2.***

Ulster Folk & Transport Museum

9

The reason for their frenzied activity was simple enough. Aside from having to sort through the mass of technical papers which would be so essential for Lord Mersey's public inquiry into the tragedy, the incomplete hull now lying idle on slip No. 2 was, in fact, the third and last Olympic-class liner to be ordered. Thus far, the work had barely progressed to the height of the tank top and before it could proceed any further it was imperative that all of the weaknesses which had been so clearly exposed in *Titanic* should be addressed. Less than five months into construction, *Britannic* was already a source of considerable anxiety to her designers.

Curiously enough, in spite of the great promise of the ship, even in conception *Britannic's* origins are somewhat obscure. The White Star Line's original plan had called for two giant liners to compete with *Lusitania* and *Mauretania*, which had resulted in *Olympic* and *Titanic*, but with the Cunard Line drawing up plans for the new *Aquitania* and the German Hamburg Amerika Line proposing a giant trio of its own, it was not long before White Star was forced into considering a third ship in order to ensure a balanced weekly service on its Southampton to New York route. As *Olympic* neared completion there seemed little doubt that the design of this third ship would continue along similar lines, and any lingering doubts were finally dispelled when, on 20th June 1911, with *Olympic* just a day away from her arrival in New York for the first time, the order for a third ship of the class was officially confirmed. Even so, it was not until the Royal Mail steamer *Arlanza* was launched on 23rd November that slip No. 2 was finally available. One week later, on 30th November 1911 the keel of yard number 433 was quietly laid on the same slip upon which *Olympic* had been built.

In keeping with White Star tradition, the design of the new vessel would take into account every conceivable lesson learnt in the construction and operation of *Olympic* and *Titanic*, so that the resulting ship would be as near perfect as possible. With all the adulation that had poured forth, it seems incredible to think that it would have been possible for Harland and Wolff to improve upon the state of 'perfection' that was *Titanic*, but in effect that is exactly what *Britannic* was

*A White Star Line publicity drawing, comparing Britannic in size to St. Paul's Cathedral.*

*Courtesy John Fleming*

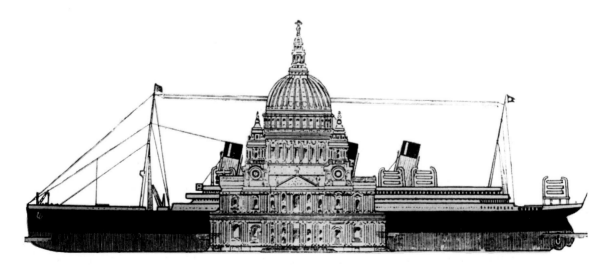

## GIGANTIC, 1,000-FOOT LINER

### To Have Golf Links, Cricket Field, Tennis Court, and Ballroom.

**By Marconi Transatlantic Wireless Telegraph to The New York Times.**

LONDON, Nov. 24, (by telegraph to Clifden, Ireland: thence by wireless.)—Remarkable details are now known of the thousand-foot liner, the Gigantic, which the White Star Line has commissioned Harland & Wolff to build at Belfast.

The beam will measure between 111 and 112 feet; the displacement will be 70,000 tons, and the gross tonnage over 50,000. The levels will be a dozen or thirteen, with the highest over seventy-five feet above the water line. The passenger accommodation will be increased in the first class from 800 to 1,000 or more, and the total passengers that can be carried will number over 4,000.

The Gigantic will not be an ocean greyhound, but a seven-day boat. She will have both reciprocating and turbine engines. The cost is to be close on to £2,000,000, or $10,000,000. She will have a cricket field, a tennis court, golf links, and reception and ball rooms, and restaurant and veranda cafés, which will be placed forward instead of aft. There will also be a plunge and all kinds of baths, and a gymnasium.

There will be a most elaborate scheme of decoration.

*Although the evidence to suggest that Yard No. 433 was originally to be called Gigantic is circumstantial at best, this cutting from a 1911 edition of the New York Times clearly shows that the press were more than happy to believe the rumours.*

*Courtesy Bruce Beveridge*

intended to be – larger and more luxurious. Following the loss of *Titanic*, however, the impact on the new ship's designs would be considerably more far reaching, and within days the first myth in her all-too-brief life was created.

For some time the rumour had been circulating in the press that the intended name of yard No. 433 was to be *Gigantic*, and that White Star was building a vessel which, at 924 feet long, 94 feet wide and some 54,000 gross tons, would rival the three giant liners being constructed for the Hamburg Amerika Line.

A closer look at the political realities of 1912, however, puts the unconfirmed reports in a more questionable light. The introduction of *Lusitania* and *Mauretania* in 1907 had provided a slap in the face for the German merchant marine which, during the previous decade, had consistently produced the world's largest and fastest ships. Faced with stiffer competition from Cunard and White Star, Albert Ballin's Hamburg Amerika Line had decided to respond in kind, and the construction of the three HAPAG liners *Imperator*, *Vaterland* and *Bismarck* meant that it was only a matter of time before they would once again regain the initiative. Quite simply, this renewed German challenge could not be ignored by the British press. Because of this, the name *Gigantic* seems to have been published frequently, and to emphasise the hyberbole associated with the press even then, the imaginary ship was endowed with even more impressive features. Typically, Lengths of 903 and 1,000 feet, not to mention a beam of 112 feet, were not uncommonly quoted.

In reality, the name *Gigantic* was by no means new. Many years before, in as early as September 1892 the *New York Times* mentioned that Harland and Wolff had been commissioned by the White Star Line to build a steamer of that name, which would be seven hundred feet long, with a beam of over sixty-five feet. Of course, the vessel never appeared, although the dimensions of *Oceanic*, which entered service in 1899, were remarkably close to those stated in the story.

But to return to 1912; the *Gigantic* controversy received further support in an article written on 15th April 1912 for the *Journal of Commerce*, which announced that one week earlier work had begun on the *Gigantic*. In this instance there was some credence to the commentary, as the new *Britannic* was indeed intended to have a 94 foot beam as stated in the report. But one has to question the validity of the reporter's sources, when it transpires that work had already been quietly progressing for practically five months before the *Titanic* went down.

The suggestion that *Britannic* was to have been originally named *Gigantic* resurfaced again as late as 26th November 1958 from a rather surprising source, when C.C. Pounder, one of the managers at Harland and Wolff and vice president of the Institute of Marine Engineers, gave a paper to that same body. The paper, *Human Problems in Marine Engineering*, was later published in the 1959 *Transactions of the Society of Naval Architects and Marine Engineers*, and Pounder's statement on page 578 was quite specific:

> "*Olympic* and *Titanic* had a sister, originally to be called *Gigantic* but, after the loss of *Titanic*, named *Britannic*."

One would have thought that as a relatively high-ranking employee of Harland and Wolff, Pounder would very likely have had some idea of what he was talking about, but the problem with his bold statement is that he does not provide it with any reference. Was it written as a result of some long lost Harland and Wolff internal memo, or could it just be that Pounder himself was as susceptible to the myths and legends of the *Titanic* as anyone else?

One thing is certain. The White Star Line was considerably less inclined to embrace the name and, in view of the embarrassing débacle of the *Titanic*, it is not difficult to see why. It could be argued that the name *Gigantic* was fairly appropriate. *Olympic*, *Titanic* and *Gigantic* all conjured up images of grandeur, power and size, but as a result of the calamitous events, far from being a major selling point the name was now a matter of great sensitivity. In May 1912 the company went so far as to publicly deny that the name *Gigantic* had ever been under consideration, and bearing in mind the fact that the transcripts of Lord Mersey's *Titanic* inquiry would also seem to suggest that at this time the name *Britannic* had indeed been allocated to the new ship, this would seem to reinforce their case. Then again, it was not unknown for ships to have their names changed during construction. A strangely appropriate example of this comes a little under forty years earlier in the company's history, when the keel of the 5,000 ton liner *Hellenic* was laid at Belfast in 1873, yet by the time the vessel was launched the name *Britannic* had been substituted.

So is there any truth to the rumours? We can immediately dismiss the suggestion that *Britannic* was any longer than *Titanic*. Even a cursory glance at the ship's registration documents shows that all three ships had an identical waterline length of 852 feet and 6 inches. As to the alleged name change; the basic problem with this argument is that no documented evidence has ever been published to suggest that the name *Gigantic* was the original choice for the ship, or for that matter, any other vessel in the White Star fleet. Any cover-up either by the White Star Line or Harland and Wolff would also have required an almost unbelievable degree of organisation and luck, when considering the vast number of people involved with the design and construction of the ship. Perhaps the rumour should not be completely dismissed, but because the available evidence in its

*Above right: By 21st February 1914 Britannic completely filled slip No. 2 in the Arrol gantry and was barely a week from being launched.*

*Right: This photograph of the Saloon deck under construction, taken in October 1913, provides an excellent example of just how vast the ship's interiors would be.*

*Ulster Folk & Transport Museum*

favour is so tenuous and based largely upon press hearsay without any documentary proof, Pounder's belated reference to the name *Gigantic* must remain open to question.

Nevertheless, it would take more than a simple name change to reassure the travelling public. It was clear that more substantial thought would have to be given to the new designs before the ship could be launched, and the resulting 270-page specification book provides adequate evidence of the fact that *Britannic's* construction would be scrutinised in the finest detail.

The book itself is a fascinating document. Not only does it itemise in almost microscopic detail the features which would transform *Britannic* into the floating palace that she was designed to be, but it also provides an interesting insight into the post-*Titanic* psyche of Harland and Wolff, for although it contains many references to fittings on *Olympic* which were to be duplicated in the new ship, the same cannot be said for *Titanic*. Instead of mentioning the ship by name, all references to the doomed liner seem to have been totally obliterated and discreetly replaced with the reference S.S. 401. Whilst the name *Titanic* was tainted with a certain ignominy throughout the marine world, within the confines of the Belfast shipyard it seems to have become almost taboo.

The specification book reveals that the internal workings of the new ship would include few alterations to the power plant which was serving *Olympic* so well. The boiler rooms were arranged in an identical manner to those of *Olympic*, with the 159 furnaces of the twenty-four double-ended and five single-ended boilers providing the necessary 215 lbs. psi of steam pressure which would drive the ship's impressive propulsion units. Two four-cylinder triple-expansion reciprocating engines, each forty feet high, would drive the two wing propellers when the ship was manoeuvring in confined waters, but once at sea, instead of being directed straight to the condensers, the exhaust steam would be diverted into an additional low-pressure turbine, which drove the centre propeller.

This system of combination machinery had actually been developed several years earlier when, in an attempt to improve both performance and economy, the White Star Line had experimented with two of its ships which were intended for the White Star-Dominion Service between Liverpool and Montreal. While the liners *Megantic* and *Laurentic* appeared to be sister ships, beneath the water line they were very different. *Megantic* was driven by two quadruple-expansion reciprocating engines, while *Laurentic* incorporated an experimental combination of two triple-expansion reciprocating engines, and an additional low-pressure turbine. Both ships entered service in 1909 and it was not long before *Laurentic* was clearly seen to be outperforming *Megantic* in both speed and economy.

At that time, however, turbine engine technology was still very much in its infancy at Harland and Wolff, largely due to the fact that few commercial shipping lines, with the exception of Cunard, had actively embraced the technology. Under these circumstances it is not surprising that Lord Pirrie had chosen not to invest in the expensive equipment required for turbine production. By 1907, however, White Star had become more responsive to the concept, but with Harland and Wolff already heavily committed to the International Mercantile Marine (IMM) and the construction of new slipways to build *Olympic* and *Titanic*, the last thing that Pirrie needed was to have to provide additional funds for the new machinery. Fortunately there was an answer to the dilemma, and in May of that year Pirrie approached the Clydebank shipyard of John Brown with the offer of a merger. This was quickly accepted and, as a part of the package, John Brown agreed to share their turbine technology with Harland and Wolff and divide the profits equally. The order for *Laurentic*'s turbine was immediately placed with John Brown, but it was clear that a turbine plant would have to be established at Belfast as quickly as possible to handle future orders. To help get things moving, John Brown subcontracted the manufacture of the turbine for the dreadnought HMS *Neptune*, then building at Portsmouth, so that by the time the turbines for *Olympic* and *Titanic* were under construction the Belfast turbine plant would be well established. As they gained experience, so refinements in turbine manufacture became

*Britannic's marine reciprocating engines would be little different to those in Olympic and Titanic, which at over forty feet in height were the largest ever built.*

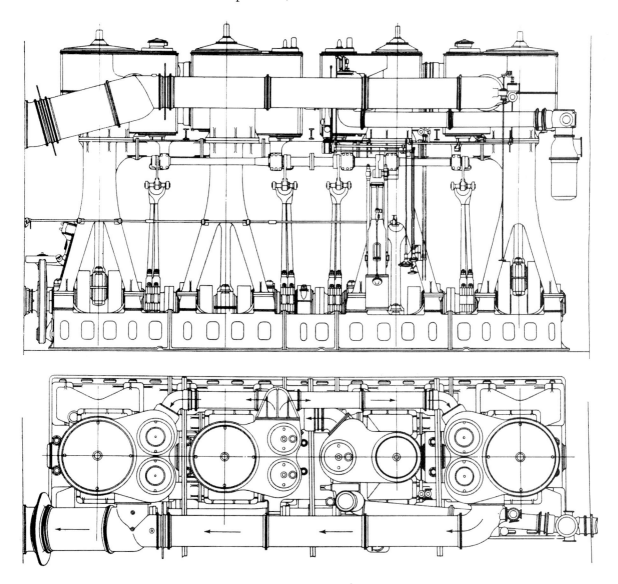

more noticeable and while the turbines on *Olympic* and *Titanic* could generate 16,000 Shaft horsepower, the turbine on *Britannic* would develop an impressive 18,000 SHP. It is interesting to note that the technical press of the day was not slow to seize upon the fact that, at 490 tons, *Britannic*'s turbine also happened to be the largest afloat.

Pirrie's investment was worth it. All told, *Britannic*'s two reciprocating engines could each develop 16,000 Indicated horsepower which, when combined with the additional 18,000 Shaft horsepower supplied by the turbine, was more than enough to maintain the ship's service speed of 21 knots.

In one key respect, however, *Britannic*'s engine and boiler rooms were very different. Externally *Britannic* may have been slightly wider than *Olympic* and *Titanic*, but this additional width would not have been noticed by the firemen labouring within the stokeholds. One of the major reasons that *Titanic* had been lost was due to the arrangement of the internal transverse bulkheads which had been shown to be woefully inadequate. As the mortally wounded ship had sunk deeper by the bow, so the rising level of water in the forward compartments had overwhelmed each of the forward bulkheads, one after the other, until the ship foundered. The solution was simple enough, and as a result five of the ship's sixteen bulkheads were raised to the height of the bridge deck, seventy-five feet above the keel and over forty-feet above the ship's deepest load line.

*Perhaps the most important feature of the new ship was the inner skin that had been so sadly lacking in the Titanic.*

Ulster Folk & Transport Museum

To facilitate the working of the ship, these bulkheads would incorporate a total of sixty-three watertight doors throughout the ship, and to further increase the margin of safety, a thirty-inch compartmentalised inner skin was fitted between frames 78 forward and 71 aft, rising to a point three feet and six inches above the middle (E) deck, six-and-a-half feet above the load line. As a result, the entire 447 ft length of the boiler and engine room compartments, accounting for fifty-two percent of the ship's waterline length was doubly protected, and when the freshwater tanks flanking the two electric engine rooms are taken into consideration, the figure actually rises to sixty percent. The result of all this internal construction meant that *Britannic* would be capable of withstanding the kind of damage which overcame the *Titanic* and, on paper at least, it was calculated that the ship would remain float with any six compartments completely flooded.

One interesting discrepancy, however, relates to the overall beam of the redesigned *Britannic*. The 1912 specification book states that the beam of the new vessel was intended to be 93 feet and six inches, yet the final beam, as recorded in the official registration documents, is 94 feet. So where did these extra six inches come from?

The technical justification for *Britannic*'s additional beam was due to a great deal more than simply the ship's new double skin. In light of the heavier top hamper and hull construction, *Britannic*'s sea-keeping characteristics would have been very different to those of *Olympic* and *Titanic*. Although the extra weight would have increased the ship's draught, making her theoretically more stable, the modified superstructure would have also resulted in a ship with additional top weight. Because of this, *Britannic*'s Metacentric Height – her "GM" – would be to some extent decreased and required a degree of compensation. In the world of naval architecture a great many other factors often have to be taken into account but essentially, the GM is the distance between a vessel's Centre of Gravity (a force acting downwards) and her Metacentre, the latter being a theoretical point formed at the intersection of a vertical line taken upwards through the waterline from the ship's Centre of Buoyancy (a force acting upwards) when the ship is in an upright position, and a similar line from the "displaced" Centre of Buoyancy caused when the ship is inclined through a small angle of heel. A large GM will cause a ship to recover from a list very quickly creating great discomfort to those on board (perhaps in extreme cases, even sweeping them off their feet), a small GM results in a slow recovery from a roll (a not unknown characteristic of the HAPAG *Imperator* class liners), while a negative GM causes the ship to remain at an angle of heel or even capsize altogether. One solution to increasing the GM is to widen a ship's beam, thereby lowering the Centre of Buoyancy without compromising her stability. To ensure that *Britannic* did not suffer from this problem it was decided to increase the ship's beam by one foot, thus restoring its Metacentric Height closer to that of the *Olympic*.

Whilst undeniably necessary, the structural modifications to *Britannic*'s designs were only part of the stratagem. All the expenditure in the world would mean nothing if the public was not reassured. In short, not only did the ship have to be safer, it had to be seen to be safer. Externally *Britannic* had more in common with *Titanic* than *Olympic*. All three ships shared the same elegant lines, but while

*Olympic's* promenade deck would always remain open, *Britannic's* forward promenade, like *Titanic's*, was enclosed with sliding windows. But there the similarities ended. *Britannic's* enclosed aft shelter deck, combined with the additional third-class smoke room beneath the raised shade deck increased the earning capacity, but also had the unfortunate effect of disrupting the aesthetic profile of the ship. As a result, *Britannic's* stern would always seem somewhat lofty and awkward when compared to the more appealing lines of *Olympic* and *Titanic*. However, this was as nothing compared with what was to come.

A major factor highlighted by the loss of *Titanic* had been the inadequate number of lifeboats. The less informed were quick to blame the White Star Line for this oversight, but the fact remains that the real villain of the piece was the British Board of Trade. Lulled into a false sense of security by the endless technological advances, the Board regulations regarding lifeboats had become increasingly outdated as larger and apparently safer ships entered service. Both *Olympic* and *Titanic* had a gross tonnage well in excess of 45,000 tons, yet the existing Board regulations regarding lifeboats had been last modified as long ago as 1894 and were so out of date that only vessels of up to 10,000 tons were considered. The Board only insisted upon the *minimum* number of sixteen boats under davits, with an overall capacity of 5,500 cubic feet. Even then it was not quite that simple. As an emigrant ship, *Titanic's* lifeboats actually needed to provide a capacity of 9,625 cubic feet, or put more simply, space for 962 persons. Fortunately for the White Star Line, the total 1,178 person capacity of *Titanic's* lifeboats comfortably exceeded the regulations.

The reasons for the lack of initiative shown by the Board of Trade are varied, but essentially, the combination of a previously good safety record, increased internal compartmentalisation and the introduction of wireless communication had lulled the Board into a false sense of security. Indeed, the loss of the White Star liner *Republic* off Nantucket in January 1909 seemed to justify this approach. Following a collision with the Lloyd Italiano liner *Florida*, *Republic's* bulkheads had kept the ship afloat for over thirty-six hours, providing more than enough time for the new Marconi installation to call up assistance from the liner *Baltic*, and for the passengers to be taken off. On that occasion only three people aboard the *Republic* had died, and none in any way due to a lack of lifeboats. But in the case of *Titanic*, the system had not worked. *Titanic* foundered almost two hours before *Carpathia* could arrive on the scene, by which time the 1,500 people who had perished in the freezing North Atlantic were little more than a tragic symbol of man's misplaced faith in technology. Now the need for complicated equations was no longer appropriate or necessary. Future regulations regarding lifeboat capacity could have only one possible outcome, and the cries of "boats for all" did not go unheeded. Immediately following the disaster, Joseph Bruce Ismay, the chairman of the White Star Line and president of the International Mercantile Marine, who had himself escaped from the sinking *Titanic* in the last boat to be lowered on the port side, ordered that no IMM vessel should ever put to sea again without a full complement of lifeboats.

As a result, after *Olympic* returned to Belfast in October 1912, Harland and Wolff spent the better part of six months rebuilding the ship. Broadly speaking, the internal modifications were an indication of the changes which would be made to

*Following the loss of the Titanic, Britannic's modified design incorporated eight sets of gantry davits serving forty-four lifeboats.*

*Ulster Folk & Transport Museum*

*Britannic*, as workmen set about gutting *Olympic's* boiler rooms before raising and strengthening the ship's key bulkheads and surrounding the vital compartments with a watertight skin. Confronting the problem of inadequate lifeboats, however, took away one of *Olympic's* key selling strengths. Previously the boat deck had been an expanse of uncluttered open space, but the replacement of the solid bulkhead with the fourteen lifeboats fitted along either side of the boat deck had severely reduced the area of open space. This reduction of open views may well be a factor in the White Star Line's decision not to enclose *Olympic's* forward promenade, in spite of the excessive spray to which this area could occasionally be subjected. If this space was to be restored on *Britannic*, the specifications of the boat deck would require considerable redrafting.

The resulting designs were unconventional in both concept and appearance. *Britannic's* intended complement of forty-four lifeboats comprised forty rigid wooden boats, each measuring 34 ft x 10 ft, and two 26 ft x 8 ft emergency cutters, with the two 34 ft wooden motorboats, equipped with their own wireless telegraphic installation. It should be said that Harland and Wolff's answer to the problem concerning the way in which so many boats were to be safely stowed while at the same time restoring the open deck space which had been lost on *Olympic*, was as unique as it was innovative.

In a major departure from the standard practice of placing a ship's lifeboats along the outer edges of the boat deck, Harland and Wolff had instead come up with a novel design which, at one stroke ensured that *Britannic* would not only carry enough boats for everyone on board, but would also restore the expanse of open space which had been lost on *Olympic*. Thus were created *Britannic's* famous gantry davits. It might have appeared that the size of these eight complex constructions with their towering davits and stacks of lifeboats was an overreaction, and when compared with the neat lines of *Olympic*, destroyed the elegance of the new ship. The new arrangements may have looked ungainly, but it was a small price to pay if the seagoing public were to be convinced that the White Star Line was taking the matter of lifeboats seriously. In fact, the company's publicity department made a particular point of featuring the merits of the new system:

"The vessel is fitted with the latest and most approved type of electrically-driven boat-lowering gear, by means of which a very large number of boats can, one after the other, be put over the side of the vessel and lowered to the water-line in much less time than was possible under the old system of davits. One of the advantages of the new system is that the passengers take their places in the boats expeditiously and with perfect safety before the boats are lifted from the deck of the vessel, and the gear is so constructed that the fully-laden boats are lowered at a very considerable distance from the side of the ship, thus minimising risk in bad weather. Moreover, the whole of the boats on board can be lowered on either side of the vessel, whichever happens to be clear, and the gear has been kept so far inboard as to give a wide passage at either side of the ship for promenading, and for marshalling the passengers in case of emergency."

Such fittings, however, did not come without cost, and aside from their aesthetic shortcomings, the gantry davits also necessitated major modifications to the ship's plans. *Britannic* had already been made wider to take into account the extra weight of a heavier superstructure, brought about by the installation of additional cabins and fittings. The inclusion of the massive gantry davits and the concentrated stacks of lifeboats forced Harland and Wolff to rethink even these modifications. As a result, *Britannic* would ultimately be some eighteen inches wider than *Olympic* and *Titanic*, instead of the originally planned twelve inches, while the superstructure itself was considerably strengthened beneath the areas where the davits were to be installed. Less noticeable, but essential nevertheless, was the rearrangement of the expansion joints within the redesigned superstructure. Instead of having two expansion joints as fitted in *Olympic* and *Titanic*, *Britannic* would have four. The superstructure itself would incorporate three such joints, while a fourth would be installed above the now enclosed aft well deck, in order to disperse the stresses in the new area of the raised deck brought on by the working of the ship and the heavier stern.

With the modified designs approved, the following twenty-two months saw *Britannic*'s giant hull gradually taking shape, but far more slowly than either the White Star Line or Harland and Wolff would have liked. Plans to have the ship in service by the end of 1913 were hopelessly over optimistic, and as one possible date after another came and went, it must have seemed as if *Britannic* would never be launched.

Inevitably, however, the great day arrived. On 26th February 1914, after twenty-seven months on the stocks (five months longer than it had taken *Olympic* to reach this point in construction), *Britannic* was finally ready to be launched. Sadly, the Irish weather did not rise to the occasion. The winter climate remained cold, depressingly overcast and particularly drizzly throughout the morning. Nevertheless, Lord Pirrie was still superintending final preparations at the shipyard as early as 5.00 a.m. for guests who would be arriving later. That same morning the Belfast Steamship Company's S.S. *Patriotic* arrived at York Dock,

*Right: **With one day to go before the launch, Lord Pirrie poses with the Belfast Harbour Commissioners beneath Britannic's stern. Captain Charles Bartlett, the White Star Marine Superintendent and Britannic's future commander, stands third from the right.***

*Ulster Folk & Transport Museum*

carrying members of the press and other guests of the White Star Line, while across the river Lagan, thousands of sightseers enthusiastically gathered along its banks, many arriving several hours early in order to guarantee a good view.

For the more important local officials and Admiralty dignitaries, however, there was no such jostling for position. A large stand had been specially erected alongside the Arrol gantry which guaranteed them a spectacular view.

In spite of the impressive guest list, two individuals were conspicuous by their absence. The great American financier, John Pierpont Morgan, whose power and money had created the International Mercantile Marine combine had died in Rome in March 1913 and while Morgan's association with *Titanic* had been less well publicised, Joseph Bruce Ismay, the hapless White Star chairman who had escaped from the sinking *Titanic* when so many others had lost their lives, was not so fortunate in evading criticism. The vitriolic campaign stirred up against him in the American press during the months immediately after the sinking had severely weakened his position within the company, so that, when it eventually came, his long-planned retirement was absolute. Had Ismay not been so closely associated with *Titanic* his subsequent request to remain as a director of the White Star Line might have fallen on more receptive ears, but by the autumn of 1912 it was clear that his days with the company were numbered. Contrary to popular belief, Ismay's retirement on 30th June 1913 as both president of IMM and chairman of the White Star Line was by no means a knee-jerk reaction to the loss of *Titanic*, and had actually been agreed as early as February 1912. His old friend Harold Sanderson was to be his chosen successor in both posts, although Ismay would remain a member of the IMM committee until June of 1916. Whether or not he was invited to *Britannic*'s launch is unclear. Ismay's absence may have been due either to over-sensitivity on the part of the company or, more likely, his own fear of being thrust back into the public spotlight which he had always conspicuously tried to avoid. Whatever the truth, with White Star and Harland and Wolff both eager to draw a line under the *Titanic* disaster the sigh of relief at Ismay's absence, if not audible, was probably heartfelt.

Shortly before high tide, a final, unexpected guest arrived. A young telegraph messenger had been allowed onto the grandstand to deliver his telegram personally to Lord Pirrie and was invited to stay to watch. Pirrie, meanwhile, had more pressing concerns, as the first rocket warning of the impending launch shot into the air at 11.10 a.m. Aside from acting as a warning for any passing vessels to stand clear, it was also the signal for work gangs crouched beneath the hull to begin dislodging the remaining shores which had supported *Britannic*'s hull for the last 819 days. Moments later, the 24,800 ton hull was being supported solely by the specially constructed sliding ways. So well was the weight distributed that the average pressure exerted on the ways was scarcely three tons per square foot. The only obstacle now holding *Britannic* back were the launch triggers, but not for long. With the river totally clear, at 11.15 a.m. a second rocket raced skyward as the valves were opened to release the pressure in the hydraulic cylinder. As the supporting rams receded, so the launch triggers were allowed to drop, and seconds later the grey-painted hull, needing no assistance from the hydraulic starting-jacks, was moving, gradually picking up speed as it slid over the twenty tons of tallow, train oil and soft soap which had been spread on the ways.

It was all over in eighty-one seconds. Having reached a maximum speed of nine and-a-half knots, the drags, consisting of three anchors and eighty tons of chain on either side of the ship, worked perfectly to slow *Britannic*'s momentum and bring the vessel to a halt long before it reached the other side of the river bank, some 2,350 feet away. The system of underwater anchors worked so flawlessly that *Britannic* had stopped moving before the hull had even travelled its own length in the water.

For now, *Britannic*'s position centre stage was over and the guests, impatient for some protection against the elements, quickly began to move away from the now vacant slip No. 2 in search of the more salubrious surroundings of the official reception. As they dispersed, the only noises to be heard were those of the launch crews as they immediately set about clearing the slipway in preparation for yard number 469, the projected 26,500 ton Red Star liner *Nederland*. In the meantime, *Britannic*'s empty hull was quietly towed into an equally grey Belfast gloom by the tugs *Herculaneum*, *Huskisson*, *Hornby*, *Alexandra* and *Hercules*, as far as her new berth in the Belfast Harbour Commissioner's deep-water wharf. From here the process of fitting out the ship would continue over the coming months.

The launch may have been over, but even at this stage *Britannic* was already more than just a new ship to the White Star Line. Coming in the wake of the *Titanic* disaster, the vessel symbolised a fresh start to the new managers of the company, while to Harland and Wolff she truly was a ship of dreams. The text in the launch booklet leaves little room for any doubt in their regained confidence:

> "I n the new *Britannic* we see, both in design and construction, as perfect a specimen of man's creative power as it is possible to conceive."

Hopefully, this time they had got it right.

# CHAPTER TWO

# RULING THE WAVES

*Britannic's* launch had gone without a hitch, but it had hardly been a gala event. One of the yard workers was so unimpressed by the lack of formality surrounding the entire affair that he was later moved to comment: "They just builds 'er and shoves 'er in."

Actually, there was nothing unusual about the lack of any christening. *Britannic's* launch had followed a well established company tradition, although exactly why the White Star Line never chose to formally christen their ships with a bottle of champagne is not clear. The Belfast superstition of alcohol being "the old evil" may well have had something to do with it, but if the launch itself lacked the accepted ceremony, the official reception at the shipyard following the launch went some way to make up for it. Harold Sanderson, Bruce Ismay's successor as chairman of White Star and president of International Mercantile Marine, had been at the launch but was unable to stay for the formal speeches due to a pressing engagement in Queenstown, where he would board the *Baltic* en route to a business trip in New York, so the usual press reception at Belfast's Grand Central Hotel was chaired by Colonel Henry Concanon. Concanon was one of the White Star Line's managers at Liverpool and his evident pride in the new vessel was clear for all to see when he announced:

> "Neither thought nor money has been spared and when you see the finished article we feel sure that we shall have your approval, as we have your good wishes today"

The other speakers were equally positive, describing the new *Britannic*, amongst other things, as comprising "the highest attainments in naval architecture and marine engineering." Of *Titanic*, however, there was practically no reference at all – at least not in public – and the ensuing press reports were all outwardly united in their attempts not to spoil the great day. The resulting press coverage also went out of its way to make no reference whatsoever to the *Titanic* disaster, choosing instead to make any comparisons with the *Olympic*. Nor did they limit themselves in any way when it came to praising the new ship itself, with such kudos as:

*Opposite: **Based on an oil painting by marine artist Charles Dixon, this publicity postcard issued by the White Star Line clearly shows how Britannic would have appeared as originally conceived.***

*Courtesy Angus Mitchell*

"… a twentieth century ship in every sense of the word,"
    or
"… the highest achievement of her day in the practice of ship building and marine engineering."

Concanon's speech had clearly struck the right note.

In return, White Star went to great pains to properly entertain the reporters. It was not until 9.35 p.m. that *Patriotic* was once again ready to depart for the

*The giant Benrather crane, specifically purchased by Harland and Wolff for the fitting out of the Olympic class liners, lowers one of Britannic's boilers into the empty funnel casings.*

Ulster Folk & Transport Museum

overnight crossing to Liverpool, where Roland J. Shelley, White Star's head of publicity, had already laid on a special train to London the next day.

With the revellers now gone, the task of fitting out could begin in earnest. The idea, of course, was to transform the ship into the company's latest seagoing palace and, as far as first-class passengers were concerned they would clearly want for nothing. The swimming bath, gymnasium, squash court, *à la carte* restaurant and Turkish bath had already proved popular successes on *Olympic*, and as an additional attraction *Britannic* would also include such features as a mechanical pipe organ at the top of the forward first-class staircase, a first-class children's playroom and an additional lift, just aft of the third smokestack, running between B and E decks. The first-class ladies would also benefit from a new hair salon and manicurist shop next to the existing gentleman's barber on B deck.

As for the established facilities, they would also be modified or improved. The three forward lifts would operate from E deck all the way up to the boat deck (on *Olympic* and *Titanic* they only operated as far up as the promenade deck), while the *Café Parisien* on B deck, which had proved such a popular attraction on *Titanic* that a similar café had later been installed on *Olympic*, was curiously done away with altogether. In its place the *à la carte* restaurant was enlarged so that it would extend across the entire width of the ship. Quite why no provision for a similar café was included in *Britannic*'s plans is a mystery as it clearly seemed to be a popular attraction on board *Titanic*, although with two veranda cafés already located on the aft promenade deck, perhaps a third café really wasn't necessary after all.

The improvements were not restricted to first-class. A new gymnasium was also installed in the aft well deck for the exclusive use of the second-class passengers, which, in turn, was covered with an extra area of open deck, enclosing the well deck altogether. Most of this additional area was also allocated to second-class, while the newly enclosed well deck now served as a covered promenade for steerage passengers who had previously no external covered areas in which to shelter during rough weather. As an additional bonus, steerage passengers also had a separate smoke room on the ship's poop deck, just below the additional shade deck.

Internally, *Britannic* was also a very different ship, with the large proportion of staterooms having their own *en suite* bathrooms. The overall layout, particularly on the bridge deck, was an interesting amalgamation of *Olympic* and *Titanic*. While *Olympic*'s bridge deck had incorporated an enclosed promenade running the entire length of the superstructure, *Titanic*'s additional cabins had resulted in a very different window arrangement. They ran

*By April 1914 the bedplates of the reciprocating engines were in position, and work could at last begin on assembling the massive high pressure cylinders.*

Ulster Folk & Transport Museum

27

from the forward end of the bridge deck to the aft first-class staircase, where the remaining open space was taken up by the *à la carte* restaurant and the *Café Parisien*. *Britannic*'s arrangements incorporated elements of both ships. The forward open promenade on the bridge deck was restored for a length of 132 ft (as far aft as the forward first-class entrance), but aft of this point the deck layout had more in common with that of *Titanic*, except that the *Café Parisien* had been removed.

A closer look at the ship's specification book, however, reveals a multitude of additional detail that few outside of a shipyard drawing office would even stop to consider. It was all very well building a ship which would be as near perfect as possible, but it also had to conform to both the Board of Trade regulations and the American Immigration Laws, not to mention the requirements of the existing Factory's Act and Port Sanitary Authority regulations. Even apparently trivial matters such as making sure that all of the removable engineering fittings and ship's keys were made from base metals instead of brass in order to prevent theft, were taken into account. While nearly every living space within the hull had its own entry in the book, right down to the make and model of every lavatory in each area of the ship, inevitably the first-class areas were planned with even more meticulous detail. Fourteen of the most expensive staterooms on B deck would be especially distinctive in their design, with six being finished in the Adams style, in white; four in the Louis XVI style, in oak; two rooms in the Louis XV style, in grey, and two more finished in the Empire style, also in white.

The real showpieces of the first-class accommodation, however, were the two private suites located on B deck. The port suite consisted of two bedrooms and a sitting room, with its own private bathroom with shower, lavatory and wardrobe rooms. The overall finish of the cabin was to be in oak with French-style oak furniture, and the London-based interior fitters of Aldham Heaton & Company would co-ordinate the entire decoration and furnishing of the cabins. Their brief included

*White Star publicity drawings of how the lounge (below) and the forward first class main entrance (right) would have looked. Overlooking the staircase clock you can clearly see the Aeolian organ intended for the ship, a feature that would have been unique to Britannic.*

brass beds, a circular table, armchairs, easy chairs, a writing desk and even a fireplace. This suite also came complete with its own private forty-foot promenade. The starboard suite was not quite so grandiose, consisting of two sets of rooms, each comprising a bedroom, a bathroom including a shower, a lavatory and wardrobe room. Each set of rooms could be entered separately and between the two rooms would be a connecting saloon and veranda. For added convenience a mahogany-panelled servant's room was also provided complete with its own bed, Pullman berth, sofa, wardrobe, folding lavatory, electric heater and even a red carpet.

So who would benefit from all this effort? Once again, the specification book is complete down to the smallest detail. With an overall crew of 950, *Britannic* would carry 785 first-class, 836 second-class and 953 third-class passengers, although these figures could vary. The first-class figures could rise to 907 in full season, while the figures for second class were considerably more complex. Only 374 of *Britannic's* berths were permanently dedicated to second-class passengers, but that figure could actually rise to 836 when taking into account the accommodations which alternated between first and second-class, and second and third-class. At full capacity the figures for the steerage passengers could rise to as high as 1,415.

In spite of all this attention to detail, the fitting out of the new ship proved to be far more difficult than anticipated. It had only taken seven months for *Olympic's* completion, and the press had not unnaturally assumed that *Britannic* would, therefore, be in service by the autumn of 1914. Unfortunately this turned out to be wildly optimistic. A combination of supply and financial problems at Harland and Wolff, which was already owed £585,000 by the IMM combine, were further hampered by an excessively full order book and declining industrial relations. With one delay after another, it was officially announced on 2nd July 1914 that *Britannic* would not be ready for her maiden voyage until the spring of 1915.

Fate would once again, however, play its part. As the European powder keg erupted into all out war in August 1914, the outbreak of hostilities was greeted with jingoistic approval by many in Britain. The effect on industry, on the other hand, was somewhat less sanguine. The war effort took immediate priority and as existing stocks of raw materials were diverted to shipyards with Admiralty contracts, Harland and Wolff was suddenly hard-pressed to obtain its own materials. Within three months of the outbreak of war over six thousand yard workers had been laid off, and even when the shipyard was eventually in a position to rehire the men, so many had rushed to the enlistment depots that it had left a severe shortage of skilled labour which would prove difficult to fill.

Nor was the White Star Line unaffected by the outbreak of war. With the port of Southampton requisitioned by the military authorities, the company had had to rely solely on its existing routes out of Liverpool to maintain a North American service. This in itself was no easy task as *Oceanic*, *Celtic*, *Cedric* and *Teutonic* were quickly requisitioned to serve as armed merchant cruisers with the 10th Cruiser Squadron, while *Laurentic* and *Megantic* had been converted to troop ships. This wasn't necessarily all bad news as the Admiralty was paying handsomely for the use of the requisitioned ships, while the understandable drop in the number of passengers since the outbreak of war meant that an improvised IMM service between Liverpool and New York was comfortably maintained by *Baltic*, *Adriatic* and the Red Star liner *Lapland*.

*Olympic*, however, was another matter. Running between Greenock in the Clyde estuary and New York, the ship was simply too important to jeopardise at sea in such an uncertain environment, and until the number of passengers had recovered sufficiently to warrant the continued risk, the White Star Line chose instead to mothball the ship at the end of October.

Far from being a straightforward affair, however, *Olympic*'s final voyage before being laid up was destined to be a memorable one. On 27th October, while off Tory Island on the north coast of Ireland, the voyage was interrupted by a distress signal from the British dreadnought HMS *Audacious*. The battleship had run foul of a German mine and in spite of the potential risk from U-boats, *Olympic*'s master, Captain Herbert James Haddock, succeeded in attaching a line before attempting to tow the damaged battleship to the safety of the naval base at Lough Swilly. Had it not been for the rising sea they might have made it, but the damaged steering gear on *Audacious* caused the ship to continually shear off into the wind, parting the towline. As one attempt after another failed, the crew of the battleship were finally evacuated to the assembling flotilla of rescue vessels. It was not a moment too soon and at 8.55 p.m., the forward magazine exploded. Within moments the *Audacious* had capsized and gone to the bottom. Following a six day internment in Lough Swilly, where for security reasons the passengers were forbidden to land, *Olympic* resumed her voyage direct to Belfast, where she finally arrived on 3rd November, to be laid up alongside her new sister ship.

In spite of the logistical problems, as the war followed its course a limited amount of work could still be carried out on *Britannic*. In September the ship was placed in the Thompson graving dock in order to have her propellers fitted. However, in October the Admiralty suddenly placed a contract with Harland and Wolff to begin work on what would come to be known as "the ghost fleet" - a flotilla of merchant vessels disguised as warships in an attempt to mislead the enemy - swiftly followed by another order for five monitors and the light battle cruiser HMS *Glorious*. As a result, all work on incomplete non-military contracts was immediately suspended.

And so, throughout the winter of 1914/15 *Olympic* and *Britannic* remained quietly laid up at Belfast, disturbed only by the presence of the maintenance crews and the occasional burst of activity when Admiralty contracts dried up. Nor did there seem to be any immediate prospect of the Transport Division becoming less wary of using larger ships. The reason for this reluctance was quite simply that the performance of the larger ships as armed merchant cruisers during the early months of the war had proved disappointing. Early experience had shown that not only were they expensive to run in terms of both coal and the necessary manpower to serve them, but their sheer size and deep draft created additional problems which had never really been taken into account. If the accidental collision between *Aquitania*, then serving as an armed merchant cruiser, and the Leyland liner *Canadian* only two weeks into the war wasn't evidence enough, the grounding and subsequent total loss of *Oceanic* off the island of Foula on 8th September 1914 was powerful proof that larger ships were both unwieldy and totally unsuitable for operations in shallow or confined coastal waters. Before long both *Aquitania* and *Mauretania* were laid up, while *Lusitania* remained the only giant liner still in commercial service with the Cunard fleet.

It was a terrible waste of resources, and the consequences for the shipping lines were no less serious. With all five of the large Cunard and White Star liners unsuitable for military duty, the Admiralty had no choice but to continue to call up an ever increasing number of the smaller vessels, placing an almost intolerable strain on the carrying capacity of the merchant marine. Furthermore, the economics of their decision were not at all satisfactory, for although it may have been cheaper to convert smaller ships on an individual basis, the cost of fitting-out several smaller vessels as opposed to one big ship which could carry the same capacity, was far greater. The shipping companies and the Admiralty clearly needed to reach a compromise and in May 1915 it seemed as if a solution to the problem had been reached. The original rates under the Cunard agreement had required the Admiralty to pay £46,000 per month for *Mauretania*, and £68,000 per month for *Aquitania*, but on 11th May Cunard agreed to a revision of the rates to 15 shillings per gross ton. On 26th June the figure was revised once again, this time to the almost unbelievable rate of £10,000 per ship per month, although in return for this deal the Admiralty agreed to be responsible for the marine and war risk insurance of the vessels, and to pay for any additional crew and fuel required to maintain speeds in excess of eighteen knots. Surprisingly, however, the Transport Division still hesitated, justifying their reservations to the First Sea Lord:

> "The number of suitable ships available and rapidity of preparing, so many ships having been taken, it is impossible to procure more ships without seriously interfering with the other services such as the food and munition supply; except by taking the large ships now laid up like the *Olympic* and *Aquitania*. These ships will accommodate large numbers – between 5,000 and 6,000 men each – but the risk of loss from submarine attack, owing to their great size and impossibility of taking them into closed harbours, is only justifiable if the emergency warrants it being taken."

Unfortunately for the Transport Division, the situation was just about as serious as it could get. In January 1915 the Russians had requested help from Britain and France to relieve the Turkish pressure in the Caucasus. The initial Allied response had been to attempt to force a passage through the Dardanelles, in the hope that a naval contingent could break through to the Black Sea and threaten Constantinople, but the operation proved to be disastrous, resulting in the loss of three battleships. After such a costly failure ground forces were then given the task of securing the Gallipoli peninsula, and at 4.25 a.m. on Sunday 25th April 1915 the first Allied troops began landing at Anzac Cove.

The operation was a foretaste of what was to come, and before long the Allies, although safely ashore, were effectively contained in several bridgeheads with over 2,000 casualties on the first day alone. With their troops pinned down on the beaches and none of the objectives taken, the idea of withdrawal was considered by the commanders of the ground forces. But once General Sir Ian Hamilton, the

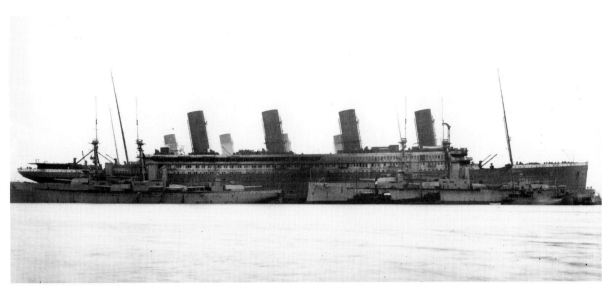

*During the winter of 1914/15, Britannic, with only one gantry davit and lifeboat fitted, lies empty at Harland and Wolff. In the distance can be seen the funnels of the S.S. Olympic, while in the foreground are the steamships Michigan and City of Oxford, disguised as the battleships HMS Collingwood and HMS St. Vincent.*

Ulster Folk & Transport Museum

Expeditionary Force commander, had rejected the suggestion, the scene was set for a renewal of the same system of trench warfare that had resulted in stalemate on the Western Front. The Allies may have got ashore, but they weren't going anywhere.

The escalation of activity in the eastern Mediterranean was the nucleus of the Transport Division's problem. The smaller ships already in service simply couldn't handle the overwhelming requests for men and supplies, and in order to ease the transport crisis *Mauretania* was finally requisitioned to serve as a troop ship in June, with *Aquitania* joining her on the Dardanelles run the following month.

Had *Lusitania* not been lost to a German torpedo on 7th May there is every chance that all three of the giant Cunard liners would have been in military service, so it is not surprising that the Admiralty was suddenly turning its attention to Belfast. Discreet enquiries regarding *Olympic*'s speed, capacity and endurance began arriving at White Star's Liverpool office in James Street as early as 19th June, although the lack of a suitable tide to transfer *Olympic* into the Thompson dock in time would result in the plan being shelved. The inactivity of such a valuable resource was not destined to continue for much longer, however, and on 1st September 1915 the Transport Division finally bowed to the inevitable, and *Olympic* was requisitioned for military service as a troop ship. Ten days later she was transferred to Liverpool, and two weeks after that *Olympic* sailed under the command of Captain Bertram Hayes for the Allied forward base at Mudros, on the Greek island of Lemnos.

Of the four remaining giant liners only *Britannic* now remained on the sidelines, and by the late autumn even Harland and Wolff, previously inundated with Admiralty orders, suddenly found the pace slackening to such an extent that a limited amount of work could recommence on the few remaining civilian projects. Yet even now the situation in the Mediterranean remained critical. Aside from the risk to life and limb from bullets and artillery shells, the medical facilities at Gallipoli were totally inadequate, hampered by the additional problem of fleas and lice. By the end of July some 200 sick were being evacuated every day. As the casualty list continued to expand, after barely two months in service *Aquitania* was converted from trooping duties to a hospital ship, with *Mauretania* following suit in September. It was only a matter of time before the increasing numbers of casualties overwhelmed even these two giants, and by November the Transport Department were once again being forced to think the unthinkable.

The big question, however, was just how ready was *Britannic* for military service? Having lain incomplete for over fifteen months, the maintenance crews had done little more than keep a close eye on the ship's machinery and other vital systems. It had still been possible to carry out some work on the fitting-out during the occasional pause in Admiralty orders, and enough work had been completed on the ship's engines by May 1915 for them to undergo their mooring trials, but little more than that. Although some work had been carried out on the interiors it would still be many months before Harland and Wolff would be in a position to hand over the completed ship. The fact remained, however, that with her engines and vital systems operational, Harland and Wolff was confident that *Britannic* could be made seaworthy in approximately four weeks should the Admiralty decide to give the ship priority. That was all the Transport Division needed to hear and on 13th November 1915 *Britannic* was finally called up for service as a military hospital ship.

After months of enforced idleness, *Britannic* was suddenly a hive of activity. The yard workers hastened to remove as many of the customary peacetime fixtures and fittings as possible, and only then could the task of turning the vessel into a hospital ship proceed. The task was by no means as simple as fitting out a trooper. Aside from the obvious areas required for wards, segregated space also had to be found for the hundreds of orderlies, doctors and nurses who would provide the essential medical services while on board. Not surprisingly, the doctors and nurses would be allocated to many of the stately first-class cabins on A and B decks, but the barrack rooms for the medical orderlies would not be quite so extravagant.

Unfortunately no detailed plans exist to give a truly detailed picture of the way in which *Britannic*'s wards were laid out. We do know that the isolation wards were located aft on C deck, probably in the area of the original ship's hospital, and that the first-class dining saloon was fully panelled and allocated as the patients' dining room. Beyond that we can only speculate. Nevertheless, even in wartime there was still space for those essential luxuries, such as an officer's smoke room aft on B deck and a gymnasium, while the five lifts which had already been installed would vastly simplify the task of getting any seriously wounded men up to the boat deck in an emergency.

Externally the ship also required to be significantly modified. After fifteen months at Belfast, *Britannic*'s dull grey hull had taken on a decidedly shabby look, and while the paint crews set about transforming the ship's drab exterior into a sparkling white hospital ship, work was also taken in hand to compensate for the fact that only five of *Britannic*'s eight planned sets of gantry davits had been installed. As a temporary solution, two lines of conventional Welin davits were fitted along the boat deck; six on either side, with each set of davits serving one wooden and one collapsible lifeboat. Two similar davits were also positioned on the aft shade deck, serving a similar number of boats so that the ship's revised lifeboat capacity would consist of a total of forty-one wooden boats and fourteen collapsibles. These figures were further supplemented by numerous stacks of Carley Floats positioned at strategic points around the boat deck, each capable of supporting twenty-five men.

As November drew to a close, *Britannic* was finally beginning to look like a proper ship. The new coat of white paint on the hull had transformed the lifeless dirty hulk into a rather sleek looking vessel that few could fail to admire, while a broad green band was painted along the full length of the hull at the level of the saloon deck, broken by three large red crosses. To complete the colourful effect, the four funnels and gantry davits sported the customary yellow paint distinctive of all British hospital ships, so that by day there could be no doubt that the ship was clearly a non combatant. So that no mistake could be made during the hours of darkness, a line of green glass-fronted boxes, each illuminated by electric lights, was suspended beneath the promenade deck from the forward end of the superstructure to the aft end of the shade deck. Finally, two electrically illuminated red crosses were placed on the outer bulkheads on either side of the boat deck.

While the work was proceeding at Belfast, back in Liverpool Harold Sanderson was more concerned with the terms under which *Britannic* would be chartered. The terms agreed for the use of *Olympic* had hardly been ideal and, as if to add insult to injury, no one at the Transport Office had thought to inform him until the deal was done that *Olympic*'s insurance value would be calculated on an annual depreciation value of 5%, rather than White Star's own figure based on a 4% annual depreciation. Much to his annoyance, Sanderson felt that they had no option but to insure the outstanding £76,279 difference between the two totals on the insurance market themselves and, bearing in mind the new nature of the ship's employment, it would be fair to assume that the premium was by no means a small one.

*Britannic*, however, provided less of an obstacle. Because the ship was coming straight from the shipyard there could be no

*Britannic as she appeared when finally completed. Beneath the bridge windows you can clearly see the ship's identification number – G618.*

Ulster Folk & Transport Museum

question of any depreciated value from an insurer's point of view. Furthermore, the Admiralty was now assuming responsibility for all of the insurance costs, without deduction from the rate of hire, for all vessels pressed into in government service. This would provide a sizeable saving to White Star.

But it wasn't all good news. When *Olympic* was called up for service Sanderson had written to the Director of Transports at the Admiralty in an attempt to have Captain Herbert Haddock reassigned to his old command. Haddock's usefulness, however, was already well known to the Admiralty, and his heroic attempt to tow HMS *Audacious* to safety had resulted in his subsequent appointment to supervise the ghost fleet. In that this "fleet" was conceived and supported by none other than Winston Churchill, then First Lord of the Admiralty, there was little chance of Haddock being released from Belfast and, not surprisingly the request was refused. Seven weeks later the situation was little changed, but, ever the optimist, on 22nd October Sanderson wrote to the Director of Transports once again:

> "The question for a commander of this ship is under consideration, and having regard to her importance it is essential that we put her in charge of the very best man in our employ. Am I to assume that the information given to me at the time a Commander for the *Olympic* was under consideration to the effect that Captain Haddock was not available still applies? as I should be very glad to know that Captain Haddock's services could be placed at our disposal, in which case we would give him command of the *Britannic*."

For almost two weeks the vexing question of whether or not Captain Haddock could be released from his post in Belfast was shuffled back and forth through the corridors of power, but eventually Sanderson was, once again, to be thwarted. On 2nd November, an abrupt twenty-seven word response finally arrived back at James Street:

> "With reference to your enquiry as to whether Commodore Haddock is available for the command of the *Britannic*; I have now ascertained that he is not available."

Sanderson now had to find a suitable alternative, and with so few commanders experienced with such a large ship, it was not a very long list. Taking this into account there really could be only one man - Captain Charles Bartlett.

Bartlett's track record with the White Star Line was a long one. After serving his apprenticeship in sailing ships, in 1888 he had joined the British India Company, with which he would remain for six years. After gaining his master's certificate in 1893, he joined the White Star Line the following year and after spending four years aboard *Doric* and *Gothic* on the company's Australian service, he transferred to the North Atlantic mail run, where the promise and opportunities for promotion were that much greater. After serving aboard *Georgic*, *Teutonic*, *Celtic* and *Oceanic*, he took his first command in October 1903, aboard the Leyland liner *Armenian*, which had been temporarily transferred to the White Star Line.

*Captain Charles Alfred Bartlett was actually the White Star Line's second choice to take command of the Britannic. Having served as the company's Marine Superintendent since January 1912, throughout 1915 he had been engaged in patrolling duties in the North Sea aboard the armed naval yacht HMY Verona.*

Courtesy Alasdair Fairbairn

Other commands followed in quick succession, including *Germanic*, *Victorian* and *Canopic*, but it would not be until 1906, when he assumed command of the 7,669 ton *Gothic*, that he would encounter his first serious challenge as a skipper. On 3rd June 1906, whilst approaching the Bay of Biscay and inbound for London from New Zealand, a fire had broken out in one of the cargo holds. The flames had been quickly extinguished but unfortunately this was only a precursor to what would follow, and when another fire broke out three days later the conflagration would threaten to destroy the ship. Fortunately the situation was kept under control long enough for *Gothic* to reach Plymouth the following morning, and by the time the flames had been extinguished the ship's saloon and staterooms had been gutted. It would be another eight months before *Gothic* was fit to put to sea again. Meanwhile, within a month Bartlett had been appointed as captain on *Republic*, before going on to command *Cymric*, *Romanic* and *Cedric*.

In January 1912 he had come ashore to accept the post of White Star Marine Superintendent. This senior position meant that he would be intimately involved with the final stages of *Titanic*'s fitting out and the subsequent redesigning of *Olympic* and *Britannic*. Although he had been allocated to patrolling duties in the North Sea aboard the armed yacht HMS *Verona* following the outbreak of war, his detailed knowledge of *Britannic* gained from his time at Liverpool and Belfast was probably a key factor which Sanderson took into account before choosing him to command Britain's largest ship.

While negotiations regarding a suitable captain continued, work at Belfast progressed quickly. On 2nd December Harland and Wolff advised White Star that *Britannic* would be ready for delivery on Tuesday 7th December, at which time the government would become responsible for the ship's insurance immediately she left port to go on her trials. Leaving nothing to chance, and in accordance with Article 2 of the Convention for the Adaptation to Maritime War of the Principles of the Geneva Convention, on 6th December the British authorities officially informed the German Government through neutral American diplomatic channels in Holland of

*Britannic*'s protected status as a non-combatant hospital ship. Two days later, after a twenty-five day refit costing some £90,000, the metamorphosis was complete. On 8th December Colonel Concanon entered the name of His Majesty's Hospital Ship *Britannic* on the Liverpool register, just as the ship was steaming into Belfast Lough to undergo a day of engine trials. With Captain Bartlett still on his way back from Aberdeen, *Britannic* was temporarily placed under the command of Captain Joseph Ranson, and while the trials may have gone unnoticed in the national press, for Richard Lee, one of the apprentices at Harland and Wolff, the great day was one that he would have more reason to remember than most:

> "It must have been the winter of 1915 that I got orders to be "pupil in charge" of the tug *Herculaneum* at Queen's Island to attend the steam trials of *Britannic*. I was then eighteen years of age. I immediately sought and found the White Star house flag to fly at the tug's main masthead, took it home and lay awake most of the night waiting for the dawn of the wonderful day. About 8:30 a.m. I got aboard the tug where the hard-bitten Liverpool skipper eyed me suspiciously. In a short time the five tugs started to move the gleaming white hull of *Britannic* with her buff funnels, green hull band and red crosses. I loved her and her new colours suited her; she had far better proportions and balance than the *Olympic* or *Titanic*, and from any angle she was aristocratic!"

As the day wore on, however, Lee's pride in the vessel was to be sorely tested and as the ship disappeared over the horizon beyond Carrickfergus, he had little idea of the ordeal that he would later face.

The first indication that something was wrong came when the *Herculaneum* arrived off Bangor at 5.30 p.m. The light was already fading and the sea conditions were far from ideal, so when a light fog began to rise he decided to signal the Morse station at Orlock Head to find out if they had any news of *Britannic*'s whereabouts. Far from providing any reassurance, the only information they could impart was that the ship had last been seen heading towards Liverpool. Sensing an early finish the tug skipper urged the inexperienced youngster to order the return to Belfast. Not one to be pressured, Lee stood his ground, but by 7.30 p.m. he was beginning to have serious doubts. With the fog thickening and the tug skipper complaining that no captain would take a ship the size of *Britannic* into the Lough at night in fog like that, Lee asked to be put ashore at Bangor in order to phone Harland and Wolff for instructions. The tug's skipper would not oblige, and in contrast to his excitement of the previous evening, Lee was now beginning to wish that he had never heard of *Britannic*, when:

> "Just then the deep pulsations of the three chime whistles of a big ship came over our heads as the tug skipper snapped the telegraph to "Full Astern," and through the fog appeared two huge white cliffs over our masthead – the *Britannic*!
>
> In a short time we made fast to her starboard side and a long shipyard ladder was let down from a service door, up which I clambered with my dispatches, the ladder gyrating and heaving to the dance of the tug.

Having delivered the dispatches to the commander, I made my way to the
engine room doors to collect a crowd of engine room officers with whom I
was to return to Belfast. I looked into a cathedral of steel; pink-tinted arc
lights softly lit the two gigantic reciprocating engines' (the largest ever
made) polished steel, brass and copper work and through it all the weird
soft wails of the feed pumps, puffing auxiliaries and sitting on the cylinder
tops and the steel stanchion rails some sixty E.R.A.s in brown boiler suits
singing, *We Are Here Because We Are Here*. Never shall I forget that scene of
power and beauty in the heart of a lovely vessel.

Within an hour we had cast off the tug and a few revolutions of the
*Britannic*'s starboard propeller sent us aswirl like a cork in a mill race."

Neither White Star nor Harland and Wolff ever published any details of *Britannic*'s
engine trials, but it seems clear that if there were any problems then they were only
minor. That same evening the ship returned to Belfast, but only for a few days. By
the evening of 11th December the work was complete and, once night had fallen,
*Britannic* finally departed for Liverpool where Captain Ranson would safely deliver
the ship the following morning. On 12th December, while lying in the Gladstone
Dock, *Britannic* was officially commissioned as a hospital ship.

As the task of taking on the medical fittings continued, *Britannic*'s own medical
officer, Dr. John Beaumont, could only sit back and look on approvingly as, one by
one, the latest and most up to date medical apparatus was put in place. As a long-
serving medical man, Beaumont would never feel particularly enthusiastic about the
military red tape and officialdom that came with working on a military hospital
ship, but by the time the 3,310 hospital cots had been installed he had no doubt that
*Britannic* was, quite simply: "the most wonderful hospital ship that ever sailed the
seas."

Everything was now in place except for the captain, and on 14th December even
that deficiency was resolved when Captain Bartlett finally arrived in Liverpool to
take command. As if to complete the family reunion, on 21st December *Olympic* also
arrived back at Liverpool, fresh from her second trooping run to the Aegean. Three-
and-a-half years after the *Titanic* disaster, the White Star Line finally had their two
greatest liners in service together, but the nature of the service in which they now
found themselves employed was a far cry from that envisaged for the original trio.
Nevertheless, with the two remaining White Star sisters now committed to the war
effort, perhaps the company could finally relegate the *Titanic* disaster to the pages of
history once and for all.

— PROGRAMME OF CONCERT —

Held on Board

HOSPITAL SHIP "BRITANNIC,"

MONDAY EVENING, DECEMBER 27th, 1915,

Under the Patronage of

Captain C, A. BARTLETT and Lieut.-Col. H. S. ANDERSON

— PROGRAMME —

| | |
|---|---|
| Song, "Show me the way to your heart" ... | Private Dixon |
| Musical Monologue, "Spotty" ... | Rev. T. W. Hancox, C.F. |
| Monologue, "The Groom's Story" ... | Capt. J. S. Morrow |
| Song, "The Sunshine of your Smile" ... | Sister Mason |
| Song, "Sincerity" ... ... ... .. | Private Lever |
| Miscellaneous Selection ... ... ... | Private Grates |
| Reminiscenses ... ... | Prof. W. St. C. Symmers |
| Song, "Till the Boys come Home" ... ... | Sister Brown |
| Song, Selected ... ... ... ... | Lieut Anderson |
| Song, "Juanita" ... ... | Sisters Henworthy and Elliot |
| Song, "The Home of the Hun" ... | Rev. W. Harrod, C.F. |
| Song, "Sweet be your Dreams" ... .. | Private Dixon |
| Musical Monologue, "The Caretaker" | Rev. T. W. Hancox, C.F. |
| Song, "When Irish Eyes are Smiling" ... | Sister Lincoln |
| Song, "The Tulip and the Rose" ... ... | Private Grates |
| Song, "In Sweet Content" ... ... ... | Private Lever |

GOD SAVE THE KING.

Accompanist  -  Lieut. T. Heywood

M.C.  -  Sergt.-Major Debney

# CHAPTER THREE

# THE MAIDEN VOYAGE

The chilly morning of 22nd December 1915 found the *Britannic*, by now officially designated as hospital ship G618, still lying in the Gladstone Dock. However, while everything may have seemed outwardly calm to an untrained observer, within the ship it was a hive of activity. Up until now *Britannic* had been an empty shell but as the last of the medical staff finally began to arrive on board that morning, at long last the ship was coming to life.

Among their number was forty-year-old Lieutenant Harold Goodman, who had held his commission in the Royal Army Medical Corps for barely a week. Even so, there was no doubting his experience. Having begun his medical training at the age of seventeen at St. Bartholomew's Hospital in London, he had moved to Barnsley in 1899 to take up a position at Beckett's Hospital, before taking over a medical practice in Hemsworth, just outside of the Frickley colliery. As the war followed its inevitable course he felt increasingly obliged to do his bit and within days of volunteering for the RAMC he was informed that his first posting would be to the largest hospital ship in commission. After spending his last night ashore in the L.N.W.R. Hotel, the following morning he took a taxi to the Gladstone Dock where, upon seeing the *Britannic* for the first time, he may well have thought himself particularly lucky to have escaped from the horror of the trenches.

As the chaotic arrangements continued, the new arrivals prepared themselves for departure. But when the ship finally pulled away from the dock at 11.00 a.m., it was only to proceed a few hundred yards out into the Mersey before immediately dropping anchor once again. The mystery was quickly solved when the news began to circulate that two hundred RAMC medical orderlies had still not arrived from Aldershot, and until they were on board the *Britannic* was not going anywhere. Not being one to waste time, as soon as Goodman had settled into cabin 51, a two-berth state room which he shared with Lieutenant Anderson from Glasgow, he decided to try his luck at finding his way around the ship which, he later wrote, was "colossal." As the afternoon wore on it became increasingly apparent that there would be no early get away, and it was only at midnight that the last of the missing men were accounted for. Twenty minutes later, *Britannic* finally headed west into the Irish Sea.

*Left: A concert programme from 27th December 1915. Although these concerts were not held on a regular basis, there was usually no shortage of theatrical talent on board. Nurses Vera Brittain and Winifred Greenwood each referred to music and dancing on board in their diaries, and Ada Garland took part in an impromptu concert in November 1916, raising £5.17.4 for the Edith Cavell Fund.*
*Unfortunately Britannic was lost three days later, so there's no record of what happened to the takings.*

*Courtesy Dr. Llewellyn Lloyd*

But where exactly was the ship going? Even now its course still remained a closely guarded secret known only to a privileged few, and inevitably rumours abounded about its ultimate destination. For some reason Australia proved to be a particular favourite in the on-board sweepstake, though Dr. Goodman was not convinced, referring to the idea in his diary as "all bunkum!" It wasn't until the following day that Colonel

Henry Anderson, the senior medical officer, gave the first indication of their route and even then he was not very specific. He merely hinted that they would only have to treat the wounded for six days before the ship would be back in England. With this information it was not difficult to work out that the destination was somewhere in the Mediterranean.

Wherever they were going, there was still very little activity on board. Goodman, having already taken the opportunity to have a look around much of the vessel, welcomed the distraction when at 10:30 a.m on the first day the doctors were paraded and allocated to their respective wards. Goodman's particular assignment, along with doctors Anderson, Pender and Bachelor, were the 426 beds of F, L, M, N and V wards, located forward on the starboard side of F and G decks. These wards consisted mostly of two tier cots, though their location was something of a mixed blessing. Situated as they were, reasonably close to the forward elevators simplified matters for embarkation and disembarkation of patients, but the combination of their location in the bowels of the ship, along with a leaking porthole and a faulty back pressure valve in the ship's tank, meant that two of the lower wards were already partially flooded. The problem might have been more manageable were it not for the fact that *Britannic* was presently pursuing a southerly course through the Bay of Biscay in the face of a strong south westerly half gale. With many of the RAMC orderlies laid low, the medical staff were hard pressed to create any order. The monotony was briefly interrupted at 5.00 p.m. when those who were not already immunised were given their obligatory cholera vaccination.

*Doctor Harold Goodman. At thirty-nine years of age, Goodman had only been in the RAMC for one week when he was appointed to the Britannic, the largest hospital ship in the world.*

Courtesy Ronald Goodman

Christmas Eve offered little respite. The continuing heavy weather kept the dining room tables thinly attended, and even the morning parade which would become a routine resulted in little more information from Colonel Anderson, save for a simple instruction to "carry on." Nevertheless, at least matters were now beginning to take shape. At midday the medical staff were treated to Professor Squires' tantalising lecture on the virtues of urea as an antiseptic, and a little later the ship's first daily run was published. *Britannic* had travelled 426 nautical miles in the previous twenty-four hours and with Cape Finisterre fast approaching it was obvious that the she was headed for Gibraltar. It would be another thirty-six hours before the ship would pass "the Rock," but the Atlantic still had one last parting gift before *Britannic* entered the Mediterranean. During the night the ship rolled so heavily that one of the tables in Goodman's cabin was overturned.

After a moderately restless night, Christmas Day dawned and, following breakfast, the dining saloon was dressed with holly and mistletoe. The Christmas service provided a brief respite from the war, but immediately afterwards it was back to reality as Colonel Anderson took the opportunity to inform the assembled medical staff of their embarkation duties. At 2.00 p.m. the first real excitement of the voyage was experienced when several tramp vessels appeared on the horizon. They were the first vessels to have been sighted since leaving Liverpool and with the ship's second published daily run totalling 443 miles it was comforting that *Britannic*'s engines were performing well.

Gibraltar was finally passed at 1.30 a.m. on Boxing Day, although few of the medical staff felt inclined to stay up to see it. By 10.00 a.m. the next morning the ship was well into the Mediterranean and, to everyone's relief, the sea conditions radically improved. At long last the RAMC landlubbers were beginning to find their sea legs, and with the situation so much better Captain Bartlett decided that the time had come to hold the ship's first lifeboat drill. As *Britannic*

**Harold Goodman's cabin on board ship. The bed is a standard White Star first-class pattern.**

*Courtesy Ronald Goodman*

would soon be entering the most hazardous part of the Mediterranean, it would not be a moment too soon.

As *Britannic* headed east so the weather continued to improve. The ship's twenty-four hour run of 416 miles on 27th December proved somewhat disappointing, especially as the previous day's run of 455 miles had been her best achievement since the voyage had begun. An evening concert in the RAMC mess provided a timely interlude, and with the first port of call now less than twenty-four hours away the routine was at last set to change.

At 8.30 a.m. on 28th December *Britannic* finally entered the Bay of Naples. Despite the haze, up on deck Goodman was taking the air and staring at the island of Capri as it passed to starboard. The war still seemed a million miles away to him at that moment, and for the time being he could still reflect on the island's colourful history. He mused upon how the Roman emperor Tiberius had lived much of his life there in the Villa of Jupiter, often amusing himself with the playful habit of dropping his victims over the cliffs to feed the lobsters. No sooner had the ship dropped anchor within the harbour, than passes were being issued for the medical staff to go ashore. On this occasion Goodman was not to be one of the lucky few and instead he remained on board observing the ceaseless hubbub of the coaling lighters which arrived alongside throughout the day.

After instructing the orderlies assigned to his wards, which were becoming more organised by the hour, Goodman was finally able to go ashore himself the following morning. As soon as the ship's motor launch dropped him and three colleagues at the Arsenal step they made to the nearest Thomas Cook bureau to obtain some local currency. Wartime restrictions on the export of gold bullion resulted in an exchange rate which came as a rather unpleasant shock. Naples, however, did not disappoint. A ride in the Bertholmi lift brought them to an hotel which provided a particularly enjoyable lunch followed by a leisurely drive back to the harbour where the launch was waiting to return them to the ship. With Vesuvius providing a spectacular backdrop, shortly before 4.00 p.m. *Britannic* weighed anchor and was once again outward bound, now on the final leg of her journey which was to be to Mudros.

*Lieutenant Colonel Henry Stewart Anderson. The son of a Belfast clergyman, Anderson originally embarked on a business career before his inability to save a man from bleeding to death drove him pursue another course. After qualifying as a doctor in 1898, Anderson immediately joined the RAMC and served in South Africa, India and Malta. Following the outbreak of war he served in France with the 1st Battalion of the North Staffordshire regiment, before being invalided home in 1915. In November 1915 he was appointed as Britannic's senior medical officer, a position he would retain for the next year.*

Courtesy Angus Mitchell

For the next twenty-fours, however, the views were spectacular, with the glowing crater of the volcano Stromboli to starboard at 5.00 a.m. the following morning looking particularly dramatic, and the Sicilian volcano Mount Etna also in sight two hours later. As *Britannic* passed between the toe of Italy and the island of Sicily, the visible ruins of the Messina earthquake might even have provided

*Just as Britannic was approaching the outer boom guarding the entrance to Mudros Harbour at 3.50 p.m., Harold Goodman took this snapshot of the monitor HMS Humber, which was about to tie up to the S.S. Strathblane before being towed on a three-day voyage to Alexandria.*

*Courtesy Ronald Goodman*

a few memories for Colonel Anderson who, in January 1909 had arrived there from Malta to assist with the British Army earthquake relief party.

With Scylla and Charibdis now astern, *Britannic* set an easterly heading as the full power of the engines could be felt for the first time. Up to that point an average speed of eighteen knots had been enough to negotiate the less hazardous western Mediterranean and conserve on-board coal supplies. But the approaching waters were fraught with new dangers. The ship was now passing through the Gulf of Taranto, and Captain Bartlett would have been aware of the increased threat posed by the German and Austrian submarines operating from bases in the southern Adriatic. With the engines now at full speed, even the medical staff were aware of the different sensation throughout the vessel.

Nor was the new year set to continue as the old one was ending. December 31st brought with it the first proper orderly duty as the medical staff made their final preparations for the arrival at Lemnos. The nurses busily made up the last of the cots, and Dr. Goodman found himself allocated to the middle watch, from 8.00 a.m. to 12.00 midday and from 8.00 p.m. to 12.00 midnight. With the impending arrival at Mudros Colonel Anderson and *Britannic*'s assistant commander, Captain Harry Dyke, started to make their first official rounds of the wards – a process which usually involved two hours of almost continuous walking.

For much of the morning the Greek coast remained clearly visible on the port side, and by 2.00 p.m. *Britannic* was passing Hagios Sprata island on the final approaches to the island of Lemnos. As the boom across the Bay of Mudros was opened to allow the monitor, *HMS Humber,* to leave, *Britannic* slipped into the bay, and at 3.35 p.m. and finally dropped anchor in thirteen fathoms of water close to the hospital ships *Dunluce Castle, Grantully Castle, Egypt, Gloucester Castle* and *Assegai*.

With the ship secured, Captain Bartlett and Colonel Anderson took one of its motor launches ashore to report to the senior transport officer and receive their instructions. With the senior personnel ashore, few expected any significant activity until they returned, so the medical staff were more than a little surprised when, at 7.00 p.m., hospital ships *Assegai* and *Egypt* suddenly arrived alongside and began discharging their patients. Dr. Goodman later recorded the procedure in particular detail:

> "The contrast in size of ships was extraordinary as their funnels only came up to our boat deck and seemed like lighters alongside. They discharged onto D deck by gangways from their boat decks which were about level. Very busy (and no dinner) until 11 p.m. Got our V ward (94) beds full and several in L and M and ten in F ward. All these latter stretcher cases, the others walked and were helped on. Whole thing apparently not arranged for and certainly should have been left until morning. Colonel Anderson and captain, I believe, both on shore and therefore this arrangement probably not in accordance with their ideas but we shall know tomorrow."

By ten o'clock the patients were settled in their wards and, after a drink of chicken broth or cocoa, the lights were turned out for the evening. It would still be more than four hours before Goodman was able to climb between the sheets himself. With the New Year about to dawn the urge to stay up and see it in had proved irresistible. When eight bells rang, across the bay hundreds of vessels sounded their whistles and hooters in a cacophony which seemed to go on for an

*A contemporary naval chart for the entrance to the Bay of Mudros, the strongly fortified Allied base in the eastern Mediterranean.*

*Hydrographic Office*

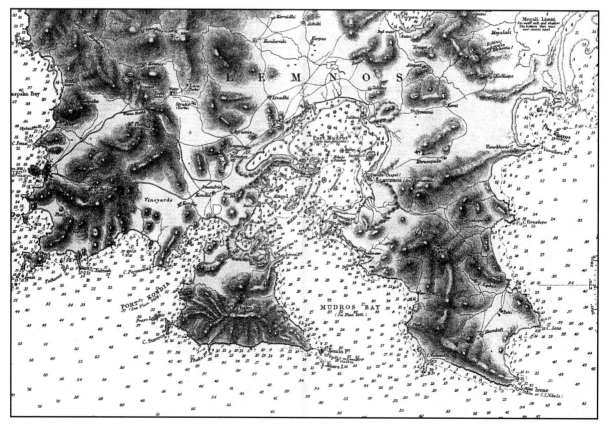

*One of the military hospitals at Mudros. The island was the main Mediterranean hub for transferring wounded from theatres of war as distant as India and South Africa.*

eternity. For a few hours the realities of the war may have been forgotten, but Dr. Goodman's final entry in his diary for 1915, hoping that the New Year would end differently, was a sentiment close to everyone's heart.

Unfortunately Goodman's diary does not make any reference to Colonel Anderson's reaction to the evening's makeshift arrangements, except to say that the transfer of invalids from *Assegai* and *Egypt* continued throughout the next day. Among the new arrivals from Cairo on *Dunluce Castle* was Private Robert Atkinson of the Essex Regiment. Atkinson was being repatriated to England after having contracted pleurisy at Suvla Bay and his first reaction at touring *Britannic* was not uncommon among the vast majority of those catching sight of the ship for the first time. He particularly remembered the covered top deck, which reminded him of Crystal Palace. More importantly, his first dinner on board had been a particularly good one, but unfortunately his positive first impressions were not set to continue. As the days passed the decreasing quality and quantity of the food would give way to considerable frustration. At one stage his rations were nothing more for breakfast than two slices of bread, while the lunch time stew was so thin that at first he mistook it for soup. The evening ration of cocoa and hard biscuits provided little relief and the continuing decline in the standard of the meals during the voyage home would result in a number of arguments between some of the patients and the stewards.

Private Walter Goodwin, who had also arrived on board via *Dunluce Castle*, would remember the voyage somewhat differently. His recollection that the trip on this splendid new vessel would be very smooth and he also took great delight in writing home that he was travelling on the maiden voyage of *Titanic*'s sister ship.

Meanwhile, the transfer of patients continued. January 2nd found the hospital ships *Asturias* and *Killman Castle* alongside, in addition to another thousand patients being transferred from the hospitals on shore. By 5.30 p.m. the hospital ship *Abdermain* was also along the port side and later that evening the day's activities were concluded by the arrival of a number of wounded officers who had been towed out from the shore on a barge. The last stage of the journey for some of these patients, however, was not a comfortable one, as a number of the immobile stretcher cases had to contend with the outlet from the ship's condensers which periodically douched them with water.

By now *Britannic*'s wards were almost full to overflowing, although the embarkation of the remaining sick and wounded was to be delayed by the ship's own motor launch. As some remaining officers were being taken aboard the engine broke down and the small boat began to drift astern, to be warped back to the ship with a rope attached to a life buoy thrown from the poop. Dr. Goodman remembered this incident in a particularly light hearted manner, describing the launch as performing "her usual antics", so it may be that the motor launches' engines were not very reliable. In spite of these problems, by three o'clock the last of the patients were embarked and the errant motor launch had been retrieved. With no further business pending, apart from landing the body of Private Arthur Howe who had died from tubercular disease the previous day, *Britannic* raised anchor and immediately made for home. Within six hours Mudros was one hundred and twenty miles astern, as *Britannic* headed in a southwesterly direction at full speed for the Kea Channel.

The return voyage was markedly different to the outward leg. In place of the empty wards *Britannic* was now home to an additional 3,300 invalids, all needing constant medical attention. Even so, many of the them were ambulent, and aside from changing existing medical dressings and monitoring their diets, treatment was reasonably straightforward. Those who were considered sufficiently mobile were often assigned to particular wards as stretcher-bearers in the event of emergency. Bearing this in mind, Captain Bartlett wasted no time in holding an immediate boat drill that first morning, and at 11.30 a.m. the general alarm was sounded as all of the watertight doors were closed and the medical staff and patients were stood to their posts.

As *Britannic* headed west, so her progress improved, with successive daily runs of 430, 497 and 496 miles. In spite of the strong winds all seemed to be going smoothly when, having skirted the southern coast of Malta and with the coast of Tunisia in sight, the onboard routine was dramatically interrupted by a call of "man overboard!"

Contrary to peacetime procedures, stopping the vessel to go back and search for the victim was not an option for Captain Bartlett. The Mediterranean was hazardous enough, but to expose his ship to the prospect of a submarine attack whilst carrying out a search at reduced speed would have been extremely foolhardy. The only option available to him was to maintain his course and speed, and carry out an extensive search of the ship to ascertain who the unfortunate individual was. While doctors checked their wards to account for everyone, the crew searched the ship from stem to stern and by the end of the morning it was discovered that a naval rating named Samuel Jones was indeed missing. In accordance with established military procedures, at 3.00 p.m. a formal court of inquiry was held on board to ascertain how and why Jones had gone overboard, but with no significant evidence pointing to either accident or suicide the verdict remained open the ship's log simply recorded: "It is reasonable to assume that he is dead."

There was, however, one positive result from the search. Three other patients reported missing from their wards the night before were located, playing cards in one of the bathrooms. The ship's log makes no mention of any action taken against the miscreants, but it's safe to assume that they were less than popular with the medical staff once they were returned to their wards.

Gibraltar was passed at 10.00 p.m. the following evening and with only 1,630 miles of sea between *Britannic* and Southampton Captain Bartlett used the opportunity to make the only legal wireless transmission which could be sent by a hospital ship. Under normal circumstances hospital ships were not allowed to send radio transmissions, as it could be interpreted as a transgression of its neutral status. The regulation was, nevertheless, relaxed at this point in order to inform the authorities of the number of casualties on board, as well as the total number of patients suffering from dysentery and enteric fever (typhoid). The information was

*On January 9th 1916 Britannic arrived at the White Star Dock in Southampton for the first time.*

of little relevance to the authorities of Gibraltar, but they were able to forward it overland to the relevant departments in England, which would then be able to arrange adequate transport by the time the ship arrived at her home port.

The remainder of the voyage looked set to pass without

*Britannic arriving at the White Star Dock in Southampton for the first time.*

incident. At midday on 7th January the ship's daily run was logged at 506 miles with an average speed for the period exceeding 21 knots for the first time, although her progress was slightly reduced to 478 miles the next day. By now, however, no one was really giving it much attention. In complete contrast to the outward leg, the Bay of Biscay was delightfully smooth and the periodic tobacco issue was of far more importance to the men as they whiled away their last hours on board. By the evening of January 8th the ship was off Ushant, and to emphasise their closeness to home, they passed the *Mauretania* on her way out to Mudros to pick up the next batch of wounded.

With the Isle of Wight almost in sight, January 9th found most of the medical staff enjoying an early breakfast, steeling themselves for a frantic day once the ship arrived in Southampton's White Star Dock. As *Britannic* arrived off the Needles lighthouse, a hydroplane arrived overhead and two minesweepers took station ahead to lead the ship into the buoyed channel, which led into the Solent. From there progress was sporadic and painfully slow, as *Britannic*, now escorted by the two patrol boats, made her way through the mist towards her berth. Southampton Water seemed especially busy and after passing several Belgian vessels *Britannic* finally arrived at the White Star dock which was already occupied by the *Aquitania* and an

Italian hospital ship. It was not until 4.30 p.m. that the six escorting tugs finally secured *Britannic* and the task of disembarking could begin in a process that would continue until shortly before midnight. At 12.30 a.m. Dr. Goodman was finally able to return to his cabin, but any thoughts of a good night's sleep were out of the question because he was still scheduled to be back in his ward at 4.00 a.m., even though the their human cargo had now left the ship,

For now, however, the work was over. *Britannic* had safely completed her maiden voyage and, for the time being at least, she was safe in her home port. The following morning saw little activity on board, save the landing of thousands of used sheets for transfer to shore based laundries. The body of twenty-one-year-old Private Charles Vincent, who had died from tuberculosis early the previous morning was also taken ashore at this time. Under normal circumstances Vincent's body would have been buried at sea, but because he had died with the English coast only hours away Captain Bartlett decided instead to take the body home to Southampton.

After six days of frantic activity *Britannic*'s bustling corridors now seemed eerily quiet. With the wounded and sick now ashore and most of the medical staff granted seven-days leave, the only activity on board was the ship's crew quietly preparing for its next voyage. While many of them may have been wondering just when that voyage might begin, few would have been aware that a sudden change in the military situation in the Mediterranean would mean that, after only one voyage, *Britannic*'s future as a hospital ship was already in doubt.

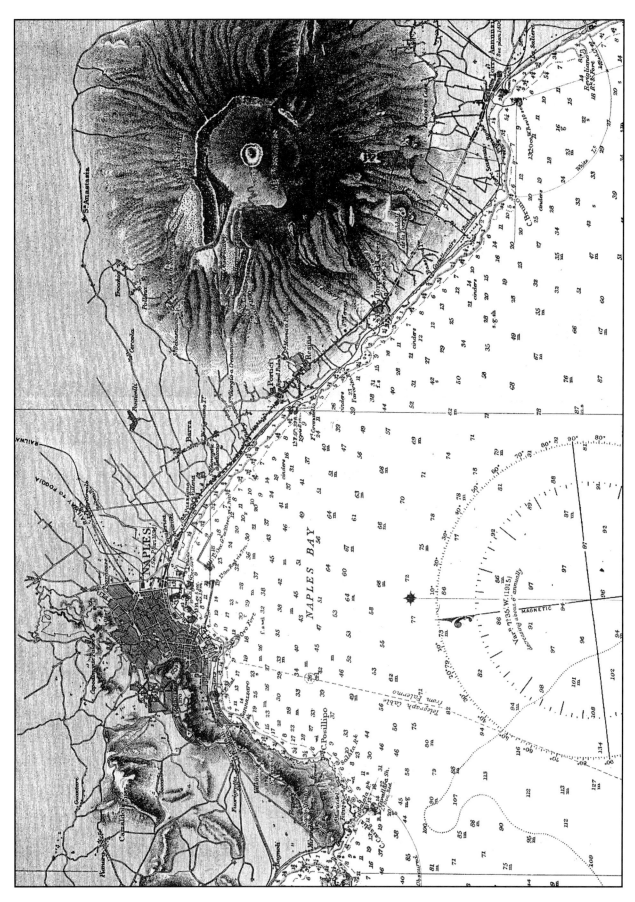

# CHAPTER FOUR

# AN ITALIAN DIVERSION

After a week with his family at Guildford and Hemsworth, Harold Goodman was back on board the *Britannic* by the morning of 16th January, to find the situation less than certain. Almost overnight the nature of the war in the eastern Mediterranean had radically changed and already there were widespread rumours that, after only one voyage, *Britannic* would not be going out again.

For months the Gallipoli campaign had been an open wound in the side of the Allied armies, which had resulted in thousands of deaths for little or no tangible gain. Following a visit to the beleaguered Allied units in November 1915, Lord Kitchener had concluded that a general evacuation was the only realistic option and, after several weeks of further hesitation, the British Government finally relented. The withdrawal was officially authorised on 7th December, although in reality the preparations had already began considerably earlier as the numbers of troops and guns were discreetly reduced.

Compared with the planning which surrounded the offensive itself, the evacuation of the Gallipoli peninsula was faultless in its execution. To maintain absolute security the troops were simply told that any noticeable reductions were in preparation for the winter, while the Turks were lulled into a false sense of security by the apparent normality. Once the official order to withdraw became known on 12th December, troops, stores and guns were gradually withdrawn each night, with the final evacuation of Anzac Cove and Suvla Bay carried out on the night of 18/19th December. So meticulous was the planning that the forward units remained in position right up until the last hours so that the Turks would not realise that an entire army was about to slip through their grasp. By dawn on 20th December the two beachheads had been successfully evacuated, without the cost of a single Allied soldier's life.

The British 29th Division held on at Cape Helles for a further seventeen days, but a similarly well-planned evacuation took place on the night of 8th January 1916, as the last Allied troops left Turkish soil for good. Churchill's obsession with the Dardanelles had proved to be a costly adventure. Of the 410,000 troops committed to the eight-month land campaign, the Allied armies had suffered over 200,000 casualties, of which 43,000 had been killed, but at long last the fighting was over – in this theatre at least.

The stabilised situation in the eastern Mediterranean, however, created an atmosphere of uncertainty aboard *Britannic*. Doubts were partially offset when Colonel Anderson informed the medical staff on 17th January that the order had come from London to carry on as normal, but with both *Aquitania* and *Britannic* lying idle at Southampton it could only be a matter of time before the Transport Division would have to make a

*Left: The naval chart for Naples showing a particularly interesting aspect of the volcano Vesuvius, which dominates the bay.*

Hydrographic Office

53

*The hospital ship Grantully Castle anchored close to Britannic in Naples harbour. In the distance you can see the Maschio Angioino, while at the top of the hill sits the Castel St. Elmo and the monastery of San Martino.*

*Courtesy Ronald Goodman*

decision. By midday on 20th January both ships were once again outward bound, and while each vessel at first assumed a westerly heading, their courses soon diverged. *Britannic* was once again bound for Mudros, while *Aquitania* was destined for Liverpool, and some long overdue engine maintenance.

As *Britannic* headed into the Bay of Biscay, she followed the now established route to Naples, with daily runs of 412 and 452 miles in quick succession. Gibraltar was passed at 2.30 a.m. on the morning of 23rd January before heading into the Mediterranean, where the bright sun provided the medical staff with a welcome change, even though the biting wind still kept most of them inside. By the evening of 24th January *Britannic* was off the southern coast of Sardinia and the crew were making final preparations for their arrival at Naples early the following morning. As anticipated, the ship anchored at 6.30 a.m., but it would be another three hours before the process of bunkering would begin. By 7.00 p.m. exactly 2,510 tons of coal had been taken on board and with fuelling complete, Captain Bartlett informed the authorities that the ship would be ready to depart early the following morning. He expected to arrive at Mudros no more than two days later, but before the day was out his schedule would undergo an unexpected alteration.

The following morning *Britannic* was still at her berth, with curiously little activity evident on board. Instead of leaving as planned, Captain Bartlett had received unexpected orders not to take on coal as usual but to await further instructions. For some unexplained reason the Principal Naval Officer at Cairo had redirected the hospital ship *Grantully Castle* from Mudros to Naples and *Britannic* was now under orders to await her arrival before proceeding as planned. But that order would never come, and with the hospital ships *Panama* and *Formosa* similarly diverted, Naples was to become the major focus of the Mediterranean Allied hospital ship activity, much to the annoyance of the Neapolitan authorities. But this is to anticipate events.

For the moment at least, the medical staff found themselves in the enviable position of being able to enjoy an extended stay in the Italian port, and very soon shore passes were being issued with Dr. Goodman taking full advantage of the leave granted:

> "Passes we got overnight and Urwick, Rentril, Marrow and I went to Cooks, changed money at 30.50 and hired *Fiat* car and guide and went to Pompeii. The roads were dreadful on the way there. We returned about 3.30 and shopped, buying coral and mother of pearl. Returned after tea at a restaurant to ship for dinner at 7 p.m. and then on shore at 8 p.m. Urwick, Saunders and myself walked down Via Roma nearly to museum and back, returning to a café where we met two Americans and then back to the ship at 10.15 in a boat, as our motor boat was *hors de combat*. Weather beautiful but not too clear."

The following day everyone was confined to the ship, although a number of the medical staff were allowed ashore in the evening to attend the opera. Dr. Goodman had chosen to remain on board because of a bad headache and it was only now that he heard the first rumours that there were hospital ships bound to Naples from Alexandria and Mudros.

**The entrance to Naples Harbour as it appeared in early 1916.**

*Courtesy Ronald Goodman*

Even though the atmosphere on board ship was outwardly relaxed, the medical facilities and wards were still maintained in a constant state of readiness. Matters were not made any easier when it was announced that the Duke of Aosta would be coming on board to visit the sick and wounded on 25th January, only for the visit to be cancelled at the last minute because there were no casualties on board at the time. The following day Captain Bartlett was also instructed by the British Consul in Naples to entertain the captain and medical staff of the American cruiser *Des Moines*. Aside from the usual exchange of diplomatic formalities, this visit also provided the British authorities with an opportunity to have *Britannic's* medical facilities inspected by nationals from a neutral country, and Colonel Anderson took the opportunity to suggest that the American ship's medical staff might wish to assist with the transfer of patients.

By now the incoming ships were getting close. On the morning of 27th January *Britannic* was still idle, though Dr. Goodman passed a reasonably productive ninety minutes examining the sterilisers in the ship's laundry, followed by a demonstration of the ship's steering gear in the stern which, it appears, he found fascinating. Clearly the apparatus had made quite an impression upon him, and in his diary he was keen to record that the gear was worked by hydraulic pressure at 230 lbs pressure (glycerine and water in copper pipes), and that the rudder itself weighed over a hundred tons. This brief technical diversion, however, would not last for much longer. During lunch the hospital ship *Grantully Castle* finally arrived and before long was secured to port. Almost immediately the transfer of her cargo of 438 sick and wounded soldiers was underway and three hours later the process was accelerated when the hospital ship *Formosa*, carrying an additional 393 patients was secured on the starboard side.

*The arrival of the hospital ship Essequibo meant that Britannic's extended stay at Naples was all but over. In the distance you can clearly see the Palazzo Reale, which dominates the northern aspect of the harbour.*

Courtesy Ronald Goodman

Today, however, Goodman would not find himself so hard-pressed. For this particular voyage he had been allocated to the port side officer's ward on A deck, and by the time *Grantully Castle* and *Formosa* had discharged their cargo only seven beds

in the warrant officers section had been filled. Clearly the effects of the Gallipoli evacuation were already beginning to tell.

*Grantully Castle* and *Formosa* both departed the following day, and although more ships could be expected at any time, activity around *Britannic* remained subdued for the remainder of the day. With little prospect of further ships arriving in the immediate future, off-duty doctors were once again allowed ashore in groups. Three uneventful days would pass in this way before the next flotilla was due to arrive, though an official visit by Nelson Page, the American ambassador to Italy, and his family provided a small diversion in an otherwise humdrum day. On the evening of 30th January Dr. Goodman and several colleagues were able to go ashore yet again and, in spite of a full house, were even able to obtain seats at the opera for a performance of *Othello*. Unfortunately their box was a little too close to the stage for their liking but the occasion, nevertheless, provided a welcome diversion from the realities of life on a military hospital ship.

Shortly after 9.00 a.m. on Tuesday 1st February the routine was interrupted once again, when the hospital ship *Essequibo* arrived alongside with another 594 patients. By now the system was functioning so well – much more smoothly than had been the case at Mudros – that the evacuation of the smaller ship was completed by 1.35 p.m., and the afternoon was so uneventful that once again Dr. Goodman was permitted to go ashore for yet another evening at the opera. This time he made particularly good use of the time, taking in both *Tosca* and the ballet *Coppelia*.

Just after breakfast the next morning it was the turn of the hospital ship *Nevasa* to come alongside, and by the time the transfer had been made *Britannic* had over nineteen hundred patients on board. The following two days provided a further lull in activity, but on the morning of 4th February the long-awaited *Panama* finally arrived alongside with the remaining 319. By midday the transfer was complete and, after an extended stay in Naples of almost eleven days, at 3.15 p.m. *Britannic* finally weighed anchor and set a course for home with 2,237 sick and wounded on board; barely two-thirds of the ship's full capacity.

In spite of the fact that the wards were far from overflowing, the voyage home was not destined to be an easy one. A strong north westerly half gale made for very heavy going, with the result that many of the medical staff and orderlies were again suffering from seasickness. For some reason the daily run went unpublished, possibly because the sea conditions had resulted in a less than impressive performance. By the following morning the ship was once again encountering beautiful weather and calm seas and not wishing to miss his chance, Captain Bartlett took the opportunity to hold one of his now customary lifeboat drills. Meanwhile, the passage to Gibraltar passed uneventfully but Biscay once again proved to be rough as *Britannic* encountered yet another north westerly half gale off Ushant. By now few on board were especially concerned about the weather. Home was now less than twenty-four hours away and, as if in celebration, a particularly successful concert was held that evening in the ship's lounge.

On the morning of 9th February *Britannic* was still inbound for Southampton, in fine but noticeably colder weather off the Isle of Wight. This time progress up the Solent seems have been a little faster than on the previous voyage, and the ship was safely berthed in the White Star Dock by 2.30 p.m. Disembarkation, however, seemed to take much longer, not that the doctors in the officers' wards would have been too hard pressed. On this occasion Dr. Goodman's task was simply to ensure that each of the officers in his care had their side arms, which had been secured below during the voyage, returned to them. Nevertheless, in spite of the fact that the wards were far from full, it was not until 10.30 p.m. that the last of the wounded had been landed.

With the wards finally emptied, the majority of the medical staff were granted seven-days leave and once again *Britannic*'s corridors were eerily quiet. Captain Bartlett was, nevertheless, kept busy. The use of Naples as a transfer point had been an interesting experiment and the Transport Division was keen to have his report. Within a day of *Britannic*'s return, Bartlett wrote to inform them as to how the procedures might have been improved. His letter leaves few details uncovered:

*On Board HMHS Britannic,*
*Southampton, 10th February 1916*

*Sir,*

*With reference to this ship's call at Naples to embark patients from smaller hospital ships, I submit the following suggestions for consideration.*

*1) Owing to there being no Naval Officer at Naples to instruct Masters of steamers bringing patients what to do, I would suggest that in their orders they be given definite instructions to proceed alongside this steamer on arrival (weather permitting) as much time would be saved, and it would be far more comfortable for patients than transferring in boats and barges.*

*2) Having obtained from the Consul General at Naples permission to use our wireless for hospital work from the Italian Admiral at Naples, I suggest that this steamer be used as a station whilst there, and messages from Malta and ships could be received which would facilitate matters for all concerned.*

*3) That the Consul General be instructed to connect the ship by telephone on arrival, as is always done with large passenger steamers calling at Naples. This would enable the Consulate to be in constant touch with the ship.*

*4) Painting the ship overside could be done at Naples by Italian labour cheaper than at home ports, the ship supplying the paint. One tender was forwarded to me through the Consul that this could be done for £80.*

*I am, sir,*

*Your obedient servant,*

*Charles A. Bartlett*
*Captain, R.N.R.*

At first glance it all looked very promising. Using Naples as a permanent base would not only decrease the dangers to which the larger hospital ships would be exposed in the eastern Mediterranean, but as far as the painting of the ships was

*By the beginning of February 1916, the empty Britannic, already with an uncertain future, lies anchored in the Solent.*

concerned, it might even save the Admiralty considerable money. The Director of Transports was certainly interested enough to forward the information to Cunard, but the project was destined to be stillborn. Behind the scenes *Britannic* was already the subject of not inconsiderable discussion in the corridors of power.

While the ship had been anchored at Naples, on 1st February, a Neapolitan representative of the Principal Provincial Sanitary Authority had gone aboard to inspect the facilities. No one had thought much about it at the time, but just as the ship was arriving back at Southampton trouble was already brewing. On 9th February the Italian authorities formally objected to Naples being used for the transfer of sick and wounded, due to the possible dangers of infection at the port. Whether or not these dangers were real or imaginary, the port of Augusta was suggested as a possible alternative, although bunkering at Naples would continue as already established.

Augusta, however, presented a somewhat less attractive alternative, and once again the Transport Division was keen to have Captain Bartlett's opinion regarding the proposal. Not being very familiar with the island of Sicily, all he could do was examine a chart of the port, and this was enough for him to advise that *Britannic* could anchor in ten fathoms of water without undue difficulty. The one drawback with Augusta, however, was that the anchorage was rather exposed and open to the southeast, and strong winds from that direction could make ship to ship transfers more difficult. Not only that, but it would also be necessary to keep a head of steam ready for immediate use at all times. On 21st February the Senior Naval Officer at

Malta also advised that Augusta would not be ideal, but the Transport Division still insisted that an officer be sent to make an inspection. On 10th March his report arrived back and it was confirmed that Augusta would be unsuitable because of the lack of facilities for coaling and watering, the lack of jetties and the possible difficulty of transfer from ship to ship in heavy weather. Unfortunately the bureaucrats seemed unwilling to have their judgement questioned by such trivial matters as operational realities, and the Transport Department officially declared that Augusta would serve as the temporary port for the transfer of war casualties until the system at Mudros could be re-established.

In any event, there didn't seem to be any particular hurry for *Britannic* to return to the Mediterranean. Shortly before midnight on 21st February, Dr. Goodman arrived back from his extended leave to find the ship still tied up at her Southampton terminal and reflecting the bitterly cold weather, feeling "like an iceberg" on the inside. *Britannic* finally vacated the White Star Dock at 1.00 p.m. the following afternoon, only to proceed slowly along Southampton Water before dropping anchor off Cowes, where *Aquitania* and *Mauretania* were both already secured. Nor were the omens for a further expedition especially positive. *Aquitania* was rumoured to have returned from her previous voyage with barely 1,500 patients on board and, bearing in mind that *Britannic's* last complement had also been less than full, their future requirement was very much in doubt.

For almost a month *Britannic* lay idle, and the temperature, both outside and in, remained decidedly cold. One of the medical staff, Lieutenant John Cropper, was hard pressed to fill the time, but he did his best to keep himself occupied, as one of his letters home reveals:

> *SS Britannic*
> *Feb 26, 1916*
>
> *Dearest Nellie,*
> *Here we are still off Cowes – the snow it snoweth every day and we are hard put to it sometimes to fill up the time. Yesterday I had one patient, two games of hockey with the V.A.D.s, one go at the gymnasium, one signalling practice, two games of chess and a study of Anglo Saxon between times. I shall soon know as much about semaphore signalling as Tom.....*

Harold Goodman similarly did his best to remain active, and seemed to be able to obtain a pass to go ashore fairly frequently, be it for shopping, walking around Cowes or even to have tea at the Marine Hotel. The routine was briefly interrupted on 3rd March, when he returned from a trip to Newport and a walk to Carisbrooke Castle to find that eight doctors, fifteen nurses and sixty orderlies had suddenly been taken off in a tug to go aboard the hospital ship *Morea*. This vessel was about to make an emergency trip across the Channel to Le Havre, but the excitement did not last long. Forty-eight hours later they were back on board after a successful trip, which had brought home another 840 soldiers.

Shrove Tuesday found Dr. Goodman ashore once again, this time in Portsmouth to collect stores. This still provided him with the opportunity for a good lunch at the

*Keppel*, after which he watched two submarines lying nearby HMS *Victory* (at this time still afloat), before returning at 4.30 p.m. through the fog and snow to *Britannic*. The situation on board was as usual, quiet, but with Captain Bartlett and Colonel Anderson both called ashore there was a strong feeling that something was now quite definitely in the air. Nevertheless, for the next ten days *Britannic* remained obstinately immobile and in an attempt to break the monotony, on Sunday 12th March Lieutenant Cropper gave one of his famous lectures on Palestine.

After weeks of inactivity the peace was suddenly broken when on 18th March the orders went out that all leave was to be cancelled and that those who were already on leave were being immediately recalled. The excitement continued into the following day, though little discernible movement could be detected. Shortly after midday on 20th March the ship was finally moving. The sense of anticipation, however, quickly turned to one of anticlimax as *Britannic* slowly inched her way through the fog and rain, only to drop anchor off Portsmouth as the pilot was put off. By 4.26 p.m., however, the ship was finally on its way.

As usual, the medical staff were not informed of the destination, although by now everyone on board was reasonably confident that the next stop would be Naples. That port was still five days away, but as the ship headed southeast towards Brittany, they could at least console themselves with the fact that the long period of uncertainty was over – for the time being, at least.

*The evening concert in the lounge on 8th February came at the end of a particularly rough crossing of the Bay of Biscay, but in spite of the hardships Dr. Harold Goodman later remembered it as being "successful."*

**Programme of Concert**

Held on Board

HOSPITAL SHIP "BRITANNIC,"

TUESDAY EVENING, FEBRUARY 8th, 1916,

Under the Patronage of

Capt. C. A. BARTLETT, C.B., and Lieut.-Col. H. S. ANDERSON

— PROGRAMME —

| | |
|---|---|
| Opening Chorus, " Are we all here, yes " | The " Dug Ups " |
| Cornet Solo, Selected | Trumpet-Major Geary |
| Serio Comic, Selected | Driver Marshall |
| Song, Selected | Corporal Hutchings |
| Comic Song, " Bobbing Down " | Private Kemp |
| Selected | Lieutenant Crawford |
| Song, Selected | C.S.M. Hogan |
| Pianoforte Solo, Selected | Private Soothill |
| Phonofiddleod lities | P.O. Pilkington |

— INTERVAL —

| | |
|---|---|
| Night Operations | Capt. Adams and Lieuts Crawford & Vines |
| Comic Song, Selected | Lieutenant Vernon |
| Song, Selected | Corporal Hutchings |
| Song, Selected | Lieutenant Feddon |
| Recitation, Selected | Captain Morrow |
| Song, " Nipper's Lullaby " | Captain Wingate |
| " Whistling Chorus " | Private Stockley |
| Song, Selected | Private Lever |
| Humorous, Selected | Private Templeton |

THE KING.

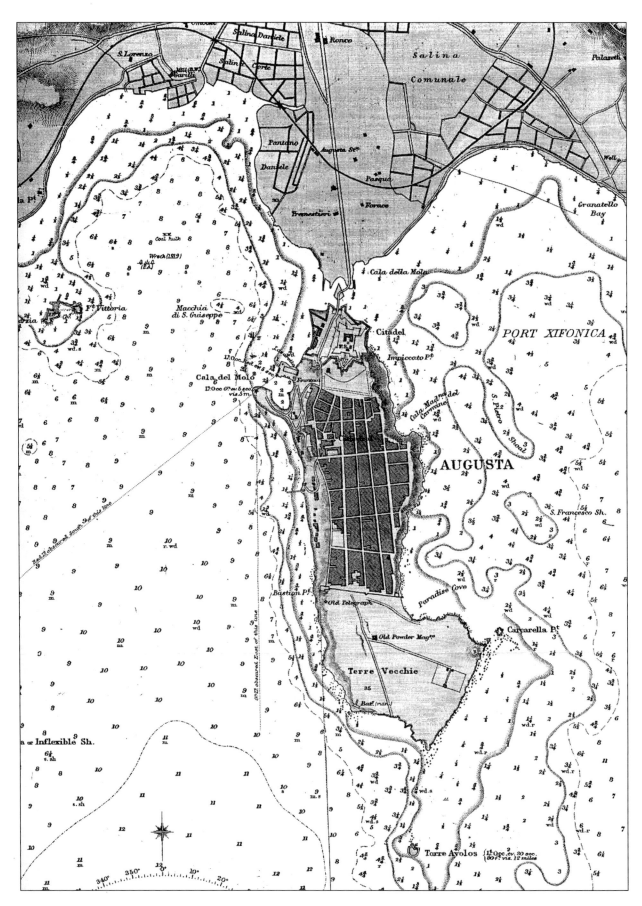

# CHAPTER FIVE

# SURPLUS TO REQUIREMENT

By noon on 21st March Southampton already lay 370 miles astern as *Britannic* sailed into an uncharacteristically smooth but rainy Bay of Biscay. As the ship continued on its southerly heading the temperature at long last began to feel noticeably warmer. Gibraltar was passed at 3.45 a.m. on 23rd March and by the time the medical staff were getting up for their breakfast later that morning the Mediterranean was looking its best. A combination of smooth seas and clear skies promised to deliver a particularly welcome hot day.

For Harold Goodman, however, that would be the last of the good news. For him the day would be spent attending to such mundane details as checking stores and ward lists, and even correcting the medical orderlies' exam papers. An evening bridge party found him feeling particularly unwell and the following morning his worst fears were confirmed – he had contracted influenza! Even so, when the ship arrived at Naples in the early hours of 25th March, he did his utmost to put his shore pass to good use. However, a busy morning of shopping and lunch at the Café Umberto proved too much, and he declined the opportunity to visit the museum. By 4.00 p.m. he was back on the ship for tea, feeling desperately tired, and the noise of the coaling throughout the night was to afford him little opportunity for sleep. To further complicate matters he awoke the following morning to find that he had developed a septic blister on his toe as a result of the previous day's exertions ashore.

On the Sunday morning *Britannic* was still anchored in the Bay of Naples with Dr. Goodman continuing to feel unwell. The cloudy weather probably influenced his decision to remain in his cabin for most of the day, although there was a short period of activity during the afternoon when the Duke of Opporto came aboard for an official visit. Aside from exchanging the usual diplomatic niceties, the Duke also brought with him a party of Italian boy scouts

While *Britannic* had been lying idle in the Solent, the White Star Line had, at the instigation of Captain Bartlett, undertaken the interesting experiment of including a troop of eight boy scouts amongst the ship's complement. Lieutenant General Sir Robert Baden-Powell, chief scout and head of the movement, was delighted that the company was offering his charges such a unique opportunity, and on 6th March Colonel Concanon had even written to him saying that not only had the boys "been very satisfactory in their signalling and other work," but that Captain Bartlett himself was also taking a great interest in them. it would now seem that the latest additions to *Britannic*'s crew were about to justify their presence on board.

Bartlett had good reason for taking such an active interest in the scouts. As one of the founding members of the RNR's Sea Urchins Club, he had always taken a great interest in training youngsters for the sea. Another reason for their presence on

*Left: Augusta, Sicily. This port was vulnerable to south-easterly winds and the lack of any suitable jetty and coal facilities proved a considerable worry to the Senior Naval Officer on Malta. His reservations must have been proved correct as Britannic would only visit this port on one occasion.*

*Hydrographic Office*

63

*This postcard of Britannic would have been quite commonly available on board. The card is an interesting (although relatively crude) adaptation of an earlier White Star publicity illustration, with the ship retaining its original davit configuration and the funnels still in their original White Star colours.*

*Paul Louden-Brown Collection*

board may well have had something to do with the fact that his only son, Midshipman Charles Sydney Ellis Bartlett, had been among the 570 crewmen killed when the British battleship HMS *Goliath* had been torpedoed off Cape Helles on 13th May 1915. With the first anniversary of his loss not far away, Bartlett's thoughts would very likely have been very much with his lost son. The scouts would not, nonetheless, have much time to enjoy a sea voyage. Captain Bartlett was also known for being a strict disciplinarian and rather than just being there for their own amusement, the eight scouts were assigned to very specific duties onboard. Their activities ranged from such mundane tasks as lift operators and messengers, through to physical drill, boat drill, swimming, Morse code and semaphore signalling. The scouts who made a particular impression on Captain Bartlett were given the captain's award for general smartness, while the White Star Line offered another prize for the scout who achieved the best results in their onboard activities. This particular call at Naples would provide them with a perfect opportunity to entertain the Italian representatives of the scout movement by showing them around the ship. By the following morning the onboard activities were back to normal as the medical staff were finally informed that Augusta was barely twenty-four hours away, and that three hospital ships were already waiting for their arrival. The ship was now a hive of activity as everyone rushed to collect their remaining stores and make the usual last-minute preparations on their wards.

After more than forty-eight hours in port, having taken on no less than 5,000 tons of coal (at the rate of 98 shillings per ton) *Britannic* departed from Naples at 4.00 p.m. on 27th March, passing between the island of Capri and the mainland as the ship turned south towards the Straits of Messina. Harold Goodman, having shrugged off the worst of his influenza, was kept busy in stores for most of the day. He must have been feeling considerably better because he was apparently strong enough to be dragged from his bed at 1.30 a.m. the following morning by Dr. Heggarty to observe the volcanic island of Stromboli which was particularly active, and glowed in the distance like a great furnace. At 6.15 a.m., just as the ship was passing through the Straits of Messina, he was back on duty, and by 10.00 a.m. *Britannic* was finally entering the Bay of Augusta.

The style of Goodman's description of Augusta itself is a little haphazard. This may well be because he still had not quite shaken off the effects of the virus, nevertheless his diary recounts *Britannic*'s one and only visit to Augusta in particularly fine detail:

"Most glorious morning. The bay is entered past a lighthouse, the houses on north side reach down to water's edge, the water a lovely clear blue. Found hospital ships awaiting us at anchor, the *Glengorm Castle* [two others]. We came to anchor and were surrounded by numerous boats selling oranges. Commenced embarking patients off the *Dunluce Castle* on port side (alongside) at 10:15 about. The *Egypt* appeared and came into bay and drew alongside at 12.15 p.m. on starboard side where I was on duty as embarkation officer with Taylor and Walsh. We got 486 all told. Embarking going on aft by barge and lighter – Canadian Hospital and equipment, so taking in at four gangways a same time. Finished at 7 p.m. with deceased officers baggage checking off, which stored in No. 3 hatch forward. Bed at 11 p.m. While we disembarked the *Egypt* the *Glengorm Castle* took *Dunluce*'s place and was disembarked and on barges the *Valderia* sent patients and the Canadian Hospital with 120 orderlies and staff to the after disembarkation ports on E deck and their equipment to the after hatches by crane."

On the following morning the Canadian hospital equipment was still being loaded, so at 11.00 a.m. Captain Bartlett took the opportunity to send a ship's officer ashore in one of the motor launches to collect some sand for cleaning the decks. This order reveals another interesting point about his character. Bartlett was sometimes referred to as "Iceberg Charlie", because of his ability to "smell" icebergs, and he was also known to his crew as "Holystone Charlie," on account of his insistence on clean decks. With most of the sick and wounded by now embarked, Goodman was at a loose end and was quickly able to gain permission to go ashore with the landing party. Before long he was aboard the motor launch and heading for the south side of the bay. Once the launch was anchored, he and one of the ship's officers transferred to a Sicilian fishing boat which they had been towing astern. With the guidance of the boat's owner and his two crewmen, they made for the beach where the British officers were carried ashore on the backs of the two Sicilians to avoid getting their uniforms wet. Once ashore the locals set about collecting the sand while Goodman took the welcome opportunity to take a leisurely stroll through the citrus groves to a nearby farm where he bought some oranges and lemons. The walk back to the beach also afforded an opportunity to capture a few lizards and pick up some seashells from the beach itself. The trip ashore could provide only a brief respite, however, and with the sand safely bagged the launch was soon being hoisted back aboard *Britannic* just in time for lunch.

At nine o'clock on 30th March the hospital ship *Formosa* finally arrived alongside. As usual, Goodman was allocated to embarkation duty, but before long he was called away to reorganise the distribution of patients as those already in L, M and N wards needed to be moved in order to make room for the orderlies of the 1st London Field Ambulance. This task alone would take over five hours, and by the time Goodman had finished *Britannic* was already homeward bound, having weighed anchor at 3.00 p.m.

Rounding the southeast corner of Sicily, the ship hugged the southern shoreline and assumed a westerly heading, while the weather remained so clear that Mount Etna remained visible until sunset. By midday on 31st March *Britannic* had travelled 444 miles in the twenty-one hours since leaving Augusta, but as the ship headed towards Gibraltar the sea conditions began to worsen. On 1st April it was

*Even war could have its more relaxing moments. Here some of the RAMC officers relaxing in the sun beneath the port gantry davits.*

*Courtesy Ronald Goodman*

raining hard, the temperature was noticeably colder and the combination of heavy seas and a strong north westerly wind was doing little to make the passage comfortable for those on board. Gibraltar was passed at 9.30 p.m. that evening, but the distance travelled for that day proved to be somewhat disappointing, with only 442 miles being logged in twenty-four hours. The sea conditions may have had something to do with this but, equally, now that *Britannic* was out of the immediate danger zone it was also likely that speed was being reduced in order to conserve coal supplies.

Once back in the Atlantic Captain Bartlett resumed his customary northerly heading for what, he hoped, would be a routine if stormy voyage home. Fortunately, as the latitude increased the weather moderated. Sadly, this particular voyage home would be clouded in the early hours of 4th April, by the death of Private Robert Pask of the VIII South Wales Borderers in the ship's infirmary. As in the case of Private Vincent on the first voyage, with the ship so close to home, it was decided not to bury the body at sea, but to land it at Southampton.

By 11.00 a.m. *Britannic* was at her berth

*A group of medical officers relax beside the motor house of the aft portside gantry davits on the boat deck.*

*Courtesy Ronald Goodman*

in the White Star Dock. On this occasion Colonel Anderson was obliged to leave the supervision of disembarkation to his subordinates, as he had to unexpectedly play host to Sir Benjamin Franklin, Surgeon General O'Donovan and several Russian princes who had unexpectedly come aboard for lunch. A visit from a surgeon general was no ordinary event and it did not take long for the rumours to start spreading. Clearly something was afoot, and within twenty-four hours it was officially announced to the crew that this homecoming would be the last. *Britannic* was to be laid up!

With the immediate future in question, the following day Colonel Anderson offered Harold Goodman the opportunity to join the medical staff of the hospital ship *Dover Castle*. In spite of the fact that the only remaining duties on board would involve the boring routine of checking through the ship's medical inventory and stores, he declined, preferring instead to remain aboard *Britannic* in order to finish the job he had started. He may later have come to regret his decision, for on 6th April the ship's matrons and VAD sisters finally went ashore, leaving only a handful of the medical personnel to sort through the mountains of bedding and linen, while the remaining orderlies off-loaded the ship's stores. This routine continued throughout the week, and by 9th April wards A through to H had been cleared. Dr. Goodman's final check list revealed that his stores and provisions were in surplus as far as practically every item was concerned. Unfortunately the stores personnel at Southampton immediately deflated his evident pleasure, when someone casually commented that it really didn't "matter a damn!"

By the morning of 11th April the ship was finally empty and at 4.00 p.m. Colonel Anderson and his three remaining medical staff, doctors Goodman, Urwick and Maclagan, stood at the end of the White Star Dock to watch *Britannic* pull away and steam down Southampton Water towards her new temporary anchorage off Cowes. Once the ship was out of sight Goodman's only remaining task was to seek out the customs officers in order to pay the duty on several bottles of Chianti which he had bought on his last visit to Naples, before catching an evening train to Guildford, where he would enjoy his promised seven-day leave.

Harold Goodman would only see *Britannic* on one more occasion, shortly after four o'clock on the morning of 17th April, from the decks of the transport *Hantonian* while en route to Le Havre. Goodman's crossing in *Hantonian* would be in stark contrast to the comfort of *Britannic*, as he remembered the transport being absolutely packed with no less than 4,000 bags of mail and people lying everywhere. Goodman was fortunate enough to have been allocated his own bunk, but in spite of the strong north westerly gale he could not resist the urge to go up on deck and observe the shadowy profile of *Britannic* off to starboard one last time. This trip down memory lane, however, was to cost him dear. As he went back inside he came across a young ten-year-old French boy shivering beneath one of the staircases in the main companionway. Taking pity on the lad, Goodman placed him in his own bunk before returning on deck where, in spite of the heavy weather, he would remain for the rest of the voyage.

*With the beaches of Gallipoli by now abandoned, after only three voyages to the Mediterranean Britannic was laid up at half rate in the Solent.*

Bruce Beveridge Collection

Harold Goodman already knew what lay in store for him, for

he had been assigned to the 76th Field Ambulance, but *Britannic*'s immediate future was less clear. For the next five weeks the ship would remain laid up in the Solent at half rate while the Transport Division ruminated over how they would go about reorganising their fleet of hospital ships. In fact the knife had already been wielded. *Mauretania* and *Aquitania* had been paid off on 1st March and 10th April respectively, and so confident was the Admiralty that the vessels would not be needed in the foreseeable future that they had even gone so far as to pay Cunard no less than £150,000 to cover the cost of refurbishing the two ships for civilian service.

For the time being *Britannic* remained, ready to be called upon at a moment's notice, but there was little doubt that the cash-strapped War Office would allow this situation to go on indefinitely. With the military situation in the Mediterranean stabilising, and intensely aware that vessels such as *Britannic* were unsuitable for any other duties, the Transport Division finally bowed to the inevitable. *Britannic* was officially discharged from military service on 6th June, although she would still remain on the Transport Division's books at half rate until 20th July. In time the White Star Line would receive a payment from the Admiralty of £76,000 towards the cost of converting the ship for peace time service, but with priority still being given to military contracts it would be some weeks before any significant progress would be made.

Six months on, *Britannic*'s situation was no different than it had been in November 1915 – unneeded, and surplus to requirement.

# CHAPTER SIX

# THE HUNTERS

While *Britannic* itself may have been temporarily redundant, the crew and medical staff who had provided the ship's essential services were urgently needed elsewhere. Within a couple of weeks most of the doctors and nurses had already been assigned to other theatres of war, while the ship's crew would have quickly found other vessels. For most of them the more secure lifestyle aboard a hospital ship would soon have been sorely missed.

As we shall later see, it was the Kaiser's love of all things maritime that had resulted in hospital ships being granted their protected status, although this concern accounted for only a small part of his maritime policy. Before the war Wilhelm's seagoing ambitions had led to an unparalleled boom in German shipbuilding that had provided a blow to British national pride. Consequently, as the early years of the twentieth century saw the German liners taking all of the honours on the North Atlantic for both size and speed, the challenge could not be ignored by Great Britain. By 1903 the competition had become so intense that the Cunard Line had even been forced into obtaining a loan from the British Government to fund the construction of *Lusitania* and *Mauretania*. But with additional pressure from the expanding American shipping companies and the Germans feeling compelled to respond in kind to every British innovation, it only provided a temporary British resurgence. In the meantime, the British press could only chafe at the upstart maritime nation that was doing so much to undermine British dominance at sea; a supremacy that had gone unchallenged since 1805.

On the face of it everyone should have been content. The resulting vessels were larger, faster and more luxurious than anyone could have dreamed only a few years earlier, and it seemed as if technology had the ability to overcome any obstacle within its path. Beneath the surface, however, this rivalry had far more sinister implications, for the rapid expansion of the German merchant marine was mirrored by the far more alarming expansion of the German High Seas Fleet.

The major German personality behind this naval expansion was Grand Admiral Alfred von Tirpitz. Even though Great Britain had the largest navy in the world he reasoned that, with so many foreign commitments this force could never be fully concentrated in the North Sea to counter Germany. Accepting that Germany would never be able to outnumber the British fleet, Tirpitz, nevertheless, set about building up a High Seas Fleet which, if called upon, could be strong enough to inflict heavy enough damage on the British Grand Fleet so that, even if Germany were defeated, it would leave Great Britain severely weakened as a maritime power. This stratagem, known as "Risk Theory," had strong support from the Kaiser and would ultimately come to dominate German naval thinking. Without realising it,

*Left: Kapitänleutnant Gustav Siess: Commander of U73 from October 1915 to April 1917, who would go on to become one of Germany's greatest submarine aces of the war.*

Courtesy Innes McCartney

*The long-range mine laying submarine U73. Not especially known for its sea keeping qualities, the U-boat was affectionately known by its crew as the "floating coffin."*

*National Maritime Museum*

however, Wilhelm was sowing the seeds of his own ultimate downfall. The accelerated German naval construction programme would so alarm the previously isolationist British Government that, in due course, it would become *the* major factor in Great Britain's ultimate decision to side with France and Russia.

Without a doubt Great Britain's declaration of war in August 1914 posed a number of unforeseen problems for Germany. It may have possessed one of the largest and most modern battle fleets in the world, but the strategic position of the British Isles was enough to ensure that it would remain effectively caged. Even when riding at anchor in its own home base at Scapa Flow the Grand Fleet was able to seal off virtually all access to the North Sea, effectively cutting Germany's trade links with the world. This did not prevent the German surface units from mounting the occasional foray into the North Sea, but the resulting damage to the German economy and hardships to the civilian population would result in a new kind of sea war that few would have considered possible only a few years earlier.

The conduct of this sea campaign ultimately proved to be a diplomatic disaster for Germany. The Allies showed little hesitation in pointing out that by waging war against British commerce the Germans were effectively trying to starve the British civilian population into surrender, and carefully released newsreel footage of sinking ships provided an invaluable propaganda weapon. Slowly but surely the Allied propaganda would help to turn the tide of neutral American opinion in their favour, although, for all of their crying foul, the rather unpalatable truth was that through their policy of distant blockade the Allies were no less guilty of waging war in the same way. The difference, however, was that the Allies' manner of achieving their aims was far less conspicuous; newsreels of unarmed merchant ships being torpedoed could only harm the German cause, while images of German civilians queuing for food could not hope to have the same impact.

For the Germans therein lay the problem. With their much vaunted surface fleet unable to gain a decisive advantage over the foe, the submarine, a development dismissed in 1901 by no lesser personage that grand Admiral Alfred von Tirpitz himself, quickly became the only weapon with which Germany could effectively wage the war at sea. The problem, however, was that by August 1914 the Imperial Navy could only field twenty-eight such vessels, of which barely twenty were operational. Nevertheless, they would quickly make their mark. The early losses of the armoured cruisers HMS *Pathfinder* and HMS *Hawke* were isolated incidents, but the sinking in quick succession of the armoured cruisers *Aboukir*, *Hogue* and *Cressy* on 22nd September 1914 by Otto Weddigen's *U9* was evidence enough that the submarine had become a force to be reckoned with.

The initial results, however, were less than impressive. Five months after the outbreak of hostilities barely ten merchantmen had been sunk, and those that were dispatched were all taken under prize rules, whereby the submarine surfaced and only attacked after warning the enemy crew, who were then allowed to evacuate their ship before it was sent to the bottom. At this stage of the war there still seemed to be a certain civility displayed in the conflict at sea, indeed, the gentlemanly conduct of some of the German officers ensured that they became respected celebrities even in Great Britain. One of the most feted German seamen was Kapitän Karl von Müller of the German cruiser SMS *Emden*. Originally a part of Admiral Graf von Spee's China Seas cruiser squadron, *Emden* was detached from the main fleet in order to operate independently, yet by the time the German ship was finally despatched by the Australian cruiser HMS *Sydney* on 9th November, Müller had cost the British Government an estimated £4,000,000 in lost shipping and cargo, without the loss of a single life.

Even the despised U-boats had their knights, such as *U53's* Kapitänleutnant Hans Rose, who had an unusual habit of sinking a foe and then towing the lifeboats to safety. Martin Niemöller, of whom we shall hear more later, even recalled an incident in early 1917 when *U39* torpedoed an Allied troop transport in the Mediterranean. As the ship was sinking the commander of the U-boat did his utmost to distract a French destroyer from the task of rescuing the survivors by occasionally raising and lowering the submarine's periscope, aware of the fact that while he did not wish to interfere with the task of saving lives, every soldier that was saved would be destined to once again fight against German troops.

While some of the Germans wrestled with their consciences beneath the waves, the Allied seamen had more immediate concerns. Officers such as Müller and Rose were the exception rather than the rule, with few other U-boat skippers showing such consideration or gentlemanly conduct. The torpedoing of *Lusitania* by *U20* on 7th May 1915 is still looked upon by many as the first modern war crime, even though much is still made of the fact that the ship was carrying war materials. The fact remains that the 1,198 civilians who went down with the ship, including 128

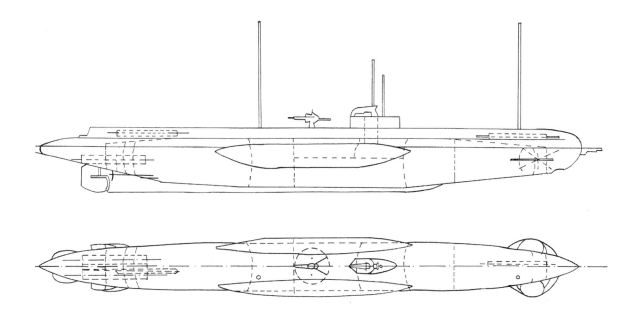

*Above: A schematic diagram of a U-boat of the U71 class. These vessels would not be unsuccessful, but experience would show that the engines of this class of U-boat were quite inadequate, while the vessels themselves would usually need extensive repairs when in port.*

Barbara Rességuier

*Left: Martin Niemöller, U73's Navigating Officer from 1916 to 1917 and the only known member of the U-boat's crew to publish his memoirs.*

Americans, amounted to a German own-goal of monumental proportions. The sinking of the unescorted White Star liner SS *Arabic* by the *U24* on 19th August 1915 left another 44 dead, and the resulting diplomatic pressure from neutral America finally convinced the German High Command that if they wished to avoid a direct confrontation with the Americans then the time had come to rein in their uncontrolled submarines.

But how much of this was actually forced upon the Germans? It didn't take long for the effects of the Allied blockade to have a serious effect in Germany. With warships of the the High Seas Fleet swinging idly at their moorings in their home ports, the British arming of merchant vessels and the introduction of Q ships (merchant ships mounting concealed guns in order to lure submarines to the surface), it soon became clear that they could no longer adhere to the policy of prize rules. Faced with this situation, on 4th February 1915 the German High Command finally declared the waters around the British Isles to be a war zone, in which any vessel might be attacked without warning. The era of unrestricted submarine warfare had arrived.

The results were immediate. In January 1915 some 48,000 tons of Allied shipping had been sunk, and with the gloves now off that figure rose to 65,000 tons by February. From then on the figures positively leapt, with no less than 120,000 tons accounted for during the first half of May alone. In August U-boats accounted for 165,000 tons and for the first time Great Britain's losses were exceeding the capacity of the shipyards to build replacements. Fortunately for the Allies the American diplomatic protests forced the Germans to revert to "prize rules," but by now the die was well and truly cast. In the future, fully aware of the hot reception that they might receive on the surface, few U-boat commanders would show any willingness to surface unannounced.

It is against this backdrop that we come to the story of the submarine *U73*, which is of particular relevance to our own story. Launched at the Kaiserliche Werfte shipyard in Danzig on 16th June 1915, *U73* was designed to complement the large number of smaller UC boats, though with an overall length of 186 feet 4 inches (56.8 metres) and a surface displacement of 745 tons (890 tons submerged), she was somewhat larger and could operate at considerably longer ranges. The two *Körting* Diesel engines could develop some 800 HP, enough for a maximum surface speed of 9.6 knots, while a cruising speed of 7-8 knots provided an operational range of up to 7,500 nautical miles. 9.6 knots was not particularly fast but this was of no major significance, as *U73* was not designed to be a fighting U-boat. She mounted two external 20 inch torpedo tubes and a single 3.5 inch gun, the latter mounted astern of the conning tower, but these weapons were of secondary importance. Far more insidious was the cargo of 34 mines contained within the submarine, which could be laid through two tubes mounted aft.

*U73*'s commanding officer, Kapitänleutnant Gustav Siess, was born in Hamburg on 11th December 1883, and had enrolled as a sea cadet in the German navy in 1902. The outbreak of war found him in command of the torpedo boat *V1*, although the routine aboard this vessel did not particularly appeal to him. Following a short spell in command of *V3*, in March 1915 he transferred to the U-boat training school and three months later he was appointed to the submarine *U41*. Clearly he must have impressed his senior officers because he was given command of *U73* in August 1915, shortly before the vessel was commissioned on 9th October

We are also particularly fortunate in that another member of *U73*'s crew, Navigating Officer Martin Niemöller, was one of the many German U-boat skippers who published their memoirs after the war. As we shall later see, the motive behind Niemöller's 1934 book *From U-boat to Pulpit* was not simply intended as a means to recount his wartime experience. Nevertheless, the resulting volume fills in a good many gaps that would otherwise exist in the story of *U73*. Niemöller had joined the German navy in March 1910 and by the outbreak of war he was serving aboard the 23,000-ton battleship *Thüringen*. Frustration at the lack of action prompted him to apply for a place at the U-boat school at Kiel on 1st December 1915, and his desire for action was to come a lot sooner than expected when, on 22nd February 1916, he was posted to *U73* to replace an officer who had been swept overboard in a storm. The omens were not all that favourable when Niemöller first met his new commanding officer. At first Siess was somewhat grim about the inexperience of his new navigating officer, asking: "How do you know I'm prepared to have you?" Niemöller was not really in much of a position to give a response, but when Siess learnt of his familiarity with wireless telegraphy and qualifications as a torpedo specialist he decided to take him on trial just the same. All must have gone well, as they sailed happily together throughout the following year.

That said, they were not destined to be going very far very quickly. The damage wrought by violent North Sea storms had left the submarine *hors de combat*, giving Niemöller plenty of time to brood on the fact that, aside from not being the fighting

U-boat for which he had hoped, the sea keeping qualities of his new vessel also left a great deal to be desired. To compound the fact that she was slow on the surface, it soon became abundently clear that once submerged *U73* could barely manage four knots, and even then only in short fifteen minute spurts. The process of diving took at least two minutes, and because the diving tanks had to be blown with the bilge-pump, it meant that surfacing could – and often did – take considerably longer. It would take an enormous stroke of luck for such a vessel to successfully position itself for a torpedo attack, let alone carry one out.

As repairs continued, rumours began to circulate towards the end of March among the crew concerning their next mission. Siess remained tight-lipped about the contents of his heavily sealed official envelope, but with every single piece of available space on board packed with supplies and Diesel oil it was clear that it was going to be a much longer voyage than usual. To make matters worse, Niemöller was less than reassured when he saw the engineer officer casting a sceptical look at his engines and commenting: "I don't mind, so long as these sewing machines don't."

With the preparations complete, *U73* finally departed from Cuxhaven on 1st April 1916, and as soon as the German coastline had dropped below the horizon Siess finally advised his men that they were bound for the Mediterranean. It would not, however, be an easy voyage. Scarcely had they cleared the Heligoland Bight than *U73* was exposed to the full fury of the North Sea, and it was not long before Niemöller realised exactly why the submarine had been given the charming sobriquet of "the floating coffin." The shortcomings of the engines were already well known and, to further complicate the situation, the saddle tanks which had been incorporated into the hull to increase the range also had the unfortunate effect of forcing the submarine to pitch rather heavily, even in moderate weather. Before long half of the crew were longing to just crawl into a corner and die, while those who were not actually sea sick spent much of the time cleaning up the now chaotic interior. Outside matters were little better, with the men of the bridge-watch having to be lashed to the rails to save them from being swept overboard. To further complicate matters the gyrocompass was not working, forcing Niemöller to navigate by dead reckoning for several days until the skies cleared and he could once again see the stars.

Ten days later, having passed around the north coast of Scotland, they entered Biscay and the weather was at last showing signs of improving. The successful sinking, by gunfire, of a British schooner was overshadowed by the fact that one of the bridge-watch had been lost overboard during the attack, but as the submarine skirted the Portuguese coast Siess could finally set about his business. Under the cover of darkness twelve mines were successfully laid off the entrance to Lisbon harbour before the U-boat made off to the west. However, the good work was very nearly undone when, the following morning, *U73* surfaced to find themselves surrounded by a Portuguese fishing fleet. The consternation amongst the Portuguese fisherman knew no bounds but, thinking quickly, Siess decided to bluff his way through the crisis by raising the French Tricolour before the alarm could be raised. The Portuguese were taken in and with calm restored Siess quickly headed off before his ruse was detected. He need not have worried, for the deception worked so well that later that day they heard on the wireless that a 5,000-ton Norwegian steamer had struck one of their mines and gone to the bottom, along with a full cargo of wheat.

On the morning of 19th April *U73* arrived off the Rock of Gibraltar and immediately, Siess, knowing that the submarine was about to enter the most hazardous stage of its voyage, was faced with a dilemma. The weather that day was especially clear, and with insufficient battery capacity to make the entire passage submerged there was nothing for it but to attempt the journey on the surface. At first all went well, but at 4.00 p.m. they suddenly came to the attention of an unidentified British steamer which began to shadow their movements, closely matching their every change in course and speed. To make matters worse engine trouble then forced the submarine to stop. Fortunately for them the unidentified steamer continued to keep its distance and with power quickly restored Siess was able to continue. By now curiosity must have been getting the better of the captain of the steamer as he attempted to make radio contact. Siess kept up his bluff by raising the Royal Navy White Ensign in the hope that this would satisfy his shadower's curiosity, but the appearance at 6.00 p.m. of another steamer fast approaching from the east finally persuaded him that discretion was the better part of valour. Submerging to sixty feet, *U73* beat a hasty retreat and remained off the Spanish coast for the remainder of the day until darkness provided them with the necessary cover to break into the Mediterranean. Later that night Siess tried again, submerging only briefly to avoid the searchlights of Gibraltar, and by the following morning *U73* had successfully negotiated the narrows and was heading eastwards.

Once in the Mediterranean their mission could begin in earnest, although it did not get off to a particularly auspicious start. An attempt to lay mines off the French Tunisian naval base at Bizerte had to be abandoned due to a combination of poor weather and technical problems, so the decision was made to proceed to their secondary target, the British base on Malta. Here, in spite of constant enemy patrols and several alarms, Siess was more successful, and was able to lay twenty-two mines

*The horned mine was the standard mine employed by the Imperial German Navy during the First World War, although the Herz Horn actually dated from as far back as 1868. The metal horn contained a glass tube filled with an electrolyte (potassium bichromate solution), which was linked to one carbon and one zinc plate. Upon contact with a passing vessel the glass tube within the horn would be shattered and the solution would leak out and connect the two plates, forming a simple battery. This battery would generate enough current to activate an electric detonator, igniting the 150 Kilo explosive charge.*

*Barbara Rességuier*

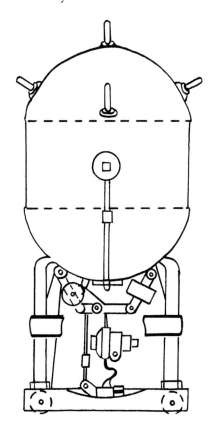

outside the entrance to Valletta. As *U73* headed northeast to the Straits of Otranto he would have had little idea of the prize he was about to bag.

*U73*'s unfortunate victim was the ageing 14,000-ton pre-dreadnought, HMS *Russell*. Having been engaged in harassing Turkish forces based at Cape Helles, blockading the Dardanelles and keeping an eye out for the German battlecruisers *Goeben* and *Breslau*, *Russell* was being rotated from her base at Imbros to Malta in order to re-supply, undergo minor dockyard repairs and give the crew an opportunity for some shore leave. Having passed the French battle fleet based at Malta the previous evening, *Russell* was scheduled to be seven miles off Valletta by 5.30 a.m. on 27th April. Suddenly the ship was rocked by two explosions, described by Admiral Sir Sydney Fremantle as "two heavy thuds under the after part of the ship, shortly followed by a burst of flame and smoke rising through the quarter-deck." *Russell* had struck two of the mines laid by *U73* and within minutes the ship had capsized to starboard, taking with her 126 officers and men. Admiral Fremantle was among the fortunate survivors to be pulled from the water, suffering nothing more serious than a couple of broken bones in his foot and wounded pride, although the loss of a treasured family heirloom, a spy glass once owned by Admiral Nelson, was not so easy for him to come to terms with.

Oblivious of their triumph, *U73* arrived three days later at the Austrian Adriatic port of Catarro, where the crew first heard of their great success. The "floating coffin" had acquitted itself so well that the Austrian emperor, Franz Josef, insisted that the entire crew be decorated for their achievement in sinking the British battleship.

A lengthy list of repairs ensured that it would be several weeks before *U73* was once again ready for active service, leaving the crew with plenty of time to enjoy some shore leave. Nevertheless, it was already clear that Germany's increased submarine commitment in the Mediterranean was very real, and with fewer neutral vessels plying these waters there was no particular reason why, in this theatre at least, the Central Powers should pull their punches and ease off on their submarine campaign.

*Britannic* may have been safe in homeport for now, but already the seeds of her nemesis were being well and truly sewn.

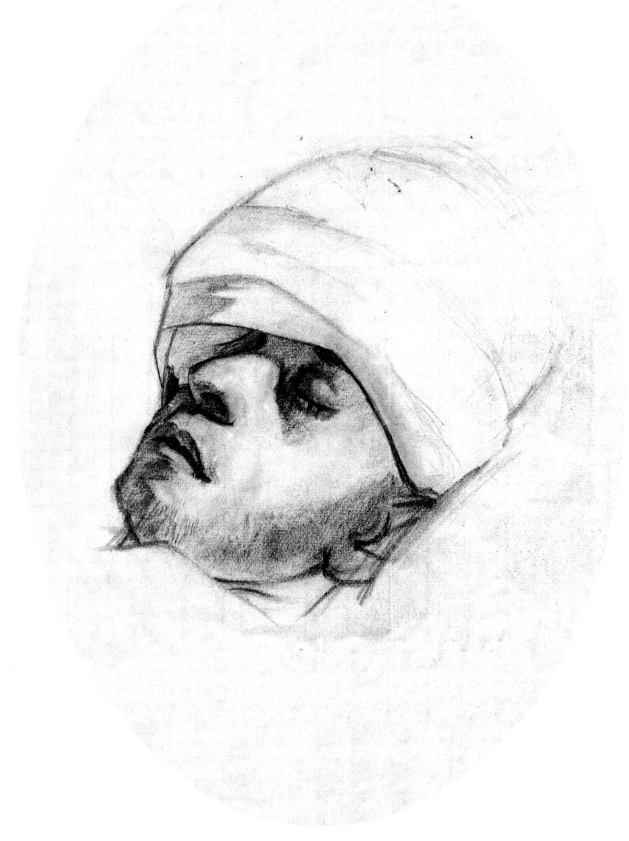

# CHAPTER SEVEN

# THE HUNTED

When Captain Arthur Rostron, the ex-skipper of the Cunard liner *Carpathia*, was appointed to command *Mauretania* in September 1915, it seems curious that in spite of the fact that he was understandably proud to command such a fine ship, he would also admit to a sense of anticlimax. As he later recounted in his memoirs:

> "I admit withal that I had a slight feeling of disappointment. We were not then tired of the chase – of the excitement of wondering whether we should get through or this time have a tin fish in our sides. One naturally imagined that a hospital ship was immune to attack. The thrills were to come, however."

It seems strange that in light of the growing number of Allied shipping casualties, more than a year into the war Rostron would still be thinking of it as an exciting chase. Nevertheless, in one respect he was unquestionably right; as a hospital ship *Mauretania* should have been immune from attack.

The Geneva Convention was very precise on the immunity that the colour scheme of a hospital ship would afford any such vessel, and the twenty-eight articles of the document signed at The Hague on 28th October 1907 left little room for any doubt. Article 1 of the Convention provided that all military hospital ships, that is to say, ships constructed or fitted out by States specially and solely with a view to assisting the wounded, sick, and shipwrecked, would be respected and immune from capture while hostilities lasted. Unlike other belligerent warships, there was no restriction placed concerning their stay in a neutral port, while their movements were guaranteed to be unhindered as long as they provided relief and assistance to the wounded, sick, and shipwrecked of the belligerents, without distinction of nationality.

For the medical and religious staff on board, their worries must also have been greatly lessened in the knowledge that in the event that they may be captured or shipwrecked, they were inviolable, and so could not be made prisoners of war. Not only that, but if they fell into the hands of the enemy they would be entitled to the same allowances to which the enemy staff of corresponding rank were entitled. This consideration, however, was not extended to the ship's crew or to the patients who were being transported. The Germans would not be obliged to return any of the sick or injured who might fall into their hands, though they could, at their discretion, repatriate them to England with the proviso that they could not serve again for the duration of the war.

*Left: A pencil drawing of a wounded soldier made during the First World War.*

*Courtesy John Fleming*

The price for this immunity was very simple. Article 4 of the Convention provided that under no circumstances were hospital ships to be used for any military purpose, and that they could not be used in any way to impede the movements of combatants. To ensure that the rules were being properly observed representatives of the belligerent powers were allowed the right to go aboard and search these vessels, but a hospital ship could only be detained if the gravity of any breaches in the Convention required it.

As with all such vessels, *Britannic's* movements were subject to these restrictions, and it would seem that those who sailed in a hospital ship would not entertain any thought at all of bending the rules. Captain Rostron's memoirs were particularly scathing when he addressed the question, noting that the enemy's suspicions were nothing more than an "idle excuse" for what followed:

> "They knew all right. They were quite aware their reason was an excuse. They understood we were only carrying wounded. What they aimed at hospital ships for was just because quite conceivably some of the wounded they took home would get well again and once more become part of the fighting army against them. Or even worse – merely to strike terror into the civilian population prompting an eagerness for peace."

Dr. John Beaumont, the first White Star surgeon to be posted aboard *Britannic*, took an equally partisan stance in his own book, *Ships and People*:

> "I never believed that the Germans would respect the Red Cross flag any more than they would a troopship; all they were waiting for was a favourable opportunity... ...a submarine could hardly miss such a huge target."

*The occupants of D Ward were among the luckier patients, as the large portholes meant that their wards were relatively bright and well ventilated. In November 1916, however, these open portholes would have a more far-reaching consequence that few would have imagined possible.*

Courtesy Angus Mitchell

While this attitude might be understandable in the circumstances, to rely solely on dubious news reporting and dramatised memoirs can, as is so often the case, result in a rather misleading picture. Dr. Beaumont's *Ships and People* was written in 1926, at a time when the memories of the First World War were far from forgotten, although his own recollection of events may have become somewhat clouded. In his book he tells an interesting tale, when he was compelled to leave *Britannic* to recover from a bout of Paratyphoid B fever, and was considered to be a possible "carrier" of the disease. Three weeks later, following his enforced departure, Dr. Beaumont was having dinner with his wife in London when he recounts the following story:

"One evening when sitting down to dinner in the hotel, my friend Genari, the manager, came over and grabbing both my hands exclaimed... "Oh, Doctor, I'm so glad you did not go on the ship." "What do you mean, Genari?" said I. "My good friend, do you not know that the *Britannic* was torpedoed this morning and sank with many lives lost?" "

If this intriguing story were true then Beaumont's affliction could indeed be looked upon as a fortunate escape, but a closer look at the facts paints a rather different picture. While it is undeniably true that the good doctor was invalided off of the ship, *Britannic*'s log states that this was actually on 19th March 1916 – a good eight months before the ship was lost! This does not mean to say that he never had such a conversation with his good friend Genari, but in the face of this evidence it seems likely that Beaumont's selective memory was either playing him false or, more likely, he had fallen back on the time-honoured technique of employing dramatic licence to embellish his story for the benefit of his readers.

Then again, it should be said that, for all of its weaknesses, there are other areas within his book to which it is easier to relate. Indeed, Beaumont leaves us with little doubt as to how he felt toward the petty officialdom that seemed to abound:

*F Ward was one of the five wards to which Dr. Harold Goodman was allocated on Britannic's first trip out. Located on the starboard side of the ship, the ward consisted entirely of fixed two-tier cots.*

*Courtesy Angus Mitchell*

"In the Army Medical Service the red tape fiend ruled with more rigour than ever I had imagined. What with signings and counter-signings of papers galore, doling out food to grains, no one daring to say or do anything without permission from a superior officer and other continuous references to chapter and verse. It seemed to me that the best interests of the patient were nothing in comparison to strict adherence to "Regulation No..., Sub-Section...!" "

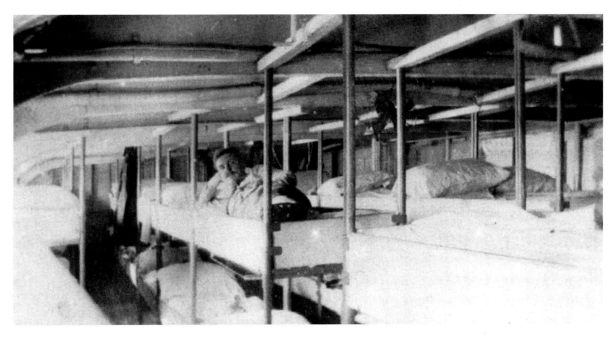

He may have had a point. The daily routine aboard one of His Majesty's hospital ships was clearly laid down in an official Admiralty guide and, although the captain and senior medical officer were given some leeway in the running of each individual vessel, it was clearly understood that the suggested guidelines were to be adhered to as closely as possible. The provisions for the journey out made little reference to the activity on board, except to ensure (as if it were necessary) that the bunks were all made ready for the incoming wounded by the time the hospital ship arrived at its embarkation point. However, once the sick and wounded were on board matters were far more clearly laid down:

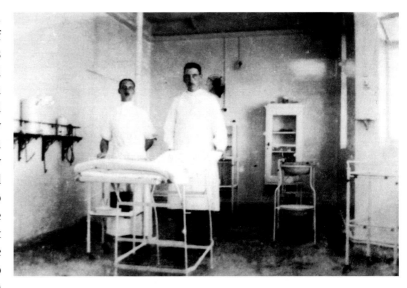

*One of the basic but functional examination rooms aboard the Britannic.*

*Courtesy Alasdair Fairbairn*

|  |  |
|---|---|
| 6.00 a.m.: | Wake patients, after which wards and passageways were to be cleaned. |
| 7.30 - 8.00 a.m.: | Patients' breakfast served, after which beds were made and the tables, benches and WCs were scrubbed. |
| 11.00 a.m.: | Captain and Senior Medical Officer make rounds. |
| 12:30 p.m.: | Lunch served, after which the wards were once again swept out, the hospital areas disinfected while the brass and paintwork were cleaned as necessary. |
| 4.30 p.m.: | Patients' tea. |
| 8.30 p.m.: | Patients put to bed. |
| 9.00 p.m.: | A ship's officer and medical officer make final round of ship, turning off all unnecessary lighting (except for identification lights). |

Even the *minutiae* were taken into consideration. The ship's guard was to consist of one NCO and nine other men, each working a relief shift of two men to police the upper decks. Their purpose on board was twofold. They were responsible for the psychiatric cases brought aboard and, in the event of an emergency, could be stationed by the lifeboats in order to keep order. Bearing in mind the nature of their duties, these men were also the only military personnel on board authorised to carry side arms.

The instructions for the preparation of food were particularly precise. Meat and "simple extras" were to be prepared in the forward galley, while the ship's chef would be responsible for all special diets and extras which were to be prepared in the saloon galley. Depending on the number of patients and their ailments, the nature of these special diets could vary considerably, so the senior medical officer was obliged to ensure that a list of the next day's requirements was provided to the ship's purser by 6.00 p.m. the night before. Needless to say, a receipt was required for absolutely everything, but at least there were rarely any questions asked when the White Star Line submitted additional accounts for payment.

Certain aspects of the prescribed guidelines were, nevertheless, particularly relevant. Few restrictions were actually placed on the movements of patients once they were on board, subject, of course, to the permission of the medical officers. On one point, however, the orders were very precise. On no account were any of the wounded permitted to go up on deck dressed in their military uniforms. The overriding consideration here was the safety of the ship. Quite simply, too many visible khaki uniforms could give the enemy the false impression that a hospital ship was being used to transport healthy troops. Because of this, as soon as sick and wounded were brought on board they were provided with standard issue blue hospital suits which would help to distinguish them from front-line soldiers. In the meantime their uniforms would be "bundled" and placed in the invalids' effects room until the ship was safely back in homeport.

*Below and overleaf: **Even in the most trying circumstances it was possible to take a more light-hearted view of life as an invalid on a hospital ward.***

Courtesy John Harvey

Even back in England the red tape of the military was evident for all to see. Hospital trains awaiting the wounded at Southampton were originally intended to take patients to hospitals that were as near as possible to their homes, yet by the autumn of 1916 there seems to have been a distinct change in

Being "done" oneself!

Watching someone else being "done"!

policy. Vivian Prideaux, a patient who returned home on *Britannic* in October 1916 tells a very revealing story:

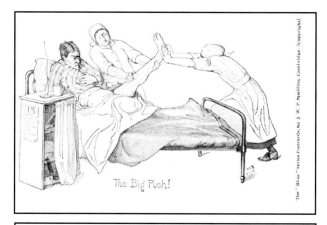

The Big Push!

> "As we waited to be disembarked I was surprised when a sergeant rushed up and said "Where do you live, Sir?" I said London. "Tell him Carlisle" came the reply!!! I was completely mystified until an army transport officer arrived with the question "Where do you live?" "Carlisle," I replied – turning to the corporal accompanying him – "4th London General" – and so I arrived at the hospital which is now known as Kings College Hospital, Denmark Hill – a twenty minutes taxi ride from home!!! Bless that sergeant!!! I have never learned yet, why it was the practise to send a casualty to a hospital as far away from their homes as possible."

The Ministering Angel.

Despite the petty officialdom, life on board did have its compensations. While their colleagues might be roughing it in the trenches of northern France, the panelled cabins aboard *Britannic* offered the medical staff a far more salubrious existence. Indeed, one of the first things that the writer Vera Brittain had noticed when she went aboard the ship en route to her posting as a VAD nurse in Malta was: "a most sumptuous first-class hotel meal in beautifully finished dining room." Another reference to her luxurious inner cabin would also seem to indicate that, although incomplete, a good deal of *Britannic*'s fine panelling was clearly in place.

Certainly, the medical staff and nurses were amongst the luckiest on board, for most of their accommodation was situated in the first-class cabins on B deck. Nurse Sheila Macbeth also recalled her homely cabin and chintz cushions with considerable affection. It is also curious how they both later recalled so distinctly one specific device employed by *Britannic*'s matron, Mrs. E. Dowse, to keep the nurses and medical orderlies apart. When writing *Testament of Youth* years later, Vera Brittain's memories of Mrs. Dowse were still as clear as ever, describing her as "a sixty-year-old dug-out with a red cape and a row of South African medals." Nor did she forget the rope barriers that had been erected by both Mrs. Dowse and their own Sister-in-Charge across the main deck, in an attempt to keep the "VAD sheep" separated from the "RAMC goats." Needless to say it didn't work, as Vera later recalled:

> "After a few days, during which the more adventurous of both sexes had edged as near to the rope as they dared, and several others had regarded one

another from a distance with eyes full of cupidity, the guardians of our virtue were astonished and pained beyond measure when one or two couples, being denied the opportunity of normal conversation on deck, were found in compromising positions beneath the gangways."

And what of the RAMC goats? Private Percy Tyler was one of the medical orderlies assigned to the *Britannic* in September 1916, and because his duties were somewhat more menial than the other medical staff, his accommodation was not nearly so luxurious. He has, nevertheless, left one of the more detailed descriptions of *Britannic*'s layout for posterity:

> "...on A deck, was the company office, the officers and nurses quarters, and the officers wards... B deck aft was the promenade portion for the RAMC, where also was the officers smoke room. Amidships were wards and for'ard some ship's quarters.
>
> C deck aft contained the isolation wards, the RAMC mess and parade ground. Amidships were more nurses' quarters and for'ard wards. D deck held the patients' large dining hall, wards and R.A.M.C. lavatories. E deck had K and H wards the two largest on the boat, and the main gallyway, which stretched from for'ard to aft known as "Scotland Road." Walking along here starting for'ard brought you to ship's quarters, and down two decks to No. 1 barrack room which held about 90 of the Corp staff; returning to Scotland Road brought you past more lavatories, scouts and stewards quarters. Passing on along the passage were crews quarters and passageways to engineers rooms and the stokeholds, lifts etc. Halfway along and again down two decks, G deck was No. 2 barrack room; back again along the road and down again to F deck found No. 3 barrack room and down to G deck No. 4 barrack room aft. There were three passenger and three cot lifts all working from Scotland Road to the boat deck six decks up. G deck was well below the waterline but air was obtained by numerous electric fans which kept a cool breeze carrying through the rooms day and night."

For one group aboard *Britannic*, however, life held few surprises. They were, of course, the ship's crew, and it would seem that despite the rigours of wartime, life on board evidently continued much as it had in happier times. Even the onset of war was not enough to stop the seamen from indulging in their time-honoured privilege of grumbling. Arthur Rostron later recalled a few amusing cases in his memoirs, ranging from a minor complaint about the margarine rations, through to a more serious refusal to obey orders. Whether or not Rostron was taking a leaf out of John Beaumont's book by embellishing his story is open to debate, but if the crew thought they could pull the wool over his eyes then clearly they didn't know their man. On one occasion when on trooping duty he accused the men of being childish and pointed out to them that there were over a couple of thousand bayonets on board and that he would not hesitate to use more "pointed" persuasion if his orders were not obeyed. On another occasion he recalled a more serious dispute that occurred on *Saxonia* while the ship was at Mudros. The story goes that a group of men had refused orders because they had expected some leave, although quite what attractions Mudros held for them is hard to imagine. Rostron went so far as to line up a squad of armed soldiers to make his point. "Whether they thought I was bluffing I don't know," he continued, "but it needs a plucky man to call a bluff while he looks down a barrel of a loaded rifle." Not surprisingly, the men reconsidered their position and the tasks were carried out.

Fortunately there is no record of any industrial strife aboard *Britannic*, though an equally interesting example of a lack of harmonious industrial relations among the crew did occur on the *Olympic* during the spring of 1916. In many ways the dispute was really something of a storm in a teacup. In order to compensate the crew for risking their lives and having to put up with the nightly black out, during the first months of the war they received a monthly war bonus of £2 from the Liverpool Shipowners' Association and the Admiralty. On 1st May 1916 Captain Bertram Hayes informed the ship's crew that, from that date onwards, the Admiralty would not be paying their bonus but that the White Star Line would be doubling their own war risk payment. Even though the bonus would, therefore, effectively remain unchanged, *Olympic*'s crew only accepted the new arrangement "under protest."

Joseph Cotter, the general president of the National Union of Stewards, Cooks, Butchers and Bakers, was not so easy to convince. He quickly pointed out that the ship's articles guaranteed a monthly £1 Admiralty bonus and that, in spite of the other increased payment, it should remain in force. Cotter took this more militant position knowing that his members were far from being amongst the highest-paid echelons of the ship's crew and the Admiralty bonus was therefore that much more significant to them. Indeed, an examination of the rates of pay contained within *Britannic*'s log shows that there may be some justification in his thinking. Aside from the £2 war bonus payable to each member of the crew, the monthly figures looked something like this:

| | |
|---|---|
| Look Out: | £6.15.0 |
| AB: | £6.10.0 |
| Leading Fireman: | £8.0.0 |
| Greaser: | £8.0.0 |
| Fireman: | £7.10.0 |
| Trimmer: | £7.0.0 |
| Ship's Cook: | £9.0.0 |
| Assistant Cook: | £6.0.0 |
| Vegetable Cook: | £10.0.0 |
| Assisant Vegetable Cook: | £6.10.0 |
| Saloon Steward: | £5.10.0 |
| Steward: | £5.5.0 |
| Scullion: | £5.0.0 |
| 2nd Class Pantryman: | £ 6.10.0 |
| Chief Laundryman: | £8 0.0 |
| 4th Butcher: | £6.0.0 |

Seen in this light, perhaps the many stewards and scullions listed amongst Cotter's members might have had grounds to feel aggrieved, although it is clear that the union's pleas on behalf of *Olympic*'s crew fell upon deaf ears. Matters became especially strained when someone at the War Office tactlessly suggested that anyone not accepting the deal might conceivably be dismissed from the ship and that, if they were not able to sign aboard another vessel within two weeks, they would risk being called up for military service. This only prompted the union to appeal to their Members of Parliament for assistance , but, fully aware that Walton Jail was already full of seamen guilty of various offences against Admiralty regulations, Cotter suggested a face-saving solution that the problem be solved by signing-off *Olympic*'s crew and re-signing them under the new agreement. His offer, alas, did not meet with much of a response. As far as the White Star Line were concerned *Olympic* was already scheduled to be laid up for an overhaul, at which time the crew would be paid off anyway, and while the Admiralty were happy to agree to this new arrangement they remained adamant that the old bonus would still not be paid beyond 1st May.

Fortunately, *Britannic*'s crew were not drawn into this rather pointless dispute as the vessel was already laid up at this time. Their situation was, nevertheless, no less precarious. On-board discipline inevitably remained the prerogative of the captain and his word was final. Any seamen returning late from leave, or absent from his post without permission was dealt with in the time honoured way by being placed on the Captain's Report. The captain was then empowered to fine them depending on the seriousness of their offence.

On 8th January 1916 the consequences of desertion became rather more serious. On that day Great Britain introduced conscription and, although the men of the merchant marine were considered exempt, desertion was no longer looked upon in quite so casual a manner. From that day forth, any deserters usually faced at least a month in prison, after which they would probably find themselves conscripted. In order to help out his crew on *Olympic*, Captain Hayes, painfully aware that the number of crewmen being put on report whilst in home port had soared, proposed to his stokehold crew a policy described by him as "Disembodied Leave." Through this means he guaranteed that as a minimal stokehold crew was required when the ship was in home port, generous leave could usually be granted on condition that anyone taking that leave would not be paid whilst they were away from the ship. Bearing in mind the large fines already run up by some absentee crewmen, this was probably no great loss, and the firemen were quick to accept the deal.

In reality, one has only to take a cursory glance at *Britannic*'s log to realise just how relevant Captain Hayes' proposal was to those on board *Olympic*, for it reveals a catalogue of breaches in discipline which, in happier times, would have had far less serious consequences for the miscreants. Three names that are particularly noticeable are those of Bertram, Thomas and Alfred Slade, the three brothers who, by stopping to allow a train pass on April 10th 1912, arrived back at *Titanic* just too late to be allowed back on board by Sixth Officer James Moody before the ship sailed. Doubtless the three men would have been cursing Moody as they left the dock that day. Four-and-a-half years later two of them would experience what it was like to be on a sinking Olympic-Class liner. Bertram Slade, however, would not enjoy even that dubious distinction, having been sentenced to one month's imprisonment in October 1916 for desertion.

The usual minor offences were almost invariably dealt with through the customary five shilling fine, but appearing with monotonous regularity are also entries of crew members who, in spite of the potential consequences, still chose to remain ashore without authority. With the introduction of conscription this now became a particularly risky practice. In the event of a ship being suddenly ordered to sea before their return, the crewmen's names would automatically be passed to the Superintendent of Merchant Marine at Southampton, who would then notify the Port Naval Transport Office and request prosecution. For those unlucky enough to be bought before the bench and not able to justify their absence, a custodial sentence was a near certainty, though in some cases offenders were able to redeem themselves by paying a fine. One such case was Fireman G. Pounder, who disappeared for seven days in February 1916. After such a long absence he was deemed to be a deserter and when finally brought before the Southampton magistrates on 22nd February he was faced with the stark

*Master at Arms James A. Milne. Aside from being responsible for onboard security, "Big Jim" (as he was affectionately known to the crew) and Master at Arms B. Coe were also responsible for the Scouts.*

Courtesy Christopher McCullogh

choice of going to prison for one month or paying a forty shilling fine. For someone on a monthly wage of £7.10.0 this was a fairly large sum of money. Pounder evidently thought his liberty worth the price. To sweeten the pill he was allowed to rejoin the ship and when the crew were paid off on April 8th his indiscretions were conveniently overlooked, with the ship's log recording that he was still given the customary V.G. (very good) rating for both ability and conduct.

Others were less fortunate. *Britannic*'s logbook contains numerous references to seamen who, for one reason or another, found themselves behind bars. in these cases their only consolation would have been that any fines levied by Captain Bartlett would be returned to them by virtue of the fact that a higher court had punished them. For those who remained on board, the captain's word was final. In spite of the apparent harshness of this regime,however, the crew were still considerably better off than a naval rating on a warship.

The defaulters who did eventually return to the fold would inevitably find themselves in front of the captain, who with few exceptions, would impose a standard company fine of five shillings and dock the men's pay for every day that they were absent from duty. Those who could provide extenuating circumstances or produce a medical certificate to explain their absence usually went unpunished, but for the others the fines stood, and once judgement had been passed, the defaulters would be allowed to make a reply which would be entered *verbatim* into the log. For the most part there was little that they could say or do, with most accepting their punishments with relatively good grace, with such recorded replies as "Quite right," "Very good, Sir" and "It's purely a mistake!" Other pleas were more in the mould of errant schoolboys trying to come up with a particularly unconvincing excuse. The logbook also records one or two responses that paint an interesting picture of the personalities of the men concerned:

> Fireman W. Etherington: "I don't see why I'm fined!"
> W. Hibberd: "No, I shan't have the 'arf a day."
> Trimmer W. Hamesworth: "I had the face ache!"
> Fireman F. Forfeit: "I'll stand the five bob fine, but not the day's pay!"
> Fireman G. Carroll: "I've paid enough. I was fined forty bob!"
> Fireman E. Donoghue: "I'm not going to have it, I've been under the doctor since Naples."
> Fireman J. Murphy: "Ugh, nuthin!"

Others were more philosophical:

> Trimmer G. Keamish: "I've got to have it I s'pose."
> H. Roberts: "I was caught fair"
> H. Ingram: "I wasn't here – I was bad."
> Fireman J. Barnes: "It's hard lines if you're late in the morning to have to wait till dinner to get your name took."

For sheer barefaced cheek, however, it's difficult to surpass Fireman W. Freestow, who, in an admirable display of matrimonial duty, replied:

> "I nearly stayed away altogether – my old woman is more to me than the ship!"

Unfortunately for Freestow, Captain Bartlett was less than impressed with this particular line of defence and wasted little time in imposing the customary fine.

In spite of his reputation as a strict disciplinarian, perhaps Captain Bartlett was not really such a hard man. If the occasion demanded it he was usually willing to grant crew members generous leave for compassionate purposes and even those who did try his patience were to discover that he had a softer side. After his return to England following *Britannic*'s sinking, he made his final entry in the ship's log at Southampton on 8th December 1916:

> "All fines and forfeitures imposed on those who were members of the crew on November 21st are cancelled on account of their excellent conduct when ship sank."

One individual who was not destined to benefit from this general amnesty, however, was Steward R. Glass. Three days after *Britannic* returned from her fifth voyage Glass left the ship without authority, and one can even detect a feeling of increasing frustration in the ship's officer who was charged with entering the name of yet another deserter in the log:

9th November:     R. Glass absent from duty without leave.

10th November:    R. Glass is again absent from duty without leave.

11th November:    R. Glass is still absent from duty without leave.

12th November:    R. Glass is a deserter.

Perhaps Glass was a touch unlucky. Other crewmen had gone AWOL for longer periods without being classified as deserters, although with *Aquitania* undergoing extensive repairs due to storm damage *Britannic*'s last turnaround of six days had been considerably quicker than normal. This would probably have been of little consolation to Glass, who would almost certainly have been faced with a custodial sentence when apprehended. During his time in prison he would at least have been able to reflect on the fact that, in view of what was to happen on that very voyage, a month behind bars was probably a small price to pay.

*Right: A bank advice addressed to Lieutenant John Cropper, awarding him a £60 gratuity for successfully completing one year of service in the RAMC. Unfortunately Cropper would never benefit from this bonus, as he would die only four days later when the Britannic was sunk.*

*Courtesy John Harvey*

HOLT & Cº

Telegraphic Address:
"MENSARIUS, WESTRAND, LONDON."

IN REPLY PLEASE
QUOTE REFERENCE
**P 53a**

ENCLOSURES

3, Whitehall Place,

London, S.W.     17 NOV 1916

Dear Sir,

   We beg to acquaint you, that the account has credit for

the under-mentioned amount, viz: -

Gratuity due on completion of a year's service     £ 60 : - : -

Less Income Tax, deducted under instructions
from the Commissioners of Income Tax, War
Office, on the ground that the gratuity
is regarded as income and therefore tax-
able.                                              £     3 : 15 : -
                                                   _____
                                                   £   56 : 5 : -
                                                   ===============

   In case you are not renewing your contract, we

avail ourselves of the opportunity to mention, that besides

acting as Bankers for Naval and Military Officers, we also

have a large number of private Customers, and if the services

of a London Banker would be of any use to you, we shall have

pleasure in continuing the account when you have relinquished

your Commission, and to afford you all the usual Banking

facilities.

          We are, Dear Sir,

          Yours faithfully,

To: *Lieut John Cropper*
       *R. A. M. C.*                      Holt Cº

                                          Exd.

# CHAPTER EIGHT

# RETURN TO THE MEDITERRANEAN

As the month of August drew to a close *Britannic* was still lying idle while the war continued to run its course, and although the military situation may have stabilised in the Mediterranean, elsewhere it was a very different matter.

The news during the preceding months had been mixed. In the east, on 29th April the 9,000 British troops besieged for five months at Kut on the River Tigris had been forced to surrender, while on 5th June the Sherif of Mecca had raised the standard of revolt against the Turkish rulers of the Hejaz, paving the way for the Arab Revolt which would ultimately make the reputation of one Lieutenant T.E. Lawrence. Elsewhere, on 4th June Russian General Aleksei Brusilov had launched his famous offensive in Galicia, forcing the Germans to divert much-needed forces from their attacking forces at Verdun, while on the Western Front the British offensive on the Somme throughout July had developed into a virtual battle of attrition. On the first day alone the British had suffered 60,000 casualties, of which 20,000 were killed.

Closer to home the news was equally grim. The Easter rising in Dublin, although quickly contained and subdued by the available British forces, had set in motion a series of events which would result in the Irish nationalist rebellion against British rule, while on 5th June Great Britain suffered a massive blow to the morale of the armed forces when Lord Kitchener was among the 655 drowned when the armoured cruiser HMS *Hampshire* was lost. *Hampshire* had struck a submerged mine off Malin Head in the Orkney Islands while en-route to Russia and the loss of the ship had, once again, provided convincing evidence of the damage that could be inflicted by a random mine.

For the purposes of our story at least, far more important than any of these events was the long-awaited confrontation between the German High Seas Fleet and the British Grand Fleet. On 31st May they finally clashed off the Danish coast at Jutland, and the engagement was to have far-reaching consequences on the future conduct of the war at sea. Even though the High Seas Fleet acquitted itself nobly, losing one battle cruiser to Great Britain's three, in strategic terms the battle had changed nothing. The Grand Fleet still retained its overwhelming superiority and it had become quite evident that if Germany were to win the war at sea the only weapon that was going to make it possible would be the U-boat. The formal resumption of unrestricted submarine warfare was still some months in the future, but the increased U-boat construction programme was evidence enough that things were set to change.

*Left:* **Vera Brittain would be one of many passengers on board after Britannic's return to service, bound for her new posting on the island of Malta.**

The activity in the Mediterranean, meanwhile, was also beginning to escalate. Following a successful German offensive in Romania, the hitherto subdued front at Salonika was about to become active and with the Allied forces preparing to advance in belated support of their Romanian and Serbian allies it did not take long for the War Office to realise that the large hospital ships would once again be required. On 21st July *Aquitania* was recalled to service and immediately the Harland and Wolff ship repair facility at Southampton set about undoing all of the work that they had carried out during the past two months to reinstate the ship as a passenger liner. With *Mauretania* already earmarked for trooping duties to Canada it was only a matter of time before *Britannic* would once again be called upon, and on 28th August the official notification arrived at the White Star Liverpool office confirming that *Britannic* would once again be requisitioned as a hospital ship.

It is curious that *Aquitania* should have taken priority over *Britannic* as the former ship had been laid up for considerably longer, with the result that she was almost completely restored to her original condition. *Britannic*, on the other hand, had lain idle for a little over two months and with Harland and Wolff's priorities understandably taken up in the construction of military vessels it is unlikely that much work would have been undertaken in the restoration of the ship. Then again, some work had certainly been carried out during this time, although the exact details remain unclear. The one thing of which we can be sure is that on 20th October the White Star Line once again contacted the Director of Transports to inform him that, for insurance purposes, *Britannic*'s first-cost had risen by over £27,000. This would therefore seem to imply that some additional work on *Britannic*'s fitting out had been undertaken during this time and, indeed, photographs do seem to indicate the appearance of an additional structure on the shade deck, which may well have been one of the motor houses for the additional gantry davits intended for the stern. As to the extent of any internal modifications, however, we can only speculate.

On 4th September Charles Bartlett once again assumed command of the ship and five days later, after taking on stores, equipment and medical personnel at Southampton, *Britannic* returned to her old anchorage off Cowes. The following two weeks would remain strangely quiet, allowing the new medical staff the luxury of being able to continue with their preparations in a relatively unhurried atmosphere. Meanwhile, the availability of such a large ship for transport purposes was not lost on the War Office. Among the many medical personnel waiting to be shipped abroad were hundreds of VAD nurses, and the availability of such a large transport was simply too convenient an opportunity to miss.

One of these lucky passengers was nurse Vera Brittain. Following the war Vera would become a famous writer and ardent pacifist, but in 1916 she was serving as a VAD nurse at the 1st London General Hospital in Camberwell, where, on 15th September, she was notified that she was being posted abroad. After a confusing week trying to obtain her additional kit while continuing to work her required hours at the hospital, she learnt that they would be leaving for their new posting on 23rd September (a week earlier than expected) aboard *Britannic*.

Departure day duly dawned, and after a last *au revoir* with her mother and brother, Vera proceeded to Waterloo Station to be met by the Principal Matron of the hospital. Clutching a bunch of violets and white heather, Vera's misery at the thought of the uncertain journey knew no bounds, but when her friend, Stella

Sharp, produced some chocolate she began to feel better. By the time the train reached Southampton they were all in much better spirits and once Vera and Stella were in a carriage bound for the docks she was beginning to rediscover the first thrill of adventure she had felt since first hearing that she was going abroad. After depositing their luggage at the docks and had checked in with the Embarkation Officer, they went to the nearby *Flower's Hotel* for a last taste of an English afternoon tea. By four o'clock they were once again assembled at the dock and before long their tender was heading south towards Cowes, where they would join the ship.

Vera would never forget her first sight of *Britannic*:

> "At last in the distance we saw the *Britannic*, a great white monster with four funnels and three large red crosses painted on her side. She was intended for the sister ship of the *Titanic*, but owing to this superstition regarding sister ships, the White Star Company ceased building her when the *Titanic* went down in 1912. But when the war broke out the Government commandeered her as a hospital ship, so that she was the *Titanic's* sister ship no longer."

Leaving aside Vera's rather innaccurate ideas regarding sister ships, she continues:

> "To us who have never been on a liner before, her size was almost terrifying, especially when I looked over A deck after night had fallen and noticed her height from the water. We waited for a long time at the bottom of the ship's main staircase while berths were being appointed; after all the staff was settled we got ours – inner cabins without portholes as we were only passengers. We were however lucky to get a cabin at all as most of the people who came next day had to go into wards. Stella and I were not together at first, but after some manipulation we managed to change with other people sharing a cabin."

With their accommodation sorted out, the VADs sat down to what Vera described as "a most sumptuous first class hotel meal in a beautifully finished dining room". In spite of all this finery she would later admit to getting extremely bored with the routine before the end of the voyage. Clearly the fear of the unknown, not to mention her feelings of claustrophobia in such confined spaces after a particularly active outdoor life, were not to her taste, so it is probably just as well that *Britannic* was not her permanent assignment. The additional restrictions imposed by the dreaded Sister Knight, whom she later remembered as "most admirable and an excellent disciplinarian," also helped to make the lives of the VADs a particular burden.

On Sunday 24th September *Britannic* remained anchored off Cowes, so Vera took the opportunity to explore the lower wards in the ship, although the sight of the swinging iron cots and the stuffiness of the lower decks only served to confirm her relief at not being permanently posted to the ship. Later she attended the Sunday morning church service at which she distinctly remembered the hymn *Jesu, Lover of my Soul*, not to mention a rather fine sermon from a little red-haired chaplain who claimed that to a certain high type of human nature "the perilous thing has always had an alluring charm." That chaplain was the Rev. John Alexander Fleming, who had only recently been transferred to *Britannic* from his post as assistant chaplain of the Tay defences at Montrose in Scotland. This particular posting aboard *Britannic,* in fact, also gave Fleming the distinction of being the first Presbyterian to serve as a chaplain on a British warship, although the predominantly Church of England congregation would also have the services of the Rev. James B. Atkinson.

The remainder of the day was spent writing a few last letters which would be sent off with the pilot, and at 5.40 p.m., escorted for the first stage of the journey into the Channel by destroyers and several seaplanes, *Britannic* was finally outward bound. After dinner, Vera went up on deck to see the last of England, which she faithfully recorded in her diary:

> "After dinner Stella and I stood again on deck, more or less oblivious of one another, and yet very thankful of each other's company. We remained there a long time watching the sunset and the green and red of the ship's lights reflected in the foam that the great liner ploughed up behind us as she sped swiftly along the Channel, going west. We seemed to sail right into a sunset of most lovely mauve and pink, the colour of one's dreams. We could not see the Needles distinct (as it was getting dark), but we passed not far from the great lighthouse there, and could see it flashing miles and miles away long after the darkness had completely fallen. After sunset we watched the orderlies singing and dancing on the deck below; it looked quite like the stage of a theatre seen from the dress circle. One man had a violin, which he played most hauntingly. I remember Tosti's *Goodbye* amongst other things. By this time we were quite out of sight of land."

The following day found *Britannic* well into the Bay of Biscay, with the condition of the sea more than living up to its reputation. It was not long before most of the medical staff were laid low with sea sickness, and even those who did attend dinner that evening did not stay for long. The following morning everyone awoke to find the ship once again in calm waters and the nurses were able to pass the morning quite comfortably up on deck. Vera's sense of monotony was briefly interrupted quite early in the morning when the inbound *Aquitania* hove into view and, coincidentally, *Britannic* picked up her first escort of the voyage – a shoal of dolphins with great shining stiff brown bodies, leaping up out of the water and falling back with "a great flop".

For the remainder of the day *Britannic* continued to navigate the Portuguese coast. At sunset the ship passed Cape St. Vincent and by 5.30 a.m. the following day the Rock of Gibraltar was in sight. Risking the wrath of Sister Knight, Stella and Vera were both up on deck to witness the event, dressed only in their night gowns. It was still quite dark at the time and all they could see was the great black rock towering above them, with a few lights right up to the top and a large searchlight working at its base. Quite close in to the shore they glimpsed what Vera thought to be the darkened silhouette of a battleship. When there was no more to be seen they went over to the starboard side to observe the lights on the coast of Africa, and as the day began to dawn, the distant mountains. For most of the day the ship remained in sight of the barren Spanish coast, but before night had fallen *Britannic* was once again in open water with the next landfall, the southern coast of Sardinia, not due to be sighted for another twenty-four hours.

The remaining passage to Naples was not destined to be a smooth one. That night the ship ran into a thunderstorm which seemed far worse than anything the medical staff had experienced in Biscay. Their predicament was not made any easier when, in the evening as they retired, they were ordered to pack up their belongings in readiness to leave the vessel in case they were to be transhipped at Naples. Vera, confident of waking early enough in the morning when she hoped it would be calmer, could not bring herself to attempt packing that night. Stella, however, was more determined. In spite of the fact that she was very seasick and virtually incapable of standing, she decided to pack what she could while lying on the floor. The sight of her crawling about in her pyjamas amongst the heaps of luggage, while trying to pull clothing down from pegs so reduced Vera to fits of laughter that Stella finally lost all patience and unceremoniously threw all of her clothes on top of her.

The following morning *Britannic* returned to the Bay of Naples for the first time in six months. By now the stormy weather had settled down, even though it was still raining, and as the ship proceeded to her customary anchorage in the area of the harbour "Reservato Navi da Guerra", it seemed to Vera as if the huge *Britannic* completely filled the harbour entrance. Her pride in *Britannic*'s size, however, was less than matched by her impression of some of the craft of the Italian Navi da Guerra. As far as she could see the Italian vessels seemed mostly to consist of ramshackle tugs with black tops and red bottoms, while a nearby training ship attracted her particular scorn, noting that in England it would probably be sold as "old iron." On the other hand, she was much more impressed by a smart grey monitor anchored nearby, particularly as the Italian crew had hoisted a collection of gaily coloured flags in honour of *Britannic*'s arrival.

Fortunately the transhipping rumour proved to be a false alarm and at midday some of the nurses were granted shore passes. After five days cooped up on board Vera was quick to make the most of this opportunity to go ashore, and before long she was treading the same paths that Harold Goodman had followed six months earlier. In spite of the rain the visions of the many coloured flowers and vegetables that she had never seen before dazzled her, though she was also quick to notice Naples' seedier side. Lines of laundry, usually in an advanced state of tatters, hung from all of the windows, while even the beggars seemed to be dressed in faded colours. The fact that nearly all of them seemed to openly exhibit their various defects with evident pride prompted her to conclude: "Italy is a corrupt country, no doubt."

The uneven paving stones that apparently passed for streets also attracted her critical eye, particularly as they were often deep with water, and in an attempt to find somewhat more hygienic surroundings Vera's group went into the Grand Arcade and then along the Via Roma. Here they would spend the first part of their visit shopping and, like any other tourist, she took the opportunity to buy as many presents as she could. For her mother she bought a small coral charm carved into the shape of a skull, for her father a wooden terracotta vase and for her brother, Edward, she found

*Britannic at Mudros, with HMHS Galeka lying alongside. Just aft of Britannic's fourth smokestack you can just see a mast belonging to the hospital ship Warilda, secured on the port side.*

*Imperial War Museum*

a couple of local water-colours. After lunch in the Arcade they hired a one-horse vehicle to visit the church of Santa Brigida, before moving on to the museum where they could see a number of Greek statues that had been excavated at Pompeii. A trip to Pompeii itself was not possible because the town had been placed off limits to visitors because of an epidemic raging there, so after tea in a café they returned to *Britannic* in the ship's launch.

Saturday morning proved to be equally uneventful and after much waiting about in watery passages at the very bottom of the ship (clearly the old problem with the back valve had not been completely solved) the ladies were once again allowed ashore. This time the weather was beautiful and after another lunch in the Arcade, where they were introduced to the complexities of eating spaghetti with a fork, they paid eleven shillings for a drive around Naples. Vera recalled that the Italians seemed particularly pleased to see the English nurses by waving and wishing them good luck, while some Italian officers even had a dangerous habit of stepping into the middle of the road and quite oblivious of the traffic, graciously saluting them. Their tour included such sites as San Martino, where the great fortress of St. Elmo provided one of the most glorious views that Vera had ever seen of the Bay of Naples, and the tour finally ended with a drive past the Aquarium and through the English quarter of the city, where she noticed that nearly all of the hotels were either closed or being used as hospitals.

Saturday was to be their last day on shore. By Sunday evening coaling had been completed and *Britannic* was once again at sea, reviving all of Vera's dormant anxieties. Her fears were not eased when she learnt that the Aegean Sea was probably the most hazardous part of the voyage, or moreover, that by now most of the VADs were beginning to get thoroughly bored with life afloat. At least they now had other matters to distract them, as the VAD passengers had been press-ganged into assisting *Britannic*'s nurses with some of the bed making. Even this was a task that Vera seemed to loathe:

> "Let no one who has never been out of England pretend she has any idea of what bed-making can be. When you are working in the convalescent wards and have the one-above-another kind to tackle, you cannot get into the middle as two rows are close alongside one another. You therefore have to stand one at the top and one at the bottom of the bed, and in order to make the top one you have to stand on a ledge fixed to the bottom one, off which you topple every time the ship rolls. The bottom one is even worse; there seems to be no alternative between nearly breaking your back or banging your head with violence. I never knew any expedient so effective in making one hot, tired, and thoroughly bad-tempered."

Fortunately her ordeal was almost over. On the morning of Tuesday 3rd October the *Britannic* was being escorted at various times by a British battle cruiser, a torpedo boat and a destroyer, and by the afternoon the ship had cleared the three rows of mines protecting the Bay of Mudros. As *Britannic* slowly proceeded to her customary anchorage, Vera noted that the bay itself was packed with all manner of shipping, including a British dreadnought and several smaller British and French battleships, not to mention seven hospital ships, most of which lay in the curve of the harbour.

As the sick and wounded came on board, the passengers remained out of the way on the upper decks. By 9.00 p.m. the

*With her decks now packed with wounded, Britannic prepares to depart from Mudros. By this time the ship's brilliant white hull is looking badly soiled by the coaling lighters at Naples; at one time these marks were even interpreted as evidence of some form of secret anti-magnetic mine apparatus.*

*Imperial War Museum*

hospital ship *Galeka* had been emptied of its human cargo and the time had come for the nurses to be transhipped. It was only now that Vera began to appreciate just how comfortable life on board *Britannic* had been, as the conditions on board *Galeka*

*With steam up Britannic prepares to depart from Mudros on 11th October 1916.*

were infinitely worse. Instead of occupying nice comfortable cabins, the nurses were now placed in two of the wards in the bowels of the ship, which had only just been vacated by the convalescing Tommies. With little privacy, primitive sanitary arrangements and only an occasional electric fan for air, perhaps it was not surprising that when *Galeka* arrived at Malta after a four-day voyage, sixteen of the VADs were suffering from a mysterious ailment that no one could isolate.

Meanwhile, the task of taking sick and wounded aboard *Britannic* resumed as if service had never been interrupted. Within two days the ship was full to capacity and once again heading for England. Sadly it was not to be an uneventful voyage. Mudros had scarcely disappeared beneath the horizon when, at 3.40 p.m. on 5th October Corporal Joseph Seddon of the 1st Manchester Regiment died in the ship's infirmary, and with England still a good six days away there could be no question of transporting the body home for burial. That same evening a service was held at the ship's stern where, at 10.30 p.m., the body was committed to the deep. Fortunately Seddon would be the only casualty on this voyage and by 11th October *Britannic* was once again safely back at Southampton, discharging her cargo of wounded.

Apart from the death of Corporal Seddon, the return voyage had gone without a hitch. The new medical staff had handled their workload with comparative ease and with *Britannic* tied up in port for the next nine days most of them would have had plenty of time to enjoy the customary seven-day leave. However, while everything appeared to be relaxed on the ship, behind the scenes at the War Office events were already unfolding which would cast a considerable shadow over the future role of the *Britannic* and of every other Allied hospital ship in service.

*Above:* **Britannic arriving at Mudros on 3rd October 1916.**

*Courtesy Alasdair Fairbairn*

*Top left:* **Britannic towers over two smaller hospital ships secured alongside at Mudros.**

*Courtesy Alasdair Fairbairn*

*Top right:* **A rare photograph of the Britannic lying at Mudros, taken from HMHS Guildford Castle on 6th October 1916 as the ship arrived from Malta.**

*Courtesy Alasdair Fairbairn*

*Right:* **It was only while lying on a stretcher on the top deck of a smaller ship such as the Guildford Castle that the patients could appreciate just how large the Britannic really was.**

*Courtesy Alasdair Fairbairn*

# CHAPTER NINE

# THE CURIOUS CASE
# OF THE AUSTRIAN OPERA SINGER

By the second week of October 1916, *Britannic* had safely completed four voyages to the Mediterranean in what, until then, had been an incident-free career. As a result, over ten thousand wounded British soldiers had been safely returned to England with the loss of only five. The Dardanelles Service had been well and truly re-established, but the mining of the hospital ship *Galeka* on 28th October, would provide the first omens of the difficult road which lay ahead, while the imbroglio resulting from *Britannic*'s next voyage would muddy the waters in a way that has never been satisfactorily resolved to this day.

The first seeds of the controversy were unwittingly sewn on 13th October 1916, when the Transport Division forwarded an innocuous request to the Admiralty from the RAMC for *Britannic* to transport medical personnel and stores to Mudros. Three days later the request was approved, but the terms of the permission, due mainly to the fact that *Britannic* was scheduled to leave in only four days time, made it clear that in future the only medical personnel to be transported in a hospital ship should be nurses.

Quite why the Admiralty should be raising these concerns at this stage is not entirely clear. Harold Goodman's diary from March 1916 mentions that Canadian Hospital personnel and equipment were taken on board at Augusta, not to mention the orderlies of the 1st London Field Ambulance, so there did seem to be an established practice for transporting medical personnel. In any event, on 17th October the orders were confirmed and over the next two days *Britannic* took on 2,762 packages of medical stores and 168 tons of other provisions destined for Egypt, Malta, Salonika, Mesopotamia and India. By the time the ship was ready to depart, in addition to its nominal medical staff there were also 484 extra medical personnel destined for various fronts, including 47 RAMC officers, 4 assistant surgeons, 8 dentists, 10 female doctors, 17 chaplains, 209 nurses, 4 British Red Cross members and 185 RAMC orderlies.

One of the additional VAD sisters was nurse Edith Moor, and her diary of the voyage to her new posting at Salonika began by painting a somewhat chaotic picture of her arrival at Southampton, which appears to have caused more than a few administrative problems for *Britannic*'s matron. An undignified scramble to retrieve her baggage at the dockside had only been the beginning of Edith's ordeal, although an RAMC officer had at least assisted her with her trunk at the platform before instructing a nearby soldier to take it on board for her. Once aboard things were little better, as she and the other passengers were then left standing for two hours at the foot of the forward staircase on D deck before they were eventually assigned to

*Left: A sunny evening on the port side promenade deck. Note the medical officer with the camera.*

*Courtesy John Fleming*

their temporary accommodation. Edith finally found herself in Y Ward, and she was happy enough with her lower cot and the fact that there were several "nice" bathrooms located nearby.

Edith was particularly dazzled by the sight of the nurses in their red capes and white caps in the ship's ornate dining room, and she clearly felt at home on *Britannic*. Other elements of her diary, such as her recollection that on the first night at sea the ship had to run at thirty knots to escape a submarine that was chasing the ship, however, are less reliable,

By 4.30 p.m. on 20th October *Britannic* was ready to depart, and as the vessel edged out of the White Star Dock the troops aboard a few of the nearby transports came up on deck to cheer off the British nurses and kept calling out "Are we downhearted, No!" To further choruses of "Keep the Home Fires Burning" and "Best Luck Go With You," *Britannic* headed south along Southampton Water and into the Solent, before assuming her now well-established course for Naples, where she arrived safely at 6.30 a.m. on 25th October.

*A typical medical card issued to patients once the ship's doctors had examined them.*

The visit to Naples once again provided medical personnel with the now customary opportunity to go ashore, but on this occasion the chaplain's decision to organise a trip to Pompeii, now apparently free from the epidemic, would turn out to be something of a disaster. In spite of the fact that they were ashore by midday, it was only at 3.15 p.m. that the special train was finally ready to leave Naples for Pompeii on a journey which was to take considerably longer than the advertised forty-five minutes. Nor was it a comfortable journey. The carriages and track shook so much that some of the nurses found it difficult to remain in their seats even at reduced speed, and once they had finally reached their destination their tour of Pompeii was severely curtailed in order to get everyone back to the ship. The journey back to Naples was equally horrendous, taking close to two hours. By the time the nurses were back on board it was well past 6.00 p.m. and to make matters worse, with their passes broken they had missed dinner. Even though they incurred the wrath of the matron, their tardiness was as nothing compared with a few of the doctors who had been issued with passes until midnight – the last man did not return on board until 2.30 a.m.

Not surprisingly, the following morning, passes to go ashore were rather scarce and instead the medical staff amused themselves by buying silks and broaches from the hordes of local traders on the flotilla of little boats which had by now surrounded the corralled hospital ship. One idle diversion involved throwing silver coins over the side to the children who would then jump from the boats into the sea and retrieve them. But for most of the nurses the distractions of the blackened, semi-naked labourers who were coaling the ship seemed to offer far greater interest. Ada Garland's concentration was clearly so intense that she even spotted some of the labourers honouring the well-established practice of deliberately dropping large lumps into the water in order to retrieve them once the ship had departed. With coal costing approximately £8 per ton at Naples it is not difficult to appreciate the financial advantages that such a practice could bring to the poorer inhabitants of the port. Despite these petty indiscretions the bunkering was complete by 5.00 p.m., and after having supposedly taken on some three thousand tons of coal and two thousand tons of water, *Britannic* was once again underway.

On the morning of 28th October *Britannic* steamed into the Bay of Mudros to conclude what had been a perfectly routine outward voyage. This good luck was, sadly, not to last. One of the first vessels to arrive alongside was the hospital ship *Wandilla*, fresh from a two-day voyage from Valletta. Among her list of passengers for transportation back to England was one Adalbert Franz Messany, an Austrian national who would in due course cause considerable embarrassment at the Admiralty.

So what was an Austrian doing on an Allied hospital ship in

*A group of nurses on the port promenade deck during embarkation at Southampton*

*Courtesy John Fleming*

the first place? Messany had actually been in Allied custody since the outbreak of war. An opera singer by profession, he had been detained in August 1914 by the British authorities at Luxor, Egypt, where he was placed under observation before a decision was made to have him interned. It was not until 1st December that he arrived in Malta, where he was destined to remain confined for nearly two years. Unfortunately for Messany he later developed a serious case of tuberculosis and the Allied authorities decided that he should be repatriated to Austria.

The repatriation itself was not a major problem, as established diplomatic channels via neutral Holland dealt with cases of this sort all the time. By the terms of the Geneva Convention hospital ships were obliged to provide relief and assistance to the wounded and sick without distinction of nationality, so transporting Messany back to England aboard *Britannic* should not have presented a problem, and on 24th October he went aboard *Wandilla* for the first leg of his journey from Malta to Lemnos.

*Barges of wounded from the shore-based hospitals arrive alongside at Mudros.*

Courtesy Angus Mitchell

It was only after *Wandilla* arrived at Mudros that things began to go wrong. Messany's repatriation was certainly carried out in line with the Geneva Convention, yet it seems curious that the security surrounding an enemy national seems to have been less than thorough. The workload may have had something to do with it, as over a forty-eight hour period *Britannic* took on over 3,000 wounded troops from a procession of hospital ships, including *Dunluce Castle*, *Glenart Castle*, *Llandovery Castle*, *Grantully Castle* and *Valdivia*. As the wounded troops came aboard, the unsupervised Messany was making a mental note of a few other activities. Being understandably ignorant of British uniforms, his untrained eye would not have appreciated that the khaki-clad troops which he saw disembarking from *Britannic* were actually RAMC orderlies, or that the dubious unidentified packages being transferred with them contained nothing more sinister than medical supplies. The mere fact that he was even allowed to witness these activities at all would haunt the Allies in the weeks to come.

By the late morning of 30th October the transfers both to and from *Britannic* were complete, and the ship sailed westbound shortly after midday. At first Messany was segregated from the wounded British troops and remained confined to the ship's mortuary. Shortly after midnight on 2nd November Corporal George Frith Hunt died from dysentery and, with the mortuary now required, Messany was moved into one of the wards. Even though Corporal Hunt was buried at sea that same evening, Messany remained in the ward for the rest of the voyage where his supervision seems to have been incredibly lax, as he remained largely free to move around and talk with whomsoever he pleased. Unfortunately it would appear that he was particularly observant. Aside from noting that a good many of the officers were allowed to retain their side arms he also struck up a number of conversations with some of the troops on board, several of whom would later become particularly relevant in the débacle that followed. Two of these soldiers were Harold Hickman, a Malaria-stricken private in the Welsh Hussars, and Private Reginald Tapley, an RAMC orderly who was also being invalided home. While their conversations may have seemed innocent enough at the time, Hickman and Tapley were about to become important pawns in the world of diplomatic brinkmanship.

On 6th November *Britannic* arrived safely back at Southampton after what seemed

*A closer view of Britannic's shade deck, one of the features which distinguished her from Olympic and Titanic. The square structure on the poop housed the ship's mortuary.*

to have been a successful voyage, with the sick and wounded disembarked in an orderly fashion. After being sent to the clearing hospital at Eastleigh, Private Hickman was transferred to the War Hospital at Carrington, near Nottingham, until he was discharged to sick furlough on 19th December, just in time

for Christmas. Private Tapley was less fortunate. Suffering from dysentery, he remained at the Second Western General Hospital in Manchester until 7th March 1917. Messany, meanwhile, would pass the remaining few weeks of his internment at Dartmouth in Devon, before the orders for his repatriation to Austria were confirmed at the end of December. Instead of disappearing into obscurity, however, Messany's arrival back in Vienna would allow the Central Powers to transform a hitherto simple routine medical repatriation into a major international dispute.

The reasons for this dispute are not all that difficult to fathom. Since May 1916, in response to American diplomatic protests, the German submarine fleet had been restricted to the practice of operating according to prize rules, whereby unarmed Allied ships were not attacked without warning. During the ensuing six months the characteristics of the war had changed beyond all recognition. The German offensive at Verdun had finally ground to a halt at the end of October, while the British attack on the Somme, although a massive drain on British resources, had seriously depleted German reserves. Even at sea the situation was one of stalemate. The High Seas Fleet had acquitted itself well at Jutland, but the outcome of that battle had changed nothing. The British Grand Fleet continued to maintain it's policy of distant blockade and with their civilian population facing increased hardship, German politicians, mindful of the dangers of antagonising neutral America, hesitated to reintroduce unrestricted submarine warfare.

For the generals at the German High Command, however, the issues were not so clouded. While Germany continued to weaken, the Allies could only grow stronger, and unless the practice of unrestricted submarine warfare was reintroduced there was little chance of an early peace with honour. Sensing the deteriorating situation, on 12th December the German Chancellor, Theo von Bethmann-Holweg, had even made a speech in the Reichstag offering peace talks with the Allies. When the offer was rebuffed one week later, the general's arguments for the reintroduction of unrestricted submarine warfare became irresistible. Before the campaign could be resumed, however, some form of justification had to be made in the unlikely hope that a still neutral America might be appeased. It did not take very long for the Central Powers to come up with their excuse - the misuse of hospital ships by the Allies.

Suddenly, Adalbert Messany's observations of what would otherwise have been a routine voyage on the *Britannic* became pivotal in Austrian and German diplomatic circles, and the timing of his repatriation could not have been more opportune. By 5th January 1917 he was back in Vienna and the information gained from his debriefing was to prove to be the icing on the cake, as Messany's allegations of the abuses on board the Allies' largest hospital ship poured fourth.

As well as his observations of the packages being taken off the ship (which according to his statement were being taken on board), two key figures in Messany's version included Privates Hickman and Tapley. Messany alleged that Tapley had claimed to be a French translator being relocated to France, while Hickman, who had also claimed to be a German interpreter, was similarly being transferred. At no time during his conversations with them had either man made any mention of being ill and, to make the situation worse, both had disclosed that there were over two thousand men kept below who were not allowed to go on deck, and being fed on different rations from the men in the wards. In apparent support of this, Messany claimed that when *Britannic* arrived back at Southampton these same troops were lined up on the quay before being marched away. He did subsequently admit that they were not actually carrying any weapons, but the same could certainly not be said of the wounded officers in the wards who had been permitted to retain their side arms for the entire voyage.

Messany's observations clearly provided enough ammunition for the German authorities to include them in a document published on 29th January 1917, detailing some twenty-two alleged cases of Allied abuses in the use and operation of their hospital ships. They also clearly had little intention of awaiting an Allied response and two days later, on 31st January 1917, Germany suddenly declared the immediate resumption of unrestricted submarine warfare around the British Isles.

Even with all their efforts to justify their decision, the international reaction against Germany was totally predictable. America broke off diplomatic relations with Germany and although this was clearly not the reaction that the Allies had hoped for, it was now only a matter of time before America finally came into the war on their side. Meanwhile, the German submarines were unleashed, and almost immediately Allied shipping casualties rocketed. 520,000 tons were lost in February 1917 alone, with the figure rising slightly to 564,000 tons the following month. By this time the losses were far outstripping the capacity of the British shipyards and, but for the American entry into the war and the belated introduction of the convoy system, there is every chance that the losses, which peaked at 881,000 tons in April, would have forced Britain to sue for peace.

Britain survived the crisis, but the diplomatic war of words still continued. It was now essential that Germany's allegations regarding the misuse of hospital ships had to be discredited, and in order to counter them the Admiralty left no stone unturned in their investigation. As *Britannic* had been specifically mentioned, it therefore seemed logical to trace Messrs. Tapley and Hickman.

Tapley and Hickman were each interviewed and their medical histories were specifically mentioned in a

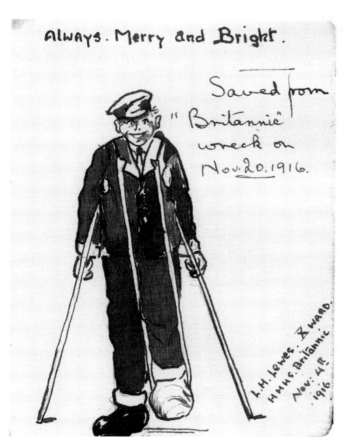

*No matter how serious their injuries, the medical staff were amazed at the courage and determination that many of the wounded often displayed.*

*Paul Louden-Brown Collection*

detailed response. It was assumed that Messany had probably claimed that they professed to be interpreters because each man had an "L" stitched onto his sleeve. This was not at all unusual, because the "L" patch was in fact the distinguishing mark given to any Allied soldier on the Salonika front who could speak a foreign language.

The two thousand mysterious troops also proved relatively simple to justify. An analysis of the 3,022 invalids embarked for this particular voyage demonstrated that only 367 men were classified as "cot cases." They would almost certainly have been on different rations to the walking wounded, depending on the instructions laid down on their individual medical cards. The remaining 2,655 non-cot cases still required constant medical attention from the medical orderlies on board. The alleged restriction of patients who were apparently not allowed on deck was also completely dismissed. As long as they followed the guidelines laid down by the Senior Medical Officer, not to mention their regulation blue hospital suits, they had the freedom to roam the allocated areas of the open deck as often as they wished.

The final allegation regarding British officers being allowed to retain their side arms, was not, however, quite so easy to validate. Nevertheless, it still had to be addressed. The side arms were the personal property of officers, and not regulation issue, and because of this it was not the practice to ship them home separately. Then again, the fact that in the earlier stages of the war these weapons would have been taken from their owners and secured below for the duration of the voyage, does seem to suggest that certain procedures might have become a little lax. The side arms should have been returned to their owners once the ship was back in homeport, but for the duration of the voyage itself the only personnel who were technically allowed to carry side arms on a hospital ship were the men of the military police. That Messany had been permitted to see these weapons at all was something of an own-goal for the Admiralty, though they continued to claim that the conveyance of weapons belonging to wounded officers was not thought to be in contravention of the Geneva Convention. Rather conveniently, the future practice was deemed to be "under consideration."

As far as *Britannic* was concerned, the matter was by this time academic. The ship had long-ceased to be a factor in the Allied war effort. Even so, British attempts to discredit Messany's allegations in the following weeks would be a lot simpler than the subsequent German attempts to justify the diplomatic consequences following the sinking of several non-combatant hospital ships in quick succession. In spite of her exalted status as Britain's largest ship, *Britannic*'s nemesis was soon to come at the hands of the humblest of weapons. A particularly intriguing coincidence, however, is that she may even have been in the area on the exact day that the seeds of her destruction were sown.

Bearing in mind that *Britannic* arrived at Mudros for the last time at 8.00 a.m. on 28th October 1916, it is reasonable to assume that the ship would therefore have been passing through the area of the Kea Channel during the early hours of that same morning. By a curious coincidence the logbook of *U73*, then in the sixth day of another voyage out of Catarro, places the U-boat in this area at the same time. In addition to several hospital ships being sighted during the day, the log includes one particularly intriguing reference, entered at 3.50 a.m. while the submarine was on the surface loading its mine tubes in preparation for the day's activities:

"Petalioli Gulf. Destroyer in gulf in sight. Hospital ship in Kea Strait."

Because of his respect for the status of hospital ships, Kapitänleutnant Siess made no attempt to interfere with the ship in any way. Indeed, *U73*'s log records that while in that area the submarine had observed no less than five hospital ships in a three-day period. Another large steamer was also spotted later that day at 2.00 p.m., headed in a north easterly direction (presumably for Mudros) and came close to being fired upon, only for Siess to abandon the attack at the last minute when the vessel was positively identified as a hospital ship.

The Kea Channel would actually prove to be a frustrating location for Siess. Between 8.07 and 8.27 a.m. *U73* laid two barrages of six mines off Port St. Nikolo, before remaining in the area for a further six hours to observe the results. Despite several near misses there was no definite evidence of any success and by 3.30 p.m. the volume of traffic seemed to have thinned out. With no further reason to stay, Siess ordered a course for the Doro Passage where the submarine surfaced at 5.15 p.m. to recharge the batteries and reload its mine tubes. Twelve hours later *U73* once again submerged and headed south for the Mykoni Channel, where the fruits of her labour would later prove equally bountiful.

With the last of the mines successfully laid, *U73* returned safely to its base at Cattaro on 7th November. With no confirmed kills the mission was at first not regarded as a particular success, but the experienced Siess knew that one of the many frustrations of being the skipper of a mine-laying submarine was that he would be extremely fortunate to see any immediate results. Nevertheless he clearly knew his business, for each of the mine barrages laid during that voyage off of the islands of Phleva, Kea and Mykonos would claim victims. Unfortunately for the Allies, however, of the more than 60,000 gross tons of shipping that was sunk as a result of this one voyage, over 48,000 tons would come in a single incident which, even today, accounts for what is still the largest single loss suffered by the British merchant marine in either of the two World Wars.

# CHAPTER TEN

# A VOYAGE TO NOWHERE

*Britannic*'s last stay in a homeport was destined to be a short one. The first indication of a change in routine had come when the ship was proceeding up the Solent. The inbound hospital ship normally passed the outbound and empty ship as it left for Mudros, so when *Aquitania* failed to make her customary appearance the medical staff knew that something was amiss. It was not until *Britannic* was well into the Solent, however, that the Cunard liner was finally sighted, anchored in Cowes Roads, and after *Britannic* had docked that the full picture was known. The heavy storms that had disrupted the final stages of *Britannic*'s homeward journey had taken an even heavier toll on *Aquitania*, and with the Cunard ship now in need of repairs *Britannic*'s turnaround in port was suddenly slashed to only six days.

For the medical staff this meant that their usual seven-day leave was reduced to only five. Nevertheless, while the preparations for the next departure continued at Southampton those who were fortunate enough to get away made the most of it. Reverend John Fleming, the ship's Presbyterian chaplain spent much of his free time visiting churches in London, but by the evening of Saturday 11th November he was back on board and pondering the spiritual needs of his own flock for the coming voyage. He didn't have long to wait and shortly after lunch on Sunday 12th November, *Britannic*, amid calm seas and clear skies, was outward bound. Once again the destination was Mudros and once again for security reasons this would not be officially confirmed to the crew until the ship had left Naples. But with the onboard routine by now so well established few even bothered to consider the possibility of going anywhere else.

By the time night had fallen the signal lights of the Channel Islands could be clearly seen to port as the ship entered the unusually tranquil waters of Biscay. From then on it was the customary course for the Portuguese and Spanish coasts. If nothing else the voyage out would be a leisurely one, and the medical staff could also console themselves with the added bonus that this time there would be no passengers on board; although it is not clear whether or not the policy had been discontinued because no more medical personnel were due to be transferred abroad, or, that the last period in home port simply had not allowed enough time to make the arrangements. The advantages for *Britannic*'s own medical staff, nevertheless were readily appreciated. As nurse Sheila Macbeth recalled:

*Left: Stewardess Violet Jessop: Having first gone to sea in 1908, Violet joined the White Star Line two years later, serving on both Olympic and Titanic before joining Britannic's crew.*

*Courtesy Margaret & Mary Meehan*

"Such a relief to find the same cabin and room-mate, and to see how homely it is now looking, with my chintz cushions and our nice jar of brown beech leaves. Everything is much nicer this voyage – as there are no passengers (These were always medical officers and nurses – going out to different hospitals in India, Egypt, Salonika, or Malta. Occasionally we took out a few Chaplains – but never any combatants) and, in consequence, we are allowed to wander all over the ship, and do not find the deck roped off at every turn with notices saying:- "Officers Only" or "Passengers Only." "

Preferring not to view the last of England from the bitingly cold promenade deck, Sheila chose instead to hold an impromptu tea party in her cabin, even though the milk (made from *Horlicks* Malted Tablets) left a particularly disgusting aftertaste.

While the medical staff could sit back and relax for the time being, it was very much business as usual for *Britannic*'s crew. For new personnel the problems of finding their way around the largest ship in the British merchant marine were as great as ever, but for one new crew member there would be no such difficulty. Stewardess Violet Jessop was already more than familiar with the Olympic-class liners.

To some it might seem bizarre that, in view of her earlier experience, the White Star Line might have thought twice before assigning Violet to the *Britannic*. Not only had she been on board *Olympic* when that ship collided with the armoured cruiser HMS *Hawke* in the Solent on 20th September 1911, but she was also among the fortunate survivors of the *Titanic* disaster barely six months later. Violet, of course, could in no

*Right: **Sheila Macbeth (back row, fifth from right) poses with the other probationers after joining the VAD.***

Courtesy Angus Mitchell

*Below: **A gusty day on the aft promenade deck.***

Courtesy John Fleming

way be held personally responsible for either of these two incidents, but if there were any particularly superstitious members among *Britannic's* crew, it just possible that one or two might have be having second thoughts about this particular voyage.

In spite of her medical training, Violet Jessop was on board in her original capacity as stewardess. Determined to "do her bit", after *Olympic* had been laid

*Britannic's portside motor launch being lowered over the side at Naples. This illustration gives a perfect example of just how far from the side of the ship the lifeboats could be lowered, meaning that even a considerable list would not effect the life saving operation.*

*Courtesy Angus Mitchell*

up in November 1914, she had enrolled as a VAD nurse and had been transferred to a hospital on the east coast. Despite the restrictive practices of Matron's rules, Violet's training at sea proved to be invaluable. She enjoyed her life as a nurse until an accident with an infected needle had resulted in a poisoned hand which, combined with general fatigue, had quickly rendered her unfit for duty. Knowing her nautical background one of the doctors had suggested that a sea trip might help her to regain her strength, so Violet immediately contacted the White Star Line, which wrote back promising her the position of stewardess aboard *Britannic* as soon as a vacancy became available. In the meantime she had been posted aboard *Cedric* to New York, but after only one voyage she was summoned to the James Street head office in order to sign Articles for *Britannic*.

One would have thought that her familiarity with both the ship and the nursing profession, should have made Violet perfectly at ease with her new assignment, yet clearly this was not the case:

> "It was like going into a new world, after being used to passenger liners, to board that stately hospital ship. For all the world, she looked like a great white swan. Soon renewed friendships made me feel more at home, for at sea you always meet someone you know."

There is little doubt that as *Britannic* continued to head south Violet would have quickly found her feet. Nor did it take long for the nurses to get back into their well-established routine, as Sheila Macbeth would recall:

> "Our days were well filled. One of the sergeants gives us a gymnastic class each morning on the boat deck, much to the amusement of the M.O.s, who come up and take snap-shots of us when looking most ridiculous and

unable to retaliate. Each afternoon we have a lecture by the bacteriologist, and, as soon as we can get away, we fly down to have that precious hour in the swimming bath... After our swim, we have tea and then either play cricket or some other game on deck."

But it was not all pleasure. All of the ship's 3,000 medical cots still needed to be made up and with no medical passengers to help, as there had been on the last two voyages, this time the nurses would have to do it all themselves. Any thoughts of shore leave would be out of the question if the bunks were not ready by the time the ship reached Naples. By breakfast time on Friday morning the last of the cots were finished just as *Britannic* dropped anchor in her customary position in Naples harbour; and with the bunkering process likely to take up the entire day, permission was granted for a number of the medical personnel to go ashore. Sheila wasted no time in making the most of the opportunity:

*The bright and well-ventilated expanse of the enclosed promenade on B deck provided an ideal area for the some of the officer's wards.*

Courtesy Angus Mitchell

"As soon as we got our passes, we went on shore. Eight of us hired two cars and a guide for the day. The guide was a good one, but, those cars – the limit! Two <u>horrors</u>, with tyres full of holes. Each driver had a boy with him, not only to occupy the Devil's seat, (in Italy, and Malta too, the people are very superstitious, and will not drive with an empty seat beside

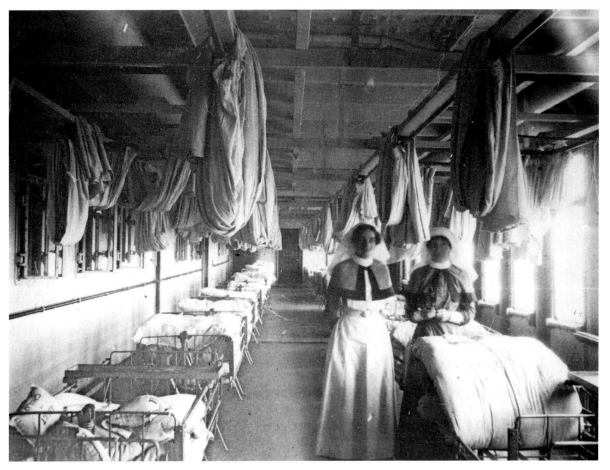

them, as they think that the Devil will occupy it) but to jump out every few hundred yards to start the engine or pick up the nuts which were shed over the road. Unfortunately, when one car broke down the other was sure to do likewise at no great distance. Still, it was great fun – except when the drivers tried to race each other on roads which were full of ruts about a foot deep.

We went to Solfatara or "Little Vesuvius," which is reached by a road running close to the sea around two bays. The views were lovely and I wished I were walking and had more time to see things.

The crater is a large one, and it is just as if the top of a large mountain had fallen in to form a huge lime pit. The guide took us over this (in the safe places) to show us some holes where the ground had caved in and exposed the boiling stream which flows from three to four feet under the entire surface. The holes are crusted with yellow sulphur crystals. It is a wonderful place and well worth going to.

From the crater we went past the old amphitheatre to Pozzvoli, where we went into the palace which Nero had cut into the cliff – like a sort of catacomb. Close to the palace was his natural Turkish Bath. I wish the guide had warned us before we went in – for although we ran all the way, we only just got out before we were quite melted away!

Some of the M.O.s were outside and when they saw us they refused to go in themselves – the cowards!

About ten minutes journey further down the road, was an old Grecian temple and, thinking we might never get another chance of seeing one, we went there instead of to lunch. We did not guess that within a week, we should be in Greece and able to see any number of old temples!

We had lunch at a little country inn – where I could not eat for watching the natives shovelling in spaghetti by the yard – a wonderful sight!"

After doing some Christmas shopping the nurses returned to the ship, but any hopes of an early departure the following morning were quickly dispelled when a storm, which had been steadily building throughout the day, finally broke. As the heavens opened Captain Bartlett found himself trapped in port, with little chance of being able to manoeuvre his massive command through the narrow opening in the harbour wall without risking serious damage to both. With little option but to ride out the storm. Reverend Fleming recalled just how uncomfortable the situation had become:

"We had hoped to leave the following morning, but during the night a great storm broke, with much damage to the shipping, and we were held fast prisoners. All the anchors were out, weighing together 37 tons, and in addition twenty great hawsers fixed the hinder part of the vessel to the quay; yet so violent was the storm that the vessel was in danger."

The situation was probably not quite as serious as Fleming depicted, but in one respect he was right. For the time being *Britannic* was going nowhere, and with no possibility of further shore leave being granted that day the medical personnel could

*Rev. John Fleming poses on the boat deck in front of the compass platform on the raised roof above the lounge.*

*Courtesy John Fleming*

do nothing but sit it out. To help pass the time John Fleming obtained permission for some of the nurses to see the ship's engine rooms and, although he was off duty, Senior Fifth Engineer, J. Scott made sure that they saw everything. Scott regularly gave guided tours which usually lasted over two hours and he always enjoyed showing off *Britannic*'s power plant to the nurses. Doubtless he would have impressed them with details of the engines, or with the fact that there was more power in the ship's engine rooms than in the whole of Birkenhead. Sheila Macbeth particularly recalled one of his more amusing anecdotes that may have reminded her of happier days:

> "After coming out of the stoke holes, and reaching a cool part of the ship, we all exclaimed, and Mr. Scott told us of an American lady who had done the same on one of the other ships he had been on. Throwing out her arms, a ship's dessert plate slipped from under her coat and smashed on the ground, much to the embarrassment of both. The only words he could say were, 'It's all right, I will steal you another one!' "

As the afternoon wore on the storm began to moderate and Captain Bartlett took the opportunity to clear the harbour while he had the chance. At 2.23 p.m. *Britannic* was once again outward bound, but within moments of the ship clearing the harbour wall the sea conditions began to deteriorate once again. In spite of the

weather the harbour pilot managed to lower himself safely on to the pilot boat, and as the ship headed south the weather gradually began to improve.

*The aft starboard gantry davits serviced one of the Britannic's two motor launches and five other rigid lifeboats. The numbering system on board would have classified them as boats 17A to 17F.*

*Courtesy John Fleming*

By the following morning *Britannic* was in the Straits of Messina, surrounded by fine weather and smooth seas. By now the ship was working up to a full head of steam and making good time, while below decks the activity was more frantic. RAMC orderlies were busy with the final preparation of equipment and medical supplies, while the pack stores orderlies were preoccupied with their own last-minute administrative details before the wounded soldiers' kit bags arrived. Even the nurses had a mountain of work to complete, for while the cots in the wards were now made up they still had to have patients' clothing kits ready before the ship reached Mudros. There was also another incentive for them to get the job done, because if the work was not completed by the end of the afternoon they would not get their usual hour in the ship's swimming pool.

It would appear that matron's threat had its effect. By the late afternoon all of the work had been completed and exhausted from their exertions both on the wards and in the swimming pool, the medical staff took the opportunity to enjoy a last relaxing evening on board before the ship arrived at Mudros. That night Chaplains

Atkinson and Fleming conducted their usual evening church service in the large dining saloon, which Percy Tyler later described as "one of the best since the boat had been in commission". As the crew dispersed to enjoy a last few hours of repose, none would have any idea of the horrors that were to occur less than twelve hours later.

The last hours of *Britannic*'s all-too-brief existence were ticking away.

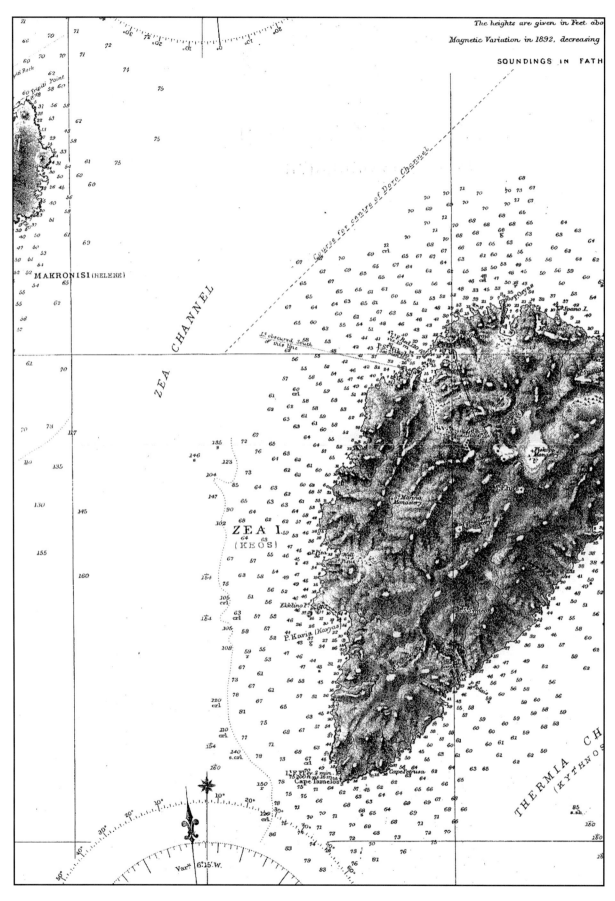

The heights are given in Feet abo

Magnetic Variation in 1892, decreasing

SOUNDINGS IN FATH

MAKRONISI (HELENE)

ZEA CHANNEL

Course for centre of Doro Channel

ZEA I.
(KEOS)

Spano I.

Marina Monastery

Fikiao Monaco

Well Point

P. Pisa

Ekklino Pt

P. Karia (Kavias)

St. Symeon

Cape Tamelos

Cape Grusa

THERMIA CH
(KYTHNOS

Var. 6°15′W.

# CHAPTER ELEVEN

# NEMESIS

At dawn on 21st November 1916 *Britannic* was steaming serenely off the Gulf of Athens, on her prescribed heading of N 48 E. High up on the bridge Chief Officer Robert Hume and Fourth Officer Duncan McTavish maintained the watch, while the exceptionally calm waters allowed *Britannic* to easily maintain her estimated speed of 20 knots. The highlight of the morning watch had probably been nothing more interesting than passing the armed merchant cruiser HMS *Heroic*, on the mail run between Mudros and Salamis.

For most of the passengers on board the atmosphere seemed equally tranquil. Rev. Atkinson was holding a well-attended morning mass in the ship's lounge for the early risers; and once the service was concluded everyone filed out, laughing and joking, before making their way below for breakfast. As eight bells sounded the ship began to come alive. Lookout, J. Conelly was relieved in the crow's nest by J. Murray, while below decks the stokehold crews were also changing watch as the firemen and trimmers walked through the forward tunnel that linked the boiler rooms to their quarters in the ship's bow. Higher up in the ship, fifteen-year-old boy scout George Perman was already at his assigned post for the day, operating the aft lift, while Violet Jessop was in one of the pantries making up a breakfast tray for one of the nursing sisters who was lying ill in sick bay.

Elsewhere on board, it was slightly more relaxed. Private Percy Tyler, having already had breakfast, was leaning against his bunk in barrack room no. 2 industriously polishing his buttons, Fifth Officer Gordon Fielding was having his morning shave in his cabin, Sheila Macbeth was running a little late and still heading for the dining room, while Rev. Fleming, also late for breakfast, was in his cabin, entranced by the sight of a little village high up on the passing island of Kea.

Kea itself was not a particularly remarkable place in the overall scheme of things, but as a student of the arts Fleming may well have been dwelling on its rich ancient history or the legends which surrounded it. Whatever he was contemplating, he was so absorbed in his thoughts that he scarcely noticed the sound of the eight o'clock gong to announce breakfast. As the minutes ticked by he remained by his window, but gradually the pangs of hunger made him realise that he was late for breakfast. He was just leaving his cabin at 8.12 a.m. when:

*Left: A map of the island of Kea. This particular chart was issued in 1916 and is the same as the one that would have been used on the bridge of the Britannic.*

Hydrographic Office

"... there was a great crash, as if a score of plate-glass windows had been smashed together; and the great ship shuddered for a moment from end to end... I had just reached the passage when the crash came. Turning back to my cabin, I snatched my life-belt, and ran down toward the station assigned to chaplains in case of emergency, one of the lowest wards in he ship; but the empty wards brought back to one's mind that there were no sick or wounded there whom one could serve, so I retraced my steps."

As he made for the dining room Fleming ran into one of the medical officers, but when he suggested that the fate of the ship might be sealed the officer remained quite calm and pointed out that it was rather unlikely as the alarm had not even been sounded. This passive response may well have been prompted by the instructions that Major Harold Priestly had just given to the nurses in the dining room. Immediately after the explosion they had all jumped up and begun to move towards the exits. As Sheila Macbeth recalled:

> "Major Priestly (of Wittenburg) took command and told us to sit down again as the siren had not sounded. It was quite the best thing to do, as the doors were few and narrow and there might easily have been a panic. As it was, there was only a most unnatural silence."

*Rev. John Alexander Fleming, one of the two chaplains assigned to Britannic in September 1916 and, coincidentally, the first Presbyterian chaplain to serve aboard a British warship.*

*Courtesy John Fleming*

As luck would have it, Priestly was quite clearly the right person in the right place at the right time. Violet Jessop later recalled him to be a modest and quiet man whom anyone could approach and, because he had managed to escape from the German prisoner of war camp at Ruhleban, he was also something of a hero to the troops. These assets inevitably made him one of the most popular men on board and the confidence that he appeared to inspire in others was about to pay dividends.

While the nurses remained silently at the breakfast tables, around the ship the response to the mysterious explosion varied. Further aft in barrack room number 2 down on G deck, Percy Tyler's reaction to the explosion was less marked:

> "... there was a violent bump, which sent me forward a few paces and back again, then the boat regularly danced. Some made casual remarks about having hit something, and others said they were more sorry for the boat we had run into, but none of us took it that seriously in that part of the boat. Aft the shock was more violent, some were thrown completely off their feet. For'ard where the boat was hit was a very different scene."

Although spread throughout the ship, the descriptions of the first seconds after the explosion are remarkably similar. Sheila Macbeth also referred to a "shiver right down the length of the ship," while eighty-three years after the disaster, George Perman, could remember the impact as if it were yesterday:

"When the thing struck us, or we struck it, the whole ship shuddered. That was my first recognition that something had happened. Oh she absolutely shuddered, and immediately the cry went round: 'The ship is sinking!' "

Violet Jessop, busy in the pantry, had more reason to suspect the worst than most on board:

"Suddenly, there was a dull, deafening roar. *Britannic* gave a shiver, a long drawn out shudder from stem to stern, shaking the crockery on the tables, breaking things until it subsided as she slowly continued on her way. We all knew she had been struck."

Unlike the loss of *Titanic*, however, there was no atmosphere of unhurried calmness. Two years of submarine warfare had left its mark on the entire crew and within seconds of the explosion the pantry was bustling:

"As one man, the whole saloon rose from their seats. Doctors and nurses vanished to their posts in a trice. The pantry where I stood, holding a teapot in one hand and a pat of butter in the other, was cleared too, as men dropped what they were doing and jumped over presses with the agility of deer. In seconds, not a soul was to be seen and not a sound had been uttered."

*Major Harold Edgar Priestley: A veteran of the Western Front, Priestley had escaped from a German prisoner camp near Wittenberg and was a hero to his men. He later said that compared to a day in a prison camp, the loss of the Britannic was "a mere picnic!"*

*Courtesy Angus Mitchell*

For a few less fortunate individuals, however, the dangers wrought by the explosion were far more immediate. One of the orderlies in the forward lavatory on E deck was nearly overwhelmed by the flow of water, which came up the hatch like a huge wave. With the boy scouts and stewards' quarters awash, he stumbled aft through the wreckage and debris towards the main staircase, just managing to get through the watertight door before it closed behind him. Private John Cuthbertson was even more fortunate. Alone in the forward barrack room on G deck, Cuthbertson was completely swept away by the massive inrush of water and, although the staircase had been destroyed in the blast, incredibly found himself washed up as far as E deck where he was able to extricate himself.

While the confusion below deck continued, the hitherto composed bridge was suddenly a hive of activity. Immediately after the explosion Captain Bartlett, still dressed in his pyjamas, rushed from his cabin to find out what had happened. His sudden presence on the bridge provided immediate reassurance to fifteen-year-old scout James Vickers, who only moments before had been standing in the wheelhouse contemplating nothing more taxing than his breakfast:

"My heart was in my mouth, but when I saw the captain standing there, cool and quiet, I thought to myself it's all right, and felt a good deal more comfortable."

Putting any further thoughts of breakfast out of his mind, Vickers moved to a nearby locker to fetch a megaphone and then, according to his orders, remained by the captain's side, ready to pass on any instructions. Captain Bartlett's cool and calm exterior, however, did not reflect the true seriousness of the situation that he now faced. Orders were immediately given to stop the ship's engines, close the watertight doors and to clear away the boats. Within minutes the damage reports began to arrive on the bridge and as the tally of bad news mounted, so *Britannic*'s chances of survival began to look increasingly bleak.

An explosion had occurred beneath the waterline somewhere in the vicinity of the bulkhead between holds 2 and 3. With two compartments open to the sea *Britannic* should easily have been capable of remaining afloat, but unfortunately it did not end there. The sealed fireman's tunnel that ran from hold number 1 through to boiler room number 6 had also been seriously damaged by the explosion, with the result that water was also flooding these two additional spaces. To make matters worse, the watertight doors which sealed off boiler rooms 5 and 6 had failed to close properly and with the ship flooding at such a rate, barely two minutes after the initial explosion the water level in the two boiler rooms was too deep for any emergency measures to be carried out. Suddenly *Britannic*'s much-vaunted six compartment safety margin was looking less than adequate.

Realising the danger now facing his ship, Captain Bartlett wasted no time in ordering the distress signal, "SOS. Have struck mine off Port Nikola", to be immediately sent out, and then issued the orders for a southerly course towards Kea. Unfortunately, this was more easily said than done. Whether or not it was the result of the original explosion, the extended shudder following the blast, or the fact that the stern had already begun to rise is unclear, but within minutes *Britannic*'s steering gear was experiencing difficulties. Fortunately, the engines were still fully operational, and by using the ship's propellers Bartlett was able to set a course for the nearby island. But his optimism was not to last for long. As *Britannic* started to move forward again, the increased stresses on the forward bulkheads

*Manufactured by the gentlemen's tailor Gieve & Co., the "Gieve Waistcoat" became an essential fashion accessory that no well-dressed Englishman could afford to go to war without. On the day of the sinking Sheila Macbeth made particularly certain that she had her waistcoat with her, but thinking it might get punctured by wreckage she then let the air out and put her ship's belt over it. Fortunately she was not called upon to test its efficiency.*

caused the forward compartments to fill even more rapidly with water.

As the ship's plight continued to worsen, the atmosphere below deck became more uncertain. In the dining room the nurses were still nervously seated at the breakfast table, but in contrast to the light chatter moments before, there was now an uneasy silence. This silence continued for what seemed like an eternity, but in reality was barely a minute before the first alarm sounded. As one, the nurses immediately rose from the table and calmly filed out of the dining room to fetch their life belts from the cabins before going up on deck.

For nurse Ada Garland it was a particularly sombre journey. As she walked quickly down the staircase and through the long corridor, with the sun streaming in through the portholes and lighting up the cabins, she could not shake off the feeling that this was goodbye to everything. Snatching up her coat, rug and lifebelt, she headed back for the staircase where she would later remember the frantic efforts of the medical staff to reach the boat deck:

> "It was a terrible sight, men who could barely walk struggling to climb the stairs. The screams and shouts could be heard all over the ship as the badly injured were being moved. We all helped until the very last minute when we heard the cry of our dear brave Matron saying "Hurry up my children." Arriving on the boat deck it appeared to be the same as boat drill, everybody was trying on their lifebelts and awaiting orders."

George Perman, realising that his electrically operated lift might fail at any time, immediately went up to his assigned lifeboat station at the stern of the ship, while another fifteen-year-old scout, Henry Pope, headed for his duty station in the purser's office. The purser, Claude Lancaster, would later recall that Pope, far from being frightened in any way, simply saluted and asked if he could do anything. Lancaster immediately responded, "Yes, just wait awhile, for I shall want you in a few minutes." He then calmly stood to his post for about ten minutes before he was given his orders and went off with the cheerful retort: "It's been a big explosion, sir, but I don't think it will do us much harm."

Violet Jessop knew better. Having already come through the nightmare of *Titanic* she knew all too well that *Britannic* was in serious trouble. Remembering her charge lying down in the sick bay, she immediately went below to see that she was safe, clearly recalling the atmosphere throughout the ship:

> "There was a hubbub of conversation on the decks below. Doors stood ajar, revealing sisters and nurses hurriedly collecting belongings and little treasures, commenting with relief at the fortunate absence of wounded on board, while they tried hard to smother their feelings of concern at Matron's command for haste."

On her way she encounteried two nurses who stopped to thank her for making them get up early to go to mass. Had they not done so, they would have been wearing their pyjamas beneath their uniforms at breakfast (a not uncommon habit amongst some of the nurses, who would lie in bed until the last possible minute).

On reaching the sick bay Violet found the sick nurse in a very agitated condition as she struggled to dress herself. Violet did her utmost to calm the nurse down, while helping her patient to finish dressing before sending her up to the boat deck with a colleague. She then retraced her steps through the now deserted corridors to her own cabin.

Elsewhere there seemed to be a less noticeable sense of urgency. Following the explosion the atmosphere in barrack room number 2 seems to have been one of complete disinterest. Percy Tyler went back to polishing his coat buttons as if nothing had happened, only to be interrupted some five minutes later when another orderly suddenly dashed in, shouting that the alarm had been sounded. With the true seriousness of the situation gradually dawning, Tyler threw down the coat on which he had previously been lavishing such attention and, after putting on his life belt, grabbed as many spare belts as he could carry before rushing up on deck.

The ship's officers, meanwhile, had sprung into action. A party of men had quickly been sent below in order to secure as many of the open portholes as possible, while up on deck Captain Harry Dyke, *Britannic's* assistant commander, stood by to organise the lowering of the boats under the aft starboard gantry davits. Sixth Officer H. Welch, oversaw the lowering of the lifeboats under the starboard Welin davits, while on the port side Fifth Officer Gordon Fielding, was responsible for the two sets of aft gantry davits, with Third Officer David Laws, taking care of the Welin's on that side. With the individual officers now at their assigned stations, the actual procedure for the lowering of the boats, however, seemed to be more confused.

*Captain Harry Dyke: Britannic's assistant commander and, on the day of the sinking, in charge of lowering the lifeboats from the aft starboard gantry davits.*

*Courtesy Harold Roberts*

According to the diary of an unnamed ship's officer (thought to be Fifth Officer Fielding), the first mention of Captain Bartlett's order to abandon ship came at about 8.35 a.m. Until then the order had simply been to uncover the boats and to have all possible ready to be sent away. Even so, a number of boats do appear to have been lowered without authority. In his book, *The Last Voyage of His Majesty's Hospital Ship Britannic*, Rev. Fleming stated that the nurses were "speedily and happily got off," yet this does not appear to be the case. In spite of her call for haste, as soon as Mrs. Dowse had ensured that all of her staff were accounted for, the nurses found themselves left hanging over the side and waiting while Captain Dyke went aft to call back a group of firemen who had taken one of the boats located on the shade deck without authority. With memories of *Titanic* coming to mind, a boat which should have held sixty-five people had barely fourteen in it and with a number of men already having jumped overboard, he yelled down instructions with his megaphone, ordering the boat's occupants to come back and pick up those who were already in the water.

While there may have been some justification for the lack of control on the isolated shade deck where only two sets of Welin davits had been installed, even the better supervised area of the aft boat deck was experiencing some early stages of panic. After swinging out two of his lifeboats, Fielding later remembered a group of stewards and a dozen or so sailors who were assigned to him promptly rushing to get into them. Reasoning that it would probably be better to get the stewards who had started the panic out of the way, Fielding managed to coax his working party back on board to stand by their stations, before lowering the boats to within a few feet of the water. At this time the ship was still moving forward and until he received a definite order from the bridge to release the boats he decided that they should remain suspended.

The situation at the aft starboard gantry davits was much the same; as nurse Sheila Macbeth later wrote:

*This photograph gives a splendid view of the lifesaving appliances onboard Britannic. In the distance the huge gantry davits each serviced up to six lifeboats, while the conventional Welin davits to the left could each handle one rigid and one collapsible lifeboat. For the less fortunate, the Carley floats stacked on the central island could were designed for twenty people, while life belt lockers were placed at strategic points around the boat deck.*

Courtesy John Fleming

"We were kept hanging over the side for a long while... We did not realise that while we were hanging over the side of the ship, the whole of the fore part of her was under water – we might have been more frightened if we had seen it."

Back on the port side the occupants of the hanging lifeboats were somewhat more vociferous. Until he received specific orders from the bridge to release them Fielding had little option but to stand by and listen to the curses of the stewards dangling below – not that it would have bothered him very much.

Meanwhile, the task of filling the boats went on. Having now reached the boat deck herself, Violet Jessop discovered to her horror that all of the women's lifeboats had already been lowered over the side. Taking her assigned position in boat number 4, forward on the port side, for the second time in her life she prepared to be lowered over the side of a sinking Olympic-class liner. Her experience on *Titanic* was, however, nothing in comparison to the ordeal yet to come.

Up to this point the evacuation had followed a reasonably orderly and recognisable pattern, but it is now that the accounts of what happened begin to vary. According to Fifth Officer Fielding, it was at about 8.30 a.m. that two of the port lifeboats located amidships were lowered into the water without the authority of Third Officer Laws. Because of the strong set of the tide and the forward momentum of the ship, these lifeboats were inexorably pulled in towards *Britannic*'s churning propellers. Violet Jessop's version of the event, however, differs to some degree. In her memoirs she recalled that at the time she reached the boat deck she was told that the nurses had already gone and she could see them steadily drawing away from the ship. This is in spite of the fact that *Britannic* was still, at that time, moving ahead. Lifeboat number 4 filled rapidly and as the boat was being lowered she not only became increasingly aware of the list to starboard, but also of the ship's propellers, which were by now revolving above the surface and churning the water further aft. One of the boats that had already been safely lowered was having difficulty in pulling away and as soon as her own boat began to drop the difficulties created by the ship's starboard list became even more apparent:

> "...our lifeboat, hooking itself on an open porthole, whose circular, brass-rimmed glass jutted out, tilted us considerably; then, righting itself, started gliding down rapidly, scraping the ship's sides, splintering the glass in our faces from the boxes, which formed, when lighted, the green lighted band around a hospital ship's middle, and making a terrible impact as we landed on the water."

In spite of the varying accounts as to how the accident came about, there was unanimity in the horrifying results. The infamous inward pull of the propellers on the Olympic-class liners, which had not only brought about the notorious collision in the Solent between *Olympic* and HMS *Hawke* in September 1911, but also *Titanic*'s near miss with the S.S. *New York* at Southampton the following year, was about to play its hand once again. With the crew of her lifeboat fighting a desperate battle to pull away from the side of the ship, gradually the boat was sucked astern. Violet continued:

> "A few minutes after the lifeboat first touched the water, every man jack in the group of surrounding boats took a flying leap into the sea. They came

thudding from behind and all around me, taking to the water like a vast army of rats.

Not a word, not a shout was heard, just hundreds of men fleeing into the sea as if from an enemy in pursuit. It was extraordinary to find myself in the space of a few minutes the only occupant of the boat; I say almost, for one man, a doctor, was still standing in silence beside me. I turned around to see the reason for this exodus and, to my horror, saw *Britannic*'s huge propellers churning and mincing up everything near them – men, boats and everything were just one ghastly whirl."

For the unfortunate souls in the boats, it was a scene of indescribable carnage. Young George Perman was able to grab a hold of a davit cable just in time and hold on, but the scene he witnessed would leave emotional scars for years to come, as the propellers scattered human bodies and shattered pieces of debris in every direction. In seconds both the surface of the water and the ship's white flanks were covered in streaks of blood.

Although Violet had never learned to swim, she quickly realised that it was a case of either jumping into the sea or suffering the same fate. Suddenly losing her life-long fear of drowning, Violet leapt overboard. At first the weight of her coat dragged her down into the depths for what seemed like an eternity, but then she felt herself rising and as the tumultuous waters continued to thrash around her, she came up beneath one of the lifeboats which prevented her from reaching the surface. Suddenly there was a terrific thump as something very solid struck her on the back of her head and as the pounding continued she instinctively reached out for something to grab in an attempt to free herself from her predicament, when suddenly...

"... joy of joys, I touched something – an arm – that moved as mine moved! My fingers gripped it like a vice, but only for a second, until my almost senseless head remembered what is said of the people drowning, that they retain their hold after death, bringing death to another. With that cheering thought, I let go."

After what seemed an eternity, but was in reality only a few seconds, Violet once again broke the surface. Grabbing hold of a loose lifejacket for support she finally open her eyes enough to be greeted by the sight of the brains of one unfortunate orderly, trickling onto his khaki tunic from his head, which had been completely split open. All around her she could see nothing but dead bodies, severed limbs and large pieces of debris, while the agonised cries of the wounded drowned out the sound of the now receding propellers. Then, just as a third boat was about to share a similar fate, the propellers stopped. The sight of the now motionless twenty-three foot blades, which had been causing bloody carnage only seconds earlier, must have been a blessed one for Captain T. Fearnhead and the few remaining RAMC occupants of a third lifeboat which had also been unable to pull away. Fearnhead wasted no time in pushing hard against the now stationary blades to get clear in case they should suddenly start up again. Also seizing the opportunity to escape from his predicament, George Perman slid down the rope to which he had been desperately clinging, badly burning his hands in the process, before dropping into the water and swimming to a nearby lifeboat.

George may well have been thanking God for his deliverance, but its timing actually had more to do with an order given by Captain Bartlett up on the bridge than any divine intervention. The halting of the engines was not to save the people in the water, for it is clear from his report that until he was picked up from the water himself, Bartlett had no knowledge of any boats being caught up in the propellers. It was simply the worsening plight of the ship that finally prompted him to order the engines to be stopped, as he would later report:

> "... the forward holds filled rapidly and water was reported in Nos. 5 and 6 boiler rooms, so I stopped the engines and ordered all boats possible to be sent away, but to stand by near the ship."

As soon as it was safe to approach the scene of carnage the nurses moved in to give what assistance they could; and there was no shortage of ingenuity to make up for the deficiencies of medical supplies. As Sheila Macbeth later wrote:

> "In our boat, we got well away from the sinking ship and busied ourselves with the wounded, whom we picked out of the water. Our brandy flasks were invaluable, also aprons and pillowcases, which were torn up as bandages. Some boats had only men in them, and if any of these contained wounded, we always went alongside and gave them some Sisters to help them."

By now it was 8.35 a.m., *Britannic* had stopped and the order to lower the boats was given. Having witnessed the earlier bloody tragedy, the curses of the stewards who had been left hanging over the side by Fifth Officer Fielding were now a good deal less vociferous and within seconds of receiving the order to lower away Fielding had dispatched his first two boats. His problems were not eased when the forward set of gantry davits under his command almost immediately became inoperable. Nevertheless, he struggled on and after successfully launching a second boat from the aft set, was about to hook up *Britannic's* port motor launch when First Officer George Oliver and Colonel Anderson arrived with orders to take the launch and co-ordinate the rescue of the two-hundred people now in the water. Scout, James Vickers, was also with them, his place on the bridge as captain's messenger now taken by another scout, Edward Ireland. As he stepped into the boat he trapped his foot between the ship and the side of the five-ton launch, later admitting with typical British understatement that it "hurt quite a bit". Filling the launch with about thirty RAMC orderlies and two or three seamen, the boat was then safely lowered into the water. By now time was getting short, and at 8.45 a.m., barely ten minutes after receiving the order to lower the lifeboats, Fielding lowered his final lifeboat, containing another seventy-five men, before the list to starboard made any further working of the boat gear on the higher port side of the ship practically impossible. He then took the remaining six seamen and the thirty or so RAMC orderlies who up to this point

*A closer view of the Carley floats and life belt lockers on the raised roof over Britannic's lounge. The skylight on the left hand side was unique to Britannic and not fitted on Olympic and Titanic.*

*Courtesy John Fleming*

had been calmly sitting in the boat fully expecting to be lowered next, to the raised island on the boat deck above the ship's lounge. Here they assisted Major Priestley's party who were busy throwing life rafts and deck chairs over the starboard side, and it was not long before Fielding began to realise that in a few minutes he would probably be using one of those very rafts to save his own life.

Elsewhere the evacuation had gone like clockwork. As soon as the RAMC orderlies had been paraded on the aft section of the promenade deck, Major Priestley went below in order to search the three barrack rooms on F and G decks for any stragglers. Meanwhile, the orderlies calmly waited until they were led up to the boats in groups of fifty. Elsewhere, the starboard davits had been working to lower the boats with almost monotonous regularity. The list to starboard allowed even the Welin davits to be used right up to the last moment, although the gap between the dangling lifeboats and the ship's deck was becoming increasingly noticeable with every passing minute.

Even in the ship's final moments people were still daring to go below. For some, the reasons were very practical. Not having had any breakfast Rev. Fleming realised that he would be very hungry after an extended period in the lifeboats, so once the nurses had been sent on their way he had gone below to the dining saloon to fill his pockets with as much bread as he could carry. Lieutenant J. Starkie of the RAMC had had a similar idea, while Percy Tyler actually made two trips below to collect as many spare lifebelts as he could carry. For Sergeant S. Halliday and Corporal S. Ogden, however, the purpose of their trip below was far more mundane, prompted solely by the need to ensure that the RAMC pay books and office records were saved – a noble thought, but hardly one worth dying for. Even Claude Lancaster, *Britannic's* purser, seemed preoccupied with his paperwork and by the time he was ready to climb into the last boat he had also made sure that most of the ship's papers, including the log, had been taken to safety.

Even at this stage it seemed that by some miracle the ship might still be saved. After the engines had stopped *Britannic* began to settle more slowly, and taking advantage of this unexpected easing of the situation, at 8.45 a.m. Captain Bartlett started the engines once again in a second attempt to reach land. For one last time

*Britannic* began to move, but once again the forward motion began to force the bow deeper into the water. When reports began to arrive on the bridge that the water had risen to the level of D deck, Bartlett knew that it could only be a matter of minutes and at long last gave the order for those remaining on board to abandon ship.

As the last remaining starboard boats were lowered away, the first signs of desperation began to emerge. Percy Tyler found one of the scouts still on deck, reluctant to abandon his post, and when all attempts at persuasion failed he had no choice but to throw him forcibly into one of the remaining boats. In spite of the fact that the boat was already heavily overloaded Tyler was also ordered to get in and seconds later the third-from last lifeboat made its descent. The eighty or so occupants packed into a lifeboat built for sixty, struggled to get away from the ship. IThey were so tightly packed within the confines of the craft that it was only possible to unship five of the lifeboat's complement of ten oars, for fear of upsetting the craft as it passed uncomfortably close to the rotating starboard propeller before finally drifting clear.

*Chief Engineer Robert Fleming. Due to an error in Sheila Macbeth's scrapbook, for many years this photograph has been wrongly identified as Captain Charles Bartlett. The error was actually spotted by Captain Bartlett's grandson, who pointed out that his grandfather did not smoke a pipe!*

*Courtesy Angus Mitchell*

With Captain Bartlett calling for haste, the rush to fill the remaining lifeboats continued apace. Coming up along the now largely deserted boat deck, Rev. Fleming and Major Priestley stood to one side as Sixth Officer Welch and a handful of seamen prepared to lower the next boat. With room to spare Fleming finally stepped into the boat, but Priestley, ignoring the pleas of the men, opted instead to have one last look around the deck for anybody who might be left behind. At 8.55 a.m., the penultimate lifeboat was lowered into the water.

Priestley's remaining moments on board could be measured in only a matter of minutes. By the time he returned to the davits, Fielding and Welch had succeeded in manhandling one last boat into position, and immediately the remaining men on that part of the boat deck took their places. Ordering Welch into the boat, Fielding and two seamen remained on deck to see it safely lowered from *Britannic's* increasingly tilting deck. Once it had touched the water Fielding steadied the lines as the two brakemen slid down the falls into the boat below before following himself. It was now 9.00 a.m.

With the few remaining minutes ticking away Captain Bartlett gave the final order to abandon ship, and with their duty now done scouts Ireland and Price, who had remained behind to act as messengers for the captain and chief officer, finally left their posts in the forlorn hope of finding a remaining lifeboat. At the same time the engines were rung off on the telegraphs, the final signal for the remaining engine room personnel to leave their stations was made, and a series of long blasts sounded on the ship's whistle. While the remaining engineers made their way up the circular staircase that would bring them to the boat deck on the port side of the fourth smokestack, the few remaining RAMC personnel were already jumping over the side. After refusing a place in a lifeboat, knowing that his portly frame would occupy enough space in the boat for two men, Captain E. Fenton succeeded in lowering himself safely into the water via a dangling rope, while scouts Ireland and Price escaped in a similar manner, shinning down fifty feet into the water before swimming another fifty yards to a nearby life raft.

Meanwhile, as his lifeboat finally got clear of the ship, Fifth Officer Fielding looked up at the *Britannic's* stern which he estimated was by now some 150 feet in the air, to see assistant Chief Engineer Joseph Wolff sliding over the taffrail and dropping into the water. Up forward he could still see Captain Bartlett, Captain Dyke and Chief Engineer Fleming standing near the bridge, by now almost level with the water as one by one they each walked along the starboard bridge wing and into the water moments before the forward section of the ship submerged completely.

Even so they were not quite the last to get off. Although the ship had been in danger of foundering at any moment, Lieutenant Starkie of the RAMC had gone below on a personal mission to find some bread and by the time he got back on deck the bridge was already submerged. Once in the water he had barely swum a hundred yards before the stern finally disappeared.

Private C. McCullogh, who had also escaped from the ship by sliding down one of the dangling lifeboat falls, was even closer. Fortunately the sight of 50,000 tons of steel poised to topple right over onto him, and the ship's propellers, high in the air, still rotating at a terrible rate, provided the incentive he needed to kick as hard as he could in the direction of a nearby lifeboat. As *Britannic* sank deeper and deeper into the water, the last moments were recalled by Rev. Fleming:

> "Gradually the waters licked up and up the decks – the furnaces belching
> forth fierce volumes of smoke, as if the great engines were in their last death
> agony; one by one the monster funnels melted away as wax before a flame,
> and crashed upon the decks, till the waters rushed down; then report after
> report rang over the sea, telling of the explosion of the boilers."

With her stem already touching the muddy seabed, *Britannic's* hull, by now almost perpendicular in the water, slowly began to settle back as the ship finally completed its roll to starboard. By the time the smoke had cleared and the noise subsided at 9.07 a.m., all that the occupants of the remaining lifeboats could see was the empty wreckage-strewn sea that only moments before had supported Great Britain's largest and finest ship.

# CHAPTER TWELVE

# AFTERMATH

With their beautiful ship now gone the full horror of the morning's events finally began to dawn on *Britannic's* dazed and scattered survivors. Like clockwork the efficient military organisation that had been so evident aboard the ship quickly sprang into action, as the medical personnel set about bringing order to the chaos that surrounded them. In spite of the emotional trauma, matters were a lot better than they might otherwise have been. It was a clear bright day, land was barely two miles distant and the warm Aegean waters were as calm as a millpond. With these conditions the chances of survival until the rescue ships arrived were very promising.

The response to *Britannic's* desperate cries for help had not gone unheeded, and within minutes the first emergency transmissions were finding their way home. Nevertheless, even though assistance was reasonably close at hand, the rescue would not be quite as straightforward as it should have been. *Britannic's* given distress position was certainly accurate enough so far as it went, but the SOS had simply stated that the ship had "struck a mine off Port St. Nikola" and made no reference to an exact latitude and longitude. Why the precise coordinates were never given to the radio operators remains a mystery, and probably stems from the fact that Captain Bartlett had assumed that because the ship was on a well-established route and in clear sight of a well-known landmark, this would be enough. Under normal circumstances this may well have been true, but had he been aware of just how common the name St. Nikola was in the Aegean, and the confusion that this would create, he would have provided more specific co-ordinates

Matters were further complicated because of a defect in *Britannic's* radio receiving apparatus, possibly caused by the explosion, which meant that none of the repeated requests for clarification from any of the rescue ships could be picked up. A potentially disastrous situation was averted simply because *Heroic* knew exactly where *Britannic* was located, as the ships had passed each other earlier that morning. Nonetheless, lessons would be learnt from *Britannic's* loss, and once the dust had settled future procedures regarding the transmission of regulation distress calls would be a lot more precise .

*Left: Lieutenant John Cropper: According to Violet Jessop, Cropper had given his lifejacket to another person and was last seen in the water after the two lifeboats had been smashed. Following the sinking Cropper was posthumously promoted to captain, and this rank is recorded in his entry on the British war memorial at Mikra, Salonika.*

*Courtesy John Harvey*

This was certainly of little immediate concern to the survivors scattered over the Kea Channel, blissfully unaware of the confusion behind the scenes. The first vessel to respond to *Britannic's* call had been the British destroyer HMS *Scourge*. Under the command of Lieutenant Commander Henry de B. Tupper, *Scourge* had been standing by to escort the Greek steamer *Sparti*, which had struck another of the mines laid by *U73*, this time off Phleva island. *Britannic's* SOS was picked up just before the towing operation could commence, and without

wasting a second Tupper set a course for the Kea Channel, with the French tugs *Goliath* and *Polyphemus* following close in his wake.

HMS *Heroic* was a little slower to receive the message. Under the command of Captain Percival Ram, RNR, *Heroic* had just turned north into the Gulf of Athens when, at 8.28 a.m., they had the first indication of *Britannic's* plight. As soon as he had obtained radio permission from Salamis, Captain Ram immediately turned his ship around and headed back for the Kea Channel.

*The auxiliary cruiser HMS Heroic was on the mail run from Salonika to Salamis, and had passed Britannic barely an hour earlier when the SOS was picked up. Curiously enough, Captain Percival Ram RNR only turned his ship around and went to the assistance of the hospital ship after obtaining permission from Salamis.*

The third vessel of the rescue flotilla was the destroyer HMS *Foxhound*. Under the command of Lieutenant Commander William Shuttleworth, *Foxhound* had been carrying out a routine patrol in the Gulf of Athens when an order from HMS *Scourge* to go to *Britannic's* assistance arrived just after 10.30 a.m. Within minutes *Foxhound* had changed course and with HMS *Foresight* and HMS *Chasseur* also converging on the Kea Channel, the scramble of vessels to go to *Britannic's* aid stood in stark contrast to the inactivity on the night that her sister ship had gone down.

Meanwhile, by the time *Britannic's* stern had disappeared into the cobalt blue waters of the Aegean over one thousand survivors were scattered across a wide area, struggling to survive and come to terms with what had happened. The immediate problem for those fortunate enough to be in a lifeboat had been to get as far away from the sinking vessel as possible to avoid being dragged down by the suction. Ada Garland clearly remembered that eight men had been detailed to her lifeboat specifically for this purpose, but as soon as it was in the water their lack of expertise was quickly evident, with nobody able to co-ordinate the oars which constantly clashed together. Ada recalls her relief that the waters were much calmer than they had been on the previous day, while Sheila Macbeth's memories of this moment were even more vivid:

> "Several of our boats had no seamen in them, and it was rather difficult for the orderlies and sisters to see to the shutting of the water-traps and the getting away from the side of the ship, as all instructions were given from so far above us (by megaphone) and were about things of which we knew little or nothing. Fortunately, several nurses knew how to row, and in several cases may be said to have saved their boats from being drawn into the propellers."

Percy Tyler's point of view was little different, though it should be said that his lifeboat was among the last to be lowered, and the rush to fill it was understandable. The occupants were only able to unhitch half of the oars which were stowed in the bottom of the boat, because it was so crowded. Any attempt to free the remaining five, if not wholly capsizing the boat, would certainly have resulted in tipping half of its load into the sea.

For over two hundred other survivors, even a place in an overcrowded lifeboat would have been a distinct luxury. The abundance of Carley Floats (each capable of supporting about twenty people), deck chairs and the other jetsam thrown overboard by Fifth Officer Fielding's party certainly helped matters, but *Britannic's* propellers had left an horrific scene of carnage in their wake. The task now facing the rescuers was a particularly gruesome one, but fortunately there were already ample medical staff on hand, and they were quick to put their training to the test. With few or no medical supplies to hand the ingenuity of the nurses to make do with available resources was severely tested and they were not found wanting. Pillowcases, blankets – even lifejackets – were all quickly torn up and utilised as makeshift bandages and slings, while a number of brandy flasks brought even more welcome relief. For those boats with no medical staff at all, Mrs. Dowse made sure that her nurses were distributed around the flotilla to help where they were needed most.

For those in the water, matters were considerably eased by the presence of *Britannic's* two motor launches. Fortunately the hitherto unreliable engines now worked efficiently, although the situation inside the port launch was far from comfortable. The twenty or thirty sodden passengers packed into the thirty-four foot vessel had not only left it chronically overloaded but a large volume of water had been shipped as survivors were pulled from the sea. Never the sturdiest of boats, the launch wallowed in the calm Aegean waters, and to guard against the possibility of it being overwhelmed, young James Vickers, his foot throbbing painfully from the injury sustained on the boat deck, was soon put to work on the hand pump. One by one, survivors were retrieved from the water and as soon as the launch was full First Officer Oliver moved from lifeboat to lifeboat, redistributing as many survivors as he could before returning to rescue more.

For others the situation was rather more gruesome. Having come through her near-death brush with *Britannic's* port propeller, and in spite of being unable to swim, Violet Jessop had far more on her mind than simply trying to remain afloat.

Clutching her extra lifebelt she did her best to stare ahead and shut out the horrific scene of carnage surrounding her until she became aware of the reassuringly fast approach of Oliver's launch. By now many were completely beyond help and their bodies were allowed to drift away. Suddenly she heard a nearby voice shouting: "There's a woman in the water here," but before she could thank the man who had called out on her behalf she could only stare helplessly as he gave a gasp and sank into the depths. Moments later the launch was alongside and she was being dragged out of the water. Her relief at being rescued was quickly forgotten when she became aware that the propeller had inflicted more damage than she had at first thought.

*The Basilisk class destroyers HMS Scourge (above) and Foxhound (right) were on patrol duty when they received Britannic's SOS and were able to respond more quickly. By 1916 these small coal-fired vessels, affectionately known as "The Mediterranean Beagles", were already bordering on being obsolete, but their three screws could still generate a maximum speed of twenty-seven knots when the situation demanded.*

Nursing a heavily gashed leg she limped to the other side of the boat with the shreds of her torn coat trailing behind. No longer could she shut out the gruesome images of the incident. One badly injured man sat to her left with both of his partly severed arms hanging by only a few pieces of skin, amazingly, still able to smile at the fact that he was lucky not to have been killed.

Others were beyond all help. In another corner of the launch seventeen-year-old scullion, L. George, and a young RAMC orderly had not been so lucky, and as the order to lower their bodies over the side was given Violet could only stare mournfully as the bodies floated away, reminding her of the images she had seen as a sixteen-year-old schoolgirl of dead bullocks being jettisoned over the side of a ship while en route from Argentina to England.

The rescue of survivors was to show a marked difference to that of the *Titanic* in one key respect. Gone were the fears of being pulled down by the suction of the sinking ship, or the possibility of being swamped by hordes of desperate swimmers, the instinct to return and help seemed almost second nature. Realising that he was in no immediate danger himself, Captain Bartlett refused an offer from the crew of the starboard launch to be picked up until they had taken care of the wounded. Instead he ordered them to take as many of the injured as they could carry to St. Nikolo. He continued to co-ordinate the rescue standing on an isolated raft, and it was not until Colonel Anderson came alongside in the port launch at 10.30 a.m. that he was finally plucked from the water.

Captain Bartlett's message to give priority to the wounded and get them ashore as quickly as possible was acted upon by Mrs. Dowse. She wasted no time in distributing her staff to where they were needed most, taking special care to make sure that six nurses were detailed to accompany the injured to Port St. Nikolo. In the meantime help had arrived in the form of Francesco Psilas, a local fisherman from St. Nikolo who, accompanied by several other Greek fishing boats which had been working nearby, was already pulling survivors from the water.

Within thirty minutes of *Britannic* slipping beneath the surface, further signs of salvation were already visible as two columns of smoke appeared on the horizon. Shortly after 9.30 a.m. the lookout on HMS *Heroic* sighted the first lifeboats floating in the distance and within half an hour HMS *Scourge* had also arrived at the scene. Moving to a different area of the channel to where *Heroic* was operating, at 10.10 a.m. Commander Tupper finally ordered the engines to be stopped and for all boats to be sent away to help pick up survivors.

Gradually order began to return as, one by one, *Britannic*'s lifeboats converged on the rescue ships. As *Heroic* was the first to arrive, over the next ninety minutes 494 survivors were taken aboard. One of them was Rev. Fleming, who would never forget

H.M.S. FOXHOUND.

the welcoming sensation of the solid deck beneath his feet or the joy at finding so many friends still alive. Fleming then went below to comfort as many of the wounded as he could. The vision that greeted him there as *Britannic's* medical staff struggled to give what relief they could to those who had sustained horrific injuries, while the crew of *Heroic* attended to the other survivors with blankets and refreshments, would remain with him for the rest of his life. For some it was already too late; Private Arthur Binks of the RAMC and trimmer Charles Phillips were both so badly injured that they were beyond help and they would be dead long before the ship reached the safety of Piraeus.

The situation on HMS *Scourge* was little different. One by one lifeboats came alongside and as the morning wore on so the winds from the African continent began to rise. Gradually the remaining survivors were taken aboard. For Ada Garland the task of getting out of her lifeboat was a lot more difficult than getting in, as the tiny craft pitched and tossed alongside the destroyer. At her first attempt Ada barely had time to throw her rug to one of the sailors before the lifeboat descended sharply only to immediately rise up on the next wave.

*Having served in Britannic since September 1916, Private Henry Freebury was one of the unfortunate occupants in one of the two lifeboats destroyed by the ship's propellers. His body was never found.*

Courtesy Jennifer A. Clarke

Just as the boat reached its highest point she jumped on to the gangway and was finally pulled to safety. Reunited with her rug she was then quickly taken to one of the cabins below. Destroyers have never been remarked upon for the spaciousness of their appointments and the tiny cabin was already so packed with nurses that Ada was forced to sit on the floor wedged between one of her colleagues and a table. Moreover, the table itself was doubling as a bed for one of the injured men and the combination of his cries of pain and the claustrophobic atmosphere was almost suffocating. Overcome by the scene, Ada could barely remember having her lifejacket and coat loosened by Sister Olford before being revived with a welcome glass of brandy and taken up on deck again for some fresh air.

Sheila Macbeth managed a little better, and once aboard HMS *Scourge* she found it easier to cope with the situation:

> "We had to wait some time whilst the sailors rowed round to make a final
> search for survivors. During this time, we saw the Captain's bridge and
> many other familiar objects float by – amongst them a notice "Officers
> Only" which made one wag wonder why we never had a notice to say that
> "Officers and Sisters must not drown on the same side of the ship!" A sailor
> pulled a chair from the water and gave me a part of the back, which I
> guarded safely under my coat."

By midday the situation on the two rescue ships was becoming critical. With 494
survivors taken aboard *Heroic* and a further 339 packed into the tiny confines of HMS
*Scourge*, space was fast running out when *Britannic*'s starboard launch arrived
alongside with the unwelcome news that over 150 survivors, many of them injured,
were still marooned on Kea. All that Tupper could do in the circumstances was place
*Scourge*'s own medical chest in the launch and send it back to Kea, although he could
at least slightly ease his own accommodation problem by placing six more nurses in
the launch to assist with the casualties on the island.

Fortunately the next wave of rescue vessels was fast approaching. HMS *Foxhound*
had been at the scene since 11.45 a.m., and with the light cruiser HMS *Foresight*,
under the command of the aristocratically named Commander Charles Tindal-
Carill-Worsely, also in sight there were now more than enough vessels on hand to
complete the rescue. Tupper finally accepted that he had achieved as much as any
man reasonably could, and after ordering *Foxhound* to join *Foresight* in one final
sweep of the channel before proceeding into Port St. Nikolo, he waited until *Heroic*
had returned from retrieving any remaining survivors or salvage from the local
fishing boats. Shortly before midday *Scourge* and *Heroic* headed west towards the Bay
of Salamis as Commander Shuttleworth on HMS *Foxhound* took over the now vacant
role of rescue co-ordinator. After an hour searching through the wreckage without
any further success, *Foxhound* dropped anchor in Port St. Nikolo while *Foresight*
continued look for survivors in the channel.

On Kea, however, it was a very different story. Strewn around the quay were over
170 survivors from the two motor launches and two of the lifeboats which had made
it ashore. Many of them had been horribly mutilated by *Britannic*'s propeller. To
make matters worse many of the available medical staff were themselves suffering
from rope burns and cuts. Nevertheless, they persevered with the meagre resources
they had to hand, even though in some cases their makeshift bandages made from
shredded lifejackets were pitifully inadequate. Violet Jessop saw one elderly man in
an RAMC uniform lying to one side with part of his thigh missing and one foot gone
altogether. Taking his hand in hers she did her best to comfort him. For others it was
already too late and just before noon Sergeant William Sharpe died on the quayside.

*Scourge*'s medical chest was already proving to be invaluable, and the timely
arrival of HMS *Foxhound* and Staff Surgeon Henry Braithwaite from HMS *Foresight*
were welcome additions. Moreover, during this time the British were not alone.
Francesco Psilas' spontaneous action in taking his boat out to rescue survivors was
by no means unique, and in spite of the language difficulties the people of Kea

rallied round to give what assistance they could. Fifth Officer Fielding who was able to speak a little French, obtained two or three bottles of brandy and some sour bread for the injured, while one woman even took Violet Jessop into her home and put her to bed while she draped her soaking uniform over some chairs outside in the midday sun. Despite the woman's best intentions the outcome was not successful, as Violet was to discover when she went out to retrieve her clothes:

> "When I slipped out later to get these, expecting they would be dry, I found
> a crowd of the ship's staff there and had to retrieve my wet corsets from
> where they had stuck to the fat backside of a colossal doctor, who sat
> swapping fantastic stories with our popular purser."

Unfortunately there was little time to finish drying the garments as the stretcher parties had by now made speedy progress in transferring the injured to *Foxhound*. Struggling into her still damp uniform, Violet squelched down to the quay before going aboard the destroyer for the journey to Salamis.

HMS *Foresight* had finally anchored alongside *Foxhound* at 2.00 p.m., and Commander Worsley offered to take the survivors to Mudros on the larger ship. Had *Scourge* and *Heroic* not already departed, Shuttleworth may well have given the idea serious consideration, but he finally decided that sending the 193 survivors, of whom 22 were seriously injured, to a different port would only confuse the situation. The simplest course of action would be to head for Piraeus as Commander Tupper had instructed, and at 2.15 p.m. *Foxhound* weighed anchor, leaving Commander Worsley to arrange for the collection of the abandoned lifeboats and the burial of Sergeant Sharpe.

By 2.30 p.m., a little over five hours after *Britannic* had gone down, the rescue was all but over as the procession of rescue ships headed toward the Bay of Salamis. Leading the field were HMS *Heroic* and HMS *Scourge*, with HMS *Foxhound* and the French tugs bringing up the rear. While some distance now divided them the activity on board each vessel was markedly similar. The Royal Navy did its utmost to rise to the occasion. The crew on board HMS *Scourge* were no strangers to disaster, having already rescued survivors from seven other ships since the outbreak of war and their experience was clearly evident. Each survivor was given a mug of tea and a welcoming cigarette as soon as they stepped on board, while those with sodden uniforms were given dry overcoats or blankets. The two scouts in Percy Tyler's boat came in for especially good treatment, and when it was discovered that they had not eaten that morning they were immediately taken below for a hearty breakfast. Nor did the others fare too badly. Ada Garland particularly remembered the cook's dainty ham sandwiches and some of the sweetest oranges she had ever tasted, followed by plates of ship's biscuits and a tin of tea, although the lack of cups meant that each tin had to be shared between a dozen or so nurses.

The sailors, unused to female company, were especially generous when it came to souvenirs. Sheila Macbeth was one of many nurses who came away with the cap ribbon of one of *Scourge*'s crew. But for her, the real highlight of the rescue was being allowed to sit up in the ship's aft gun turret, known to the crew as "the bus." There she could see everything going on around her and her eye quickly spotted eight of

*Britannic*'s lifeboats being towed behind, although by the time *Scourge* had reached twelve knots the destroyer was throwing out such a wake that only three of the boats survived the journey to Salamis.

On board HMS *Heroic* it was a little more spacious, while even the cramped compartments of HMS *Foxhound* seemed more orderly. It was not long before the destroyer was travelling at a speedy twenty knots at the beginning of a journey that Violet Jessop would never forget:

> "A journey on a destroyer must always be a thrilling adventure for a
> civilian, and certainly my battering did not prevent me realising this to the
> full as she flew over the waves, her nose parting the flying spray."

The highlight of the journey, or so she thought, came when one of the crew asked if she would like to take a bath. Still clutching her damp corset, Violet followed the sailor on what seemed like an endless excursion through the entire length of the ship, until they arrived at a tiny cabin where a tin hip bath had already been filled with hot water. Entrusting her precious clothes to the sailor who promised to have them dried in the engine room, Violet immersed herself in the steamy water and scarcely had she began to relax when her eyes started to wander around the room. The first thing she noticed were the piles of neatly folded clothes placed there for her use, right down to a beautifully darned hole in a woollen undershirt. But the homely images of the wife or mother who might have done the work quickly vanished when she looked up to see a sign above another door alerting her to the fact that she was right next to the ship's magazine. The sudden realisation that she was lying only a few feet away from tons of cordite and explosive seemed to dim her enthusiasm for the hitherto soothing bath, as she made her speedy exit from the hip bath. She hastily dressed and hobbled up to the top deck, where her nerves were partly revived by a cup of thick navy cocoa. The cocoa did not last long, with most of the liquid being spilt as the ship pitched and tossed as she sped through the water.

By mid afternoon the focus of activity had moved from the Kea Channel to the Bay of Salamis, and in particular to HMS *Duncan*, the flagship of the British Adriatic Squadron. The sudden rush of activity would probably have been very welcome to the men of *Duncan*'s crew. Up until that moment the daily on board routine had been relatively dull. From six o'clock that morning the crew had been employed in the task of cleaning the ship with the usual morning break for Divisional Prayers at 9.10 a.m. Afterwards the fore turret personnel were put through their paces while other members of the crew were subjected to the tortures of physical exercises. All this was to change at 3.45 p.m. when HMS *Heroic* finally arrived alongside with the first survivors, followed fifteen minutes later by HMS *Scourge*. Now over eight hundred survivors were clamouring for attention and *Duncan*'s surgeon, Nelson J. Roche, who was already having to contend with nine of *Duncan*'s own crew on the sick list, found his sick bay overflowing. His problems, however, were as nothing compared to those of Rear-Admiral Arthur Hayes-Sadler, who now had to organise food and accommodation for over a thousand unexpected guests.

Fortunately, Admiral Darrieus, the commander of the French Third Squadron, immediately offered to place all of the French resources at his British ally's disposal.

*HMS Duncan, sister ship to HMS Russell, another victim of the U73, was the venue for the investigation into the loss of Britannic.*

Before long, boats from the French Squadon were busily moving back and forth between *Heroic* and *Scourge*, ferrying the uninjured survivors to locations in all corners of the port. Yet even at this early stage there were clearly the makings of a plan of action. Not surprisingly, the 76 nurses quickly found themselves centre of attention on board the flagship as young naval officers, starved of female company, went out of their way to provide them with overcoats and anything else that they might require, and were even treated to tea with Admiral Hayes-Sadler in his sitting room. The ultimate destination of *Britannic's* crew and RAMC orderlies would be more of a lottery. The luckier ones found themselves accommodated either on board *Duncan* or assigned to berths in a number of the French ships, but for some three hundred men their destination would turn out to be the ex-Greek depot ship *Kanaris*. As Percy Tyler would later recall, his new quarters would be very different to those he had known on board *Britannic*:

> "Being the last we were less fortunate than the others. Ours was a very poor boat, which smelt from end to end as much like a sewer as could be, and looked very much as though it had never had a clean up since it was launched ... It was also very unfortunate that our two scouts were with us and for their own sakes we made them sleep up on deck with us, sleeping below was out of the question from a health point of view and the language of the crew was not fit for them..."

In spite of the conditions and the language, Tyler's observations were not totally negative:

> "The treatment of all the survivors on these boats is beyond my powers to set down here. The sailors gave to all that had lost clothing, everything that was needed, tobacco we never had to ask for, while at night they gave up their hammocks and slept on the floor so that we should be comfortable. They insisted in waiting on us at meal times and in fact there was nothing

they would let us do for ourselves. On one boat a jolly little marine,
knowing apparently a sentence or so in English, continually shouted "Is
everybody happy?" and since it has been a byword amongst the boys."

The medical officers and nurses fared considerably better. After gathering up on deck in the evening twilight for a roll-call, at 6.00 p.m. the French ferry *Marinos* transferred them to Piraeus where Lieutenant William Rogers had been able to arrange for their accommodation in the Phalére and Aktaion hotels at Phaleron.

Meanwhile, the situation on board HMS *Foxhound* was more critical. The destroyer, carrying by far the largest number of injured, finally anchored alongside *Duncan* at 5.30 p.m., by which time the medical facilities on board the flagship were already stretched to breaking point. Colonel Anderson would probably have had a far clearer understanding of the conditions on board *Duncan* than most, having spent several days on the ship in December 1908 when, as an RAMC captain, he had been a part of the British earthquake relief party from Malta to Messina. Nevertheless, until the remaining 171 uninjured survivors had been disembarked the destroyer was simply unable to move. That process alone would take a full hour and it was not until 6.30 p.m. that *Foxhound* was finally able to weigh anchor and proceed to the Piraeus grain wharf, which also happened to be serving as a military pier. Once ashore the wounded were steadily taken off in ambulances arranged by the overworked Lieutenant Rogers, and transported to the nearby Russian hospital. The lack of ambulances meant that it would not be until half past midnight that *Foxhound* was finally cleared to depart.

By 7.00 p.m. the commotion in the Bay of Salamis had settled down, although the evening tranquillity was briefly disturbed when a motor launch from the flagship arrived alongside *Heroic* at 7.25 p.m. to collect the bodies of Arthur Binks and Charles Phillips, having already retrieved the body of fireman Joseph Brown from the French tug *Goliath*. Fifteen minutes later HMS *Scourge* was also on the move as Commander Tupper finally headed out at ten knots to return to his original patrol line off the island of Phleva. The frantic activity in Piraeus, however, told a very different story, and even now the tireless Major Priestly continued to oversee the transfer of the injured to the hospital. Throughout the day he had been a tower of strength from the second he sat down to his breakfast seventeen hours earlier to the moment the last of the injured had been transferred, and it is perhaps appropriate that the final paragraph of Colonel Anderson's report into the episode should be used to sum up what would probably be one of the most traumatic days in any normal man's life:

> "The highest praise is due to Major Priestly for his quiet and determined
> courage. After his gallant conduct on board, he took a prominent part in
> tending the injured at St. Nikola and later remained alert until the last
> patient had been admitted to hospital about 1 a.m. on the 22nd November,
> 1916. He remarked that it was a mere picnic compared with a day in a
> prisoners camp."

Some picnic!

# CHAPTER THIRTEEN

# A GREEK TRAGEDY

At dawn on the morning of Wednesday 22nd November 1916 HMS *Scourge* and HMS *Foxhound* were once again back in the Kea Channel, where, in a classic case of trying to shut the stable door after the horse had bolted, they would spend the better part of two hours sweeping for further mines. The logs of the two destroyers do not record any successes on that particular morning, although a further two mines would later be found there following *Britannic's* loss.

Meanwhile, the calm situation in the Bay of Salamis was in stark contrast to the tumult of the previous afternoon. Sunrise found little or no activity around HMS *Duncan*, save for *Britannic's* now empty lifeboats bumping gently against the sides of the ageing pre-dreadnought. Yet, in spite of the calm atmosphere, it is unlikely that either Captain Bartlett or his officers got very much sleep that night.

The predicament for those on shore was a little less secure. The medical officers lodged in the Phalére Hotel had quickly discovered that they were not particularly welcome guests and Rev. Fleming later recalled that the hotel staff were not supporters of Eleutherios Venizelos, the prime minister of the pro-Allied Provisional Greek Government. Instead their loyalties lay with the Greek king, Constantine I, who due to his German ancestry and education was considered by the Allies to be somewhat more biased in favour of the Central Powers. Fleming felt neither welcome nor safe in his hotel, but fortunately the situation for the nurses at the Aktaion Palace was a little better. Several of the staff there were Venezelists and they could not do enough to make the nurses feel welcome. Even though many of the Aktaion's rooms had been closed up for the winter the owner was still willing to make room for the them. Nevertheless, Sheila Macbeth recalled that in spite of this hospitality, communications were quite often less than perfect:

> "Instead of expecting 80 of us, they had only made preparations for 18 – so as most of the rooms were shut up for the winter, we just wandered about and took any rooms we could find, many of us sleeping four in a room. B. and I shared a room. She had a small bed and I had a mattress on the floor. The sheets were impossible, being very damp, so my eiderdown came in very usefully."

Because she knew a little French, Sheila was able to speak with some of the women at the hotel and obtain some nightclothes, a brush and some soap. The soap became a particularly highly prized luxury amongst her colleagues, so Sheila used the jack knife she kept in her Gieve waistcoat to cut it into eight pieces, which were then shared amongst the rest of the company.

*Left: **Britannic's surviving medical staff photographed on the steps of the Aktaion Hotel at Phaleron.***

*Courtesy Angus Mitchell*

One survivor, however, had shown a little more forethought. As the ship was sinking, Violet Jessop, being no stranger to

*151*

shipwreck, had remembered that the one thing she had craved more than anything after *Titanic* had gone down was her toothbrush. Following her return to England her brother Patrick had often teased her "Never undertake another disaster without first making sure of your toothbrush," and the irony that on this occasion her first priority had been to retrieve so humble an item was not lost on her. Not that it did her much good; after a supper consisting of a lukewarm liquid purporting to be tea, and a slice of bread spread with a white, frothy, vile-smelling substance which was allegedly butter made from goat's milk, Violet was in her room cleaning her teeth when the assistant matron looked in. Instead of a reassuring enquiry about her injuries, she simply looked in amazement and said: "Wherever did you get that toothbrush?" In her weakened state Violet replied that she had brought it with her, but she would never get over the look of suspicion on the assistant matron's face, as if she suspected that's Violet's forethought was the result of her somehow being in league with the enemy. After all, who but a spy would have a weekend bag already packed?

The first priority for the nurses after dinner had been to arrange for telegrams to be sent to let their families in England know that they were safe, and although the military authorities would later decide for security reasons not to send the cables, it did provide some relief for them. Unaware of the embargo, they then settled down wherever they could for the night, but for some even the opportunity of a good night's sleep was not to be. Sheila Macbeth's thoughts of a warm comfortable bed for the night were very quickly thwarted:

> "I had not been in mine more than half an hour, when I was knocked up to go to the Russian Hospital at Piree. I was to act as a sort of Nurse-Interpreter as the Staff were all Greeks and Russians, one or two of whom were able to speak French. I had gone with our Assistant Matron and two of the Charge Sisters, so naturally felt rather embarrassed when one of our M.O.s greeted me with: 'You are the one who speaks French? Then you must be Matron here, please.' "

Sheila's linguistic talents were to prove invaluable to the injured men lying helplessly in the wards, where the well-meaning but incomprehensible local hospital staff had done their best to help. Even a few French patients already in the hospital were pleased that they could at last speak to someone. In spite of this progress the evening would bring with it one last moment of sadness as one of *Britannic*'s lookouts, G. Honeycott, became the final casualty to die from his injuries. For the remaining survivors the night passed uneventfully.

Wednesday brought with it the sad duty of having to arrange for the burial of the dead. It took most of the morning to assemble the *Britannic*'s scattered crew and medical orderlies, as by now they were spread around the French fleet or on the poky *Kanaris*. A few of the more fortunate crew members had, nonetheless, managed to find space aboard the ex Austrian Lloyd steamer *Marienbad*. Captain Bartlett and his officers had remained on HMS *Duncan* in order to be on hand to assist with the inquiry into the sinking, but at 1.20 p.m. the routine was interrupted when *Duncan*'s ensign was lowered to half mast as the bodies of Arthur Binks, Charles Phillips and

*Some of the nurses relaxing on the verandah at the Aktaion hotel.*

*Courtesy Angus Mitchell*

Joseph Brown were taken ashore by the funeral detail. Rev. Fleming would later record his memories of the occasion in particular detail:

"We gathered in the afternoon amid glorious sunshine on the grain quay of the Piraeus. The friends on the flagship had added to their many kindnesses the gift of lovely wreaths inscribed "To the heroes of Britain." Surely there never was a stranger or more touching funeral procession! The allied fleets were represented there, and a firing party was furnished from the flagship. Greek sympathisers joined, and our own fellow countrymen whose homes were in these parts came down to mingle with ours their sorrow for the loss of the brave.

The streets were densely packed with men, who looked on with strangely conflicting expressions; but all were reverent towards us, as we carried our burden to the tomb. The great wreaths which had been sent in sympathy our orderlies carried in front of the coffins. These men and the other orderlies who followed, were a touching sight, dressed in all varieties of uniform – naval and military, French and British, a strange reminder of the losses and the trials of the day before..."

With the services concluded, at 3.00 p.m. *Duncan's* ensign was once again raised to the top of the mast as the routine on board began to return to normal, as Admiral Hayes-Sadler now pondered the question of what to do with the salvaged lifeboats which were choking the waters around the flagship. His dilemma was not made any easier when at 4.00 p.m. another four boats were returned from the French battleship *Vérité*, and he finally decided that before movement around the flagship became all but impossible the lifeboats should be transferred to the Salamis dockyard. Someone else could work out what to do with them later.

Meanwhile Captain Hugh Heard, HMS *Duncan*'s commanding officer, and Commander George Staer, the flagship's chief engineer, had more important matters to consider. Unlike Lord Mersey's *Titanic* investigation back in 1912, where time and money had been no object, the resources available in the Aegean to an already over-stretched Royal Navy were considerably more limited. Their task of collating the information was not made any easier by the fact that of the 1,032 survivors scattered around Piraeus barely a handful were in a position to contribute anything close to meaningful evidence, and even then much of that would be contradictory. Everybody knew why *Britannic* had foundered, but exactly what had caused the explosion?

From a propagandists point of view the torpedo theory would have suited many, and the two strongest protagonists of the torpedo theory would be steward Thomas Walters and baker Henry Etches. Unfortunately their testimonies bore little resemblance to each other. Walters, who had been standing forward on the starboard promenade deck since 8.00 a.m. on the morning of the sinking, takes up the story:

> "… my eyes caught sight of a white stream coming at a great speed towards the ship's bow. The thought flashed to my brain that this was a torpedo. On the instant I gripped the rail and leaned inboard to await the explosion which seemed to occur immediately. I then looked down at the water but had to hold my nostrils on account of the fumes which were stifling. I could see what appeared to be a great disturbance of the water occurring aft."

Further aft, Etches' more colourful account paints a somewhat different picture:

> "… I was on the after poop, when the crash occurred, starboard side, I at once ran over to port and standing just forward of after bridge, I saw small gimps [sic] in water approaching at great speed about four hundred yards from side of ship, where I was standing, but what caught my eye most was a long straight line following it, reaching as far as my eye could follow causing a slight displacement of a darker coloured water, no one being near me at the time, I ran forward to my boat."

Although not claiming to have seen the explosion itself, an additional statement given by engineer's writer Thomas Eckett adds more interesting fuel to the controversy. Following the alarm he had proceeded to his assigned station at lifeboat no. 19 on the starboard side of the poop deck, when, about twenty minutes later he noticed:

> "… on looking across the water I saw, about a quarter of a mile away (or at the most no more than a half a mile), about five or six points off the

*In spite of their duties at the Russian hospital, there was still time for Britannic's medical staff to visit the Parthenon at Athens.*

Courtesy Angus Mitchell

starboard bow, what appeared to be a small narrow mast sticking out of the water about three or four feet, there was a wash of water both fore and aft of this object – the wash being greatest at the after end – as if something was just awash, it was also moving along slowly, the direction it was going in would take it across the course the *Britannic* was then making."

Eckett was not the only one to see it. Fireman, E. Biffen, was standing right next to him at the time, and commented that it looked as if a submarine had come up to shell them. Luckily Biffen was to be proved wrong, as the mystery object apparently remained in view for approximately four minutes before gradually sinking beneath the surface. At face value, therefore, the torpedo theory seemed to have at least two strong proponents.

Unfortunately it was not that straightforward. Immediately after the explosion Captain Bartlett had signalled that *Britannic* had struck a mine, and in that none of the personnel either on the bridge or on lookout had reported any sign of a torpedo track it is not hard to see why. To further muddy the waters, lookout, J. Conelly, on being relieved in the crow's by J. Murray at 8.00 a.m., had reported that two "suspicious objects" were in sight – an observation which Rev. Fleming later expanded on in his book, describing them as "moving objects resembling barrels." The final piece of evidence that Heard and Staer took into consideration was a theory of their own, noting that at the time of the explosion no one had reported the

column of water usually thrown up by an exploding torpedo. Walters and Etches may have genuinely believed that they had seen torpedo tracks, but more and more the inquiry was tending towards the mine theory and the uncomfortable realisation that the German U-boats now seemed capable of laying mines in far deeper waters than had previously been thought.

*Some of Britannic's surviving crew aboard HMS Lord Nelson at Salonika on 26th November 1916. Scout George Perman (wearing white seaman's cap) can just be seen standing on top of the battleship's 'A' turret.*

While Heard and Staer weighed the available evidence *Britannic*'s crew passed the time as best they could. Lieutenant Rogers had already ensured that transportation was constantly on hand for the nurses at the Aktaion hotel so that they could commute back and forth to the Russian hospital, although their presence was not greatly appreciated at first by the Greek staff. Far from taking advantage of their services, it seemed as if they resented that the British nurses were there at all. Initially, one may understand why, as none of the VAD sisters had any idea where anything was kept and tended to get in the way, but as the local doctors gradually came to realise that the British nurses had a greater degree of training than their Greek counterparts they began to rely more heavily on them. As a result, over the course of the following week Sheila Macbeth remembered that the Russian hospital underwent a complete transformation:

"When we first arrived at that hospital, we found an English, a French, and

several Russian officers, none of whom had ever had their beds made, and
they had only had their hands and faces washed about once a week – but
that state of affairs was soon altered. I hunted three wash-basins out of the
Sister's rooms and after a few days the Greeks began to copy us and to wash
their patients and make their beds. They also became most friendly with us,
offering us the use of their baths, beds and clothing. If we had stayed there
another month, I guess it would have been the best hospital in Greece, for it
certainly was already a fine building, beautifully kept, besides having some
very clever surgeons who worked extraordinarily hard. With a few good
Sisters, it would have been a perfect place to work."

Conditions at the Russian hospital may have been improving by the day, but the
fact still remained that a survivor's lot in Athens was not necessarily an easy one.
Many had escaped from the ship only half-dressed in their uniforms, while over two-
hundred others had had their clothes either badly torn or soaked from their
immersion in the salt water. The garments provided by the British and French sailors
had provided a temporary stop-gap, but if the crew were going to remain in Greece
for any length of time then they would need more than the clothes in which they
were standing. Fortunately Mr. and Mrs. Anastasiali at the Serbian relief stores
provided by the United States Government came to the rescue, and Rev. Fleming
would clearly recall the lengths to which some people would go just to make
themselves look more presentable:

"The nurses, who had been so gallant in the hour of danger, revealed their
gallantry in a new, and no less real way, when we safely reached the shore.
We had lost all our belongings, and the only clothes we retained were those
in which we stood when we escaped. Our immediate needs were heartily
met at the Serbian relief stores, and we were able, in a peculiar way, to
appreciate the work of the United States on behalf of our stricken allies. But
the clothing available needed adjustment, and for the next few days the
hands of the nurses were busied with all manner of wonderful garments ...
if the truth will out, many a dignified officer returned to England wearing a
collar made from trousers meant by our American friends to clothe a little
Serbian boy."

Fleming's own contribution came in the form of a khaki handkerchief he had
bought in Athens, which he gave to the nurses so that they could make a tie for
*Britannic*'s Church of England Padre. A pair of boy's khaki trousers from the Serbian
stores provided enough material for a collar and by the time they had finished Rev.
Atkinson was once again looking a little more dignified.

Once suitably attired the distractions of Athens could be enjoyed by all. The
ship's scouts found themselves the honoured guests of their Greek counterparts and
were given a tour of the ancient city that days before they could have only dreamt
about, while Sheila Macbeth enjoyed every minute of her time in Greece. In spite of
the scandalous £4 price tag for a pair of much needed boots, (an offer which, not
surprisingly, she felt unable to accept) she would have given anything to stay there,
and in spite of the uncertain political situation she felt safe wherever she went.

Athens was clearly a city in which Sheila Macbeth felt at ease, although not all of her colleagues were as enamoured. Ada Garland remembered attending a Sunday church service and the walk back to the hotel had been more eventful than she had wished. As they passed through the market square where traders were busily attracting custom she suddenly became aware of *"crowds and crowds of dirty little men"* selling all manner of goods, and as they nervously moved through the market the sounds of the occasional bottom being pinched and the odd slap considerably quickened their pace.

Away from the blue skies of the Mediterranean the outlook in London was decidedly grey. *Britannic's* loss had been a severe enough blow, but there were still several thousand wounded to be brought home and the resulting pressure on the hospital ship service was providing a considerable headache for the Transport Division. *Aquitania* was still safe and lying at Southampton but she could not be in the Mediterranean for at least a week, so as a temporary measure the hospital ships *Warilda, Herefordshire, Wandilla, Llandovery Castle, Dover Castle* and *Glenart Castle* had all been ordered to return to England with as many casualties as they could carry. This would certainly have relieved the immediate pressure on the hospitals, but the resulting dearth of available hospital ships in the eastern Mediterranean would result in a major logistical problem for the foreseeable future. The situation was further complicated when, two days after *Britannic's* demise, HMHS *Braemar Castle* also ran foul of a mine laid by the *U73*, this time in the Mykoni Channel. Employing the same tactics that Captain Bartlett had used, Captain Ernest Mais of *Braemar Castle* managed to beach his ship before it foundered in deep water. Now with the Dardanelles service temporarily denied the use of eight hospital ships *Britannic's* loss was clearly going to have a severe effect for weeks to come.

The question also remained as to how and when the loss of such an important vessel should be officially admitted, and on Thursday 23rd November the Admiralty finally announced the news in the press. The response by the British press was totally predictable. As far as the naval correspondent of *The Times* was concerned, the Germans had already been tried and convicted:

> "... a deliberate opportunity was made by the Germans to exhibit their disregard for the laws of nations and at the same time to get rid of a vessel likely to be a formidable competitor for passenger traffic after the war."

*The Times'* Athens correspondent was also quick to take the moral high ground. claiming that the ship had been deliberately torpedoed in a *"new act of German barbarity"*, while not content with the mere facts, the creative reporter for *The Daily Mirror* went all out for maximum propaganda value, noting that *"...every effort was made to save over one thousand sick and wounded,"* in spite of the fact that there was none on board at the time. Headlines aside, perhaps it is a little unfair to totally condemn the bias of the press in wartime, particularly as the entire affair provided a golden opportunity to put further pressure on the still neutral United States to enter the war. It is quite clear that even the survivors themselves were not above embellishing the story. George Perman later recalled hearing rumours in Athens that

HM.T. HUNTSEND.

Paul Louden-Brown Collection

*Based in the Mediterranean, HMT Huntsend transported the surviving medical orderlies on a six-day voyage from Malta to Marseilles in December 1916. Unfortunately Huntsend's days afloat were also numbered and the ship was torpedoed off Crete on 3rd January 1917.*

*Britannic*'s engineers had been kept below until the last minute by the authority of the chief engineer's pistol. The story, of course, had no foundation and not surprisingly it never found it's way into the newspaper columns, but the fact remains that if the survivors were not above exaggerating their story then what chance did the press have of reporting it accurately?

By the following day the reports had calmed down just a little. Inaccurate details of the wounded troops on board had been quietly dropped as cooler heads prevailed. The accusations had, nevertheless, stung the Germans enough for them to consider an immediate response through a communiqué from Berlin published in *The Times*:

"According to reports so far at hand, the ship was on its way from England to Salonika. For a journey in this direction the large number of persons on board is extraordinarily striking, which justifies the forcible suspicion of the misuse of the hospital ship for purposes of transport. Inasmuch as the ship carried distinguishing marks of a hospital ship, in accordance with regulations, there can naturally be no question of a German submarine in connection with the sinking."

This unambiguous statement set the cat well and truly amongst the pigeons, with the result that the Admiralty now had to justify the high numbers of personnel on board the ship. Publishing their response in the same edition of *The Times*, the Admiralty stated that of the 1,125 on board at the time of the sinking, 625 were members of the crew, while the ship also transported a permanent medical staff consisting of twenty-five officers, seventy-six nurses and 399 medical orderlies, lab attendants and clerical staff. The figures announced in Athens of 1,062 personnel told a slightly different story, and comprised a total of 673 crew, 313 RAMC staff and 76 nurses. To further confuse matters the final report delivered to the shipping casualties register on 7th December 1916 indicated a crew of 1,074, made up of 673 crew, twenty-two surgeons, three chaplains, seventy-seven nurses and 299 RAMC orderlies.

Despite these albeit slight variations, whatever the final tally the Admiralty could at least count themselves fortunate that on this particular voyage *Britannic's* complement did not include the 500 medical personnel transported on the previous voyage. Had this been the case then not only could the number of casualties have been significantly higher but they might also have been faced with the embarrassing task of justifying the use of *Britannic* as a medical transport.

Away from the diplomatic fracas Captain Heard and Commander Staer quietly continued their task, unshackled by either the editorial bias of the British press or the inevitable propaganda of the German High Command. By Friday 24th November they had completed their preliminary investigation, although compared with the copious volumes of text created by Lord Mersey's inquiry into the loss of *Titanic* the 726 word document and three crude sketches submitted by Heard and Staer would seem almost perfunctory by comparison. For the most part the report dealt with a simple summary of the event, but in its key final sentence it would appear that the Germans had been exonerated from deliberately torpedoeing the ship:

> "The effects of the explosion might have been due to either a mine or a
> torpedo. The probability seems to be a mine."

After adding his own despatches to the report, along with accounts given by the commanding officers of HMS *Scourge* and HMS *Foxhound*, Admiral Hayes-Sadler passed the paperwork to Vice Admiral Cecil Thursby, the Senior British Naval Officer in the Eastern Mediterranean at Salonika. That same morning *Britannic's* 605 surviving officers and uninjured crew were transferred to the RFA *Ermine* which would take them on the first stage of their journey home. Escorted by HMS *Foxhound*, *Ermine* proceeded into the Makronisos Channel and headed for Salonika, where they arrived at 11.00 p.m. the following evening. It was only at 7.00 a.m. the next day, however, that the ship finally came alongside Admiral Thursby's flagship, HMS *Lord Nelson*. Only then were the men finally able to get their first decent bath in days, followed by a good meal. The visit aboard *Lord Nelson* also allowed Vice Admiral Thursby to examine the despatches and interview the key personnel mentioned within its pages. The discussions did not last long and by 3.30 p.m. *Ermine* had transferred to the town quay where the survivors went aboard the transport HMT *Royal George*.

With *Royal George* secured at the wharf overnight, a number of the crew took the opportunity to go ashore and pay a visit to the White Tower Theatre and, although it seems quite absurd, two men actually took the opportunity to desert. When *Royal*

*After six days in Athens the nurses were rushed aboard the hospital ship Grantully Castle and transferred to Malta.*

Courtesy Angus Mitchell

*George* finally departed at 3.30 p.m. the following afternoon Firemen W. Kelly and J. Curly had both failed to return to the ship and as a result Captain Bartlett had no choice but to enter their names in the log as deserters and forward the facts to the transport authorities for eventual prosecution.

The five-day journey to Marseilles was largely uneventful, save for many of the survivors suffering from bouts of dysentery. Captain Bartlett utilised the time as best he could to compose the report which he would in time present to the Admiralty Transport Office. *Royal George* arrived at Marseilles on the morning of Saturday 2nd December and it was here that he finally bade farewell to his crew as he took a faster scheduled overland train. For the remainder of the men the journey north would be far less comfortable.

The nightmare journey began shortly after 5.30 p.m. on 4th December as the men were packed into unheated carriages, in spite of the near-freezing temperatures. Brief stops at Louvre, Lyon, Macon, Dijon and Nantes provided only the simplest of refreshments, such as a mug of black tea, and by the time the train reached Louvre the men had become so desperate that they were virtually fighting for the meagre bully beef and biscuit rations being issued there. A few of the ship's officers who had some French money were able to obtain a reasonable meal at a nearby hotel, but

*One of Rev. Fleming's prayer meetings aboard the Grantully Castle.*

*Courtesy John Fleming*

many had to go without altogether. Nor did things improve. The men had to practically beg for some bread and cheese from the Red Cross nurses on the platform at Lyon, Macon provided little more than bread, cheese and tea, while at Dijon they were lucky if they even got that. The 9.00 p.m. stop at Avillon enabled a few of the officers to buy some wine bread, cake and garlic sausage, but the sausage was so strong that few could actually bring themselves to eat it, in spite of their hunger. The fifty-hour journey finally ended shortly after 8.00 p.m. on 6th December at Le Havre. Even then the men still had to undergo a five mile walk to the No. 1 Rest Camp and endure a freezing night under canvas, stretched out on duck boards without even the luxury of a blanket. No breakfast was supplied on the following morning and it would not be until 3.00 p.m. that a meal of hot stew and bread was finally served.

Barely an hour later they were on the move again with a six-mile walk to the dock where they finally began to embark on the transport *Caesarea*. By this time many of the crew were so weakened by their ordeal that they were close to collapse and one man even fell into the freezing water. Once on board the ship they could at least content themselves with the fact that, for the first time in a week, they would be sleeping in warm bunks. Not surprisingly, few stirred on the overnight journey and as the *Caesarea* arrived back at Southampton at 9.00 a.m. on 8th December, Captain Bartlett was waiting on the quay to welcome them. Each man was granted the usual two week period of survivor's leave and, in spite of his reputation as a disciplinarian, Bartlett also announced that he had arranged with the White Star Line to cancel the fines and forfeitures that had been imposed on the more errant members of the crew. In effect, the slate had been wiped clean.

The odyssey surrounding the medical staff was a little more drawn out. After lingering in Athens for a few days after the ship's crew had been shipped out, on 27th November they and the wounded survivors finally went aboard the hospital ship *Grantully Castle*. This time, however, their initial destination was Malta where they eventually landed at the Hamilton Landing Wharf shortly before midday on 30th November. Their arrival provided former *Britannic* passenger Vera Brittain with the opportunity to renew old acquaintances, although her trip to Floriana Hospital to visit one of the nurses whom she had befriended on the *Britannic* gave her quite a shock. Instead of the cheerful young girl she remembered, she found a nervous and distressed shadow of the person she had previously encountered, constantly on the verge of bursting into tears. Vera's description of her experience on the ship seemed to help her colleague, and then as the nurse unfolded her own story, so Vera began to reassess the character of *Britannic*'s hitherto feared matron:

> "In one of the boats sat the Matron, looking towards the doomed *Britannic*, while the rest of its occupants, with our friend amongst them, anxiously scanned the empty horizon. She saw the propeller cut a boat in half and fling its mutilated victims into the air, but, for the sake of the young women for whom she was responsible, she never uttered a sound nor moved a muscle of her grim old face. What a pity it is, I meditated as I listened, remembering the rope across the deck, that outstanding heroism seems so often to be associated with such unmitigated limitations! How seldom it is that this type of courage goes with an imaginative heart, a sensitive intelligent mind!"

Malta was probably the ideal location for the medical staff to recuperate and in time they even became something of a curiosity to the local inhabitants, who marvelled at their ragtag clothing comprised of Serbian boy scout hats and ill-fitting, borrowed uniforms. Needless to say, the nurses fared better than the men, as Sheila Macbeth would later recall:

> "The M.O.s and Orderlies were also billeted in a hospital where each had his temperature taken twice daily and a chart marked "Torpedo Shock!" The day after landing we went into Valletta and met these poor men all hunting for a good place to get a solid meal, as they had been put on a milk diet! (This being the rule for all new patients for the first 24 hours.) We were not quite so badly off as that, but as we had only two tiny sardines for breakfast, and that very early in the morning, we did not hesitate to follow their example."

Sheila's only real problem was that by staying in a hospital she felt at a loose end because she was not working there. It was a situation with which she would have to cope for seventeen days, but for the men of the RAMC it was very different. Percy Tyler's journal of his visit to Malta and the subsequent journey home tells a particularly detailed and all-too-familiar story:

"At 2.00 p.m. we disembarked and were taken in lorries to Fort Manoel Hospital where we were admitted as patients suffering from nerve shock. We fell in for more good treatment here. Several of the boys were unfortunate enough to get a touch of dysentery but soon got over it. On November 30th the whole of the hospital staff had a group taken just as we were dressed when we boarded the *Grantully Castle*. Next day we left for All Saints Active Service Camp to await embarkation to England.

December 8th saw 77 of our number leave for home on a Transport going that night. We remained another day at All Saints and then taken to the overflow camp, All Souls.

At 7.30 a.m. on December 10th we marched off for home and boarded H.M.T. *Huntsend* (captured German vessel *Lutzow*) at about 11.00 a.m. leaving the nurses and sisters to follow later on one of the hospital ships. It was a very slow and tedious journey, partly on account of the zigzag course and also the roundabout way we had come. We met very bad weather in the Gulf of Lyons and it was exceedingly cold all the way. We eventually arrived at Marseilles 5.30 in the evening of the 16th. Much to our relief we were not taken off that night so the band of the survivors of H.M.T. *Minnewaska* gave us some selections on deck.

Next evening we disembarked and left for the station where we entrained about 7.30 p.m. and left for Le Havre at 10.00 p.m. It was now nearly a month since the sinking and we were still making our way back to England and although we had an exceedingly rough time, we little thought what was in store for us.

We were packed into carriages 4 feet 6 inches wide and 8 feet 6 inches long, five on one and four seated on the other side. In these narrow compartments we had to travel for three nights and two days, with one blanket per man, travelling at a very slow pace over snow-clad country, each man numbed with the cold. We were on short rations, which on the 18th consisted of three tins of beef, two tins of beans, one tin of jam and twenty-seven biscuits for nine men to last twenty-four hours. This of course was really only a one meal ration. At 5.30 a.m. the train put in at a siding where we were served with tea; two small canteens for the nine of us.

We got nothing more hot to drink until 9.30 p.m. On the 18th we stopped at 2.30 a.m. for more tea and had the same amount of rations issued for the day and made a further stop at 1.00 p.m. for more tea. Here we were fifty miles from Paris and the warm drink was very welcome as everybody was very cold, the air freezing at the time. While we were here the boys ran races on the platform to get up circulation.

We arrived at the suburbs of Paris about 2.00 p.m. and Versailles 4.30 where the French Red Cross gave us refreshments, cigarettes, etc, which were very acceptable. We then, slowing down to a crawl, passed through Rouen about 11.50 and arrived at Le Havre at 3.30 a.m. on the morning of the 20th December.

We stayed there until 10.30 a.m. when we were marched to a rest camp, arriving there at 11.00 a.m. We got our first meal, and the only one, of beef and biscuits at 3.30 p.m. We fell in again at 4.30 p.m. and marched off for the docks where we boarded H.M.T. *King Edward* for Southampton. We were packed so close here that we slept on top of one another. After a rough crossing we came alongside the quay at 10.30 a.m. where we hung about until 2.30, when we once again got our one and only meal of the day at the R.A.M.C. barracks there. We hung about the sheds here until 5.30 p.m. when we entrained for our final destination, Blackpool, at which place we arrived about 9.00 a.m.

We got to Preston at 5.00 a.m. where we were very well treated by ladies at the Sailors and Soldiers Refreshment Rooms, where they gave us hot tea, food and cigarettes, which kept us going for a bit. We left for Blackpool at 7.15 and by 10.30 a.m. we were in billets with the prospect of a good breakfast and a soft bed before us."

The RAMC orderlies, unlike *Britannic*'s crew, would not be granted the automatic two weeks survivor's leave. The fact that it was also Christmas meant that the men particularly resented this decision, but it appears that the War Office had come to the conclusion that their sojourn on Malta had been enough. In a letter home, written from Blackpool on 2nd January 1917, Private C. McCullogh could only lament on the fact they were getting leave in batches of twelve and that it would probably be at least a month before it was his turn. His letter did, nevertheless, end on an optimistic note:

"I wonder where our next act will be staged. France, Salonika, Egypt, or Mesopotamia? However, we must wait and see! The war will soon be over!"

To be spared the discomfort and hardships of the overland route, the nurses and stewardesses remained on Malta until a vessel was ready to transport them directly to England. For Violet Jessop this was a particular bonus as it allowed her plenty of time to visit her brother, William, who was recovering from a bout of malaria in a Maltese hospital. It was only on their seventeenth day on the island that the nurses were suddenly roused from their tranquil existence and rushed aboard HMHS *Valdivia*. Once again the vessel was a pale shadow of the nurses' former floating home, but the important thing was that the ship was bound for England and they still had a chance of being home in time for Christmas. Sadly it was not to be, and Sheila Macbeth records that the nurses ended up experiencing a voyage, which, if not as arduous as the journey experienced by the men, was no less frustrating:

"In peace time it is probably a nice boat to sail on, but without cargo and empty water tanks, it was a beast and rolled about as much as it could, without rolling completely over. We slept (or at least tried to do so with very little success) in different wards. I was with my friends in a ward with about a hundred Sisters. The ward contained three baths, all out of use for lack of water and three small wash-basins. We started to get up at 5 a.m. so that each one might get a "sponge." As I went to the second breakfast, I seldom got a look at the washing place until late, when the Orderlies were running about – so I had to wash with one hand and cling to the screen with the other for fear of being left high and dry after each roll!!!"

*On 4th December the surviving orderlies and medical staff gathered to be photographed at Fort Manoel.*

*Courtesy Angus Mitchell*

*Valdivia's* lack of fresh water was only the start of the problem. Malta had held insufficient supplies to replenish the ship's tanks and an unscheduled stop at Gibraltar to rectify the situation had proved equally fruitless. By the end of the voyage the passengers had been reduced to making tea with salt water. The nurse's plight was made even worse when, after being deluged twice in the wards, orders were made to ensure that all portholes on the lower decks were kept firmly shut. This turned some areas into virtual ovens and it was little better on deck. There was plenty of fresh air, but there were only a dozen or so deck chairs available for the 150 passengers. Furthermore, it became increasingly obvious as the voyage continued that *Valdivia*, in an attempt to avoid contact with U-boats, was hugging the Biscay coastline and would clearly not get them home in time for Christmas. Nevertheless, when December 25th dawned the ship's passengers were determined to make the best of it. Christmas stockings found a host of objects mysteriously appearing in them, ranging from soap, cigarettes, chocolate oranges and a leather belt, through to nail brushes and even half a comb. Even Sheila's *"dear old Matron,"* better known to Vera Brittain as the *"sixty-year old dug-out,"* had a present for each of the nurses which she had obtained on Malta. That evening, with the ship close to home any of the *"stodgy"* girls who refused to get excited were treated to the indignity of being dumped unceremoniously in the ship's ice chests.

*Valdivia* finally docked at Southampton at 9.00 a.m. on Boxing Day and remained in port for barely a few hours to replenish her woefully depleted water tanks before departing for France. The nurses, meanwhile, were packed on to a scheduled train to Waterloo Station where they were met by the Matron-in-Chief and permitted to return home to await further orders. Sheila's days as a refugee were finally over.

With the loose ends now finally drawn together, it seemed as if the short history of the hospital ship *Britannic* was very much concluded. The dead had been buried, the survivors had been brought home and all that remained to be done was for the British Government to forward a cheque to the White Star Line to cover the loss of the ship. With two years of the war still to run there were clearly other more important priorities, and it is not difficult to understand why the files should be relegated to a forgotten corner of a dusty office. Now, all that remained to be done was to ensure that the crew found new vessels and the medical staff were sent to other theatres of war.

However, while the lives of the doctors, nurses, orderlies and crewmen on board the hospital ship would soon become little more than distant memories, time would later reveal that *Britannic*'s story was still very far from over.

# CHAPTER FOURTEEN

# TIME AND THE SURVIVORS

In the February and March 1917 editions of the United Free Church of Scotland magazine, Rev. John Fleming published a two-part article in which he told the story of his last days aboard *Britannic*. His article provoked so much interest that it was later reissued as a booklet, yet in spite of the overall positive theme of his story he concluded the first instalment with a curiously negative outlook:

> "The memory of the glorious ship will soon fade away, even the pathos of
> its passing will quickly be forgotten, but a gracious work went on aboard
> that vessel, whose fragrance will cling to our every memory of her…"

Sadly, his fears turned out to be all too prophetic. In spite of the fact that *Britannic* would remain the largest British ship to be built prior to the commissioning of the *Queen Mary*, in the intervening years the ship has somehow been erased from the memory of the British public with a precision bordering on surgical. Yet a closer look at the many coincidences and events over the five year period during which the ship existed shows that *Britannic*'s star was eclipsed practically from the start.

It all began to go wrong on 15th April 1912. Although work had been progressing quietly on *Britannic*'s hull over the preceding five months, the *Titanic* disaster resulted in work on the hull being dramatically reduced while Harland and Wolff set about rethinking *Britannic*'s designs. Meanwhile, the White Star Line was tackling the more immediate problem of salvaging what remained of the company's reputation in the courts, and the less pressing consideration of publicising the company's new vessel could wait. By the spring of 1913 attention was firmly concentrated on the reconstructed *Olympic* which incorporated such innovative ideas as a double skin and lifeboats for all, while work on *Britannic* quietly continued in the background.

It was not until February 1914 that *Britannic*, having taken five months longer than *Olympic* to reach the launching stage, was finally ready to enter the public spotlight, and even then the launch on a particularly grey and drizzly day seemed to diminish the occasion. Had *Britannic* also been able to make a glamorous maiden voyage of her own then perhaps matters would have been different, but storm clouds of a different kind ensured that even this would be denied to the ship. Following the outbreak of the First World War *Britannic* would spend the better part of fifteen months tied up at Belfast before desperation rather than sentiment forced the War Office to call on her services, only for the ship to suffer the indignity of being sunk on her sixth voyage after less than a year in service.

In the world of publicity timing is vital, but somehow the guardian angels who oversaw *Britannic*'s brief life span never

*The war memorial at Mikra, Thessalonika. This is the only memorial listing the names of those who died on the Britannic but whose bodies were never recovered.*

*Courtesy Jennifer Clarke.*

quite seemed to get the hang of it. Certainly, the loss of the ship was reported, and the British press did their utmost to exploit the event for their own reasons of propaganda, but at the end of the day it was just another news item which was quickly forgotten by a civilian population that would have to endure another two years of similar losses and horrific casualty lists. As if to hammer the final nail into *Britannic's* coffin, even at her passing the great ship was beaten to the headlines by Austrian Emperor Franz Josef I, who died at Bad Ischl in Austria that same evening. At a stroke, the death of Austria-Hungary's longest ruling emperor would dominate both the headlines and probably the topic of conversation for days to come.

As far as the War Office was concerned, the legacy of *Britannic's* demise had developed into a considerable crisis. The ship may well have been lying at the bottom of the Aegean but the military activity in the Eastern Mediterranean was still very real and threatened to overwhelm the medical facilities if the wounded could not be shipped home. Within days *Aquitania* was once again en route to the Mediterranean, although by now the lesson had been well and truly learnt and the painful loss of their largest hospital ship had forced the Admiralty to rethink its strategy. No longer would large hospital ships be exposed to the increasing dangers of the Aegean; from now on Port Augusta would once again serve as a temporary centre for the transfer of sick and wound until a more permanent solution could be devised.

There were other equally pressing concerns. *Britannic's* loss had also highlighted a number of procedural problems. The fact that the ship's radio call for assistance had been less than precise, combined with the coincidental break-down of its receiving apparatus which had prevented the ship's radio operators from being able to receive any enquiries from the rescue ships, needed to be urgently addressed. To Admiral Thursby at Salonika the situation was wholly unsatisfactory and, concerned that a similar situation should not occur in the future, he later issued recommendations that wireless operators should be routinely advised of the ship's position; once every hour for ships travelling at twelve knots or less, and every thirty minutes for ships travelling over twelve knots. As to the faulty receiver, a further recommendation was issued in January 1917 that a back-up "stand by" receiving circuit, permanently tuned to 600 metres and capable of immediate connection to the aerial, should be fitted on all hospital ships.

Interestingly, the question of the ship's radio highlighted another small problem. Namely, the not uncommon practise by masters of hospital ships to order their radio operators to *"take the press."* This operation involved operators tuning in to a different frequency in order to get the news headlines, which would then be printed up in the ship's newspaper. In itself it was a harmless enough practice and it did not in any way conflict with a hospital ship's permitted usage of the radio, but it did have the unfortunate side effect of compelling the operator to shift from the standard 600 metre wave length, with the result that distress signals and other urgent messages could be delayed or even missed altogether. Thursby's solution to the problem was admirable in its

*Right: The graves of four of Britannic's dead in the British Naval and Consular Cemetery, Piraeus.*

Courtesy Frank Guttman

*Right (inset): The names of the eight RAMC personnel whose bodies were not recovered are included on the war memorial at Mikra, Salonika.*

Courtesy Jennifer A. Clarke

33647 PRIVATE
A. BINKS. MM.
ROYAL ARMY MEDICAL CORPS
21ST NOVEMBER 1916

G. HONEYCOTT
SEAMAN. MV.
H.M.T. "BRITANNIC"
21ST NOVEMBER 1916

H. S. BRITANNIC
ROYAL ARMY MEDICAL CORPS
CAPTAIN                    PRIVATE
CROPPER J.           BOSTOCK G.J.
                     FREEBURY H.
SERJEANT             JONES T.
SHARPE W.            KING G.W.
                     SMITH L.
                     STONE W.
H. S. BRAEMAR CASTLE
ROYAL FUSILIERS
PRIVATE BUSHILL R.W.M.
ROYAL DUBLIN FUSILIERS
PRIVATE DOYLE J.
H. M. S. SENTINEL
ABLE SEAMAN ALLAN G.F.P.

FIREMAN
J. BROWN
H.M.T. "BRITANNIC"
21ST NOVEMBER 1916   AGE 41
R.I.P.

CHARLES J.D. PHILLIPS
TRIMMER. MM.
SS. "BRITANNIC"
21ST NOVEMBER 1916   AGE 23

*The entrance to the British War Cemetery at Drapetsona, Piraeus, where the four recovered bodies were buried on 22nd November 1916.*

*Courtesy Frank Gutmann*

simplicity, and within days instructions were being sent out to the masters of all hospital ships that on no account were they to listen for any press news while at sea.

In spite of his incisive observations, Admiral Thursby was to be proved wrong on one important point. Assuming that a more thorough investigation into *Britannic*'s loss would be held in England he chose not to convene a formal court of enquiry at Salonika to avoid Captain Bartlett and his officers being unnecessarily detained. Yet after the crew arrived back home nothing further was heard on the matter. On 4th December Bartlett submitted his report to the Admiralty Director of Transports at Southampton and on 7th December the loss was duly entered in the Board of Trade's shipping casualties register. The document was endorsed by the Admiralty three days later and on 18th December *Britannic*'s name was officially cancelled on the Liverpool ship registry. After that little more was heard.

The important matter of *Britannic*'s insurance was largely taken care of on 23rd January 1917 when the British Government made a £1,750,000 down payment to the White Star Line until the initial cost of the ship could be finally calculated. By the time Harland and Wolff was able to deliver its final account in March 1917 the sum had been calculated at exactly £1,947,797 5s 10d. The inclusion of the last five shillings and ten pence would seem to suggest that the White Star Line was determined to get back every penny that they had spent on the *Britannic*, although the accidental discovery of a Steinway piano that had been placed in storage when the ship was requisitioned prompted the company to offer to buy it back for the sum of £45.

By that time, however, *Britannic* was no longer an isolated case for the White Star Line. Within weeks Germany's reintroduction of unrestricted submarine warfare would result in the build up of a large backlog of correspondence between the Admiralty and the shipping companies, so that by the end of May 1917 Harold Sanderson was

once again writing to the Transport Office to request payment. Along with the outstanding *Britannic* paperwork, Sanderson also had to take into account the loss of *Laurentic* which had been sunk on 25th January 1917 after running foul of a mine off Lough Swilly, while on 12th February *Afric* had been struck by a torpedo from the *UC66* and gone down twelve miles off

*Above: This advertisement for one of the auctions of Britannic's fittings after the war would seem to confirm that a considerable amount of the wooden panelling originally intended for the ship had not been installed by the time hostilities broke out. Britannic may have been seaworthy, but internally large areas of the ship were clearly incomplete.*

*David Hutchings Collection*

the Eddystone light. The Admiralty very quickly made additional down payments on both of these other vessels, but by the end of May 1917 the White Star Line was still over £600,000 out of pocket. Sanderson's polite entreaties ensured that a further £100,000 was advanced to the company in June, although it would still be several months before the accounts were settled in full.

And there were other loose ends. At the end of April 1917 the Foreign Office approved the small matter of a £4 payment to Francesco Psilas, the Port St. Nikolo fisherman, in return for his help in rescuing the survivors from the Kea Channel, which goes some way to show that the insinuations that local fishermen were more concerned with picking up salvage than rescuing survivors were not entirely justified. Six months later a further £2 was paid to a Mr. Charilaos Mandouvalos who claimed to have salvaged two of *Britannic's* lifeboats at Xeronisi on Petali island. The boats were recovered and towed to the island of Syra where they were placed in the care of the British Consul, and it is here that the trail of *Britannic* finally goes cold.

There was a revenge of sorts. On 21st November 1918, exactly two years to the hour that *Britannic* had been lost, the British Grand Fleet met the German High Seas Fleet in the North Sea for the last time as the German fleet steamed to internment and ultimate self-destruction at Scapa Flow. The end of the war also brought with it the break-up of the Kaiser's merchant marine, as the once great German ships became the war prizes of the Allies. In spite of the White Star Line's wartime services the Admiralty was at first unwilling to offer any of the captured tonnage for sale to the company. The agreement which J.P Morgan had made with the British Government, which ensured that British ships of the International Mercantile Marine combine remained on the British registry, was due to expire in August 1922. After this date IMM simply needed to give five years notice of their intention to transfer vessels to foreign registries. Understandably, therefore, few officials at the Admiralty had any interest in selling hard-won British war prizes to a fleet which may, within ten years, be transferred to the American register.

It would not be until 2nd September 1919 that a final agreement would be hammered out, whereby IMM agreed to extend the original agreement by twenty-five years in return for the continuation of the existing agreement. With this final sticking-point resolved, Harold Sanderson now found himself in a position to restore the White Star Line to its pre-war glory at a stroke, and, considering the massive rise in the cost of shipbuilding, at a fraction of the anticipated cost. Because of this Harland and Wolff would never be given the opportunity to build replacements for either *Titanic* or *Britannic*, and the White Star Line would take full advantage of the available prize tonnage. The company bought three vessels on the list. The former Norddeutscher Lloyd liner *Berlin*, the ship which had laid the mines that sank the battle cruiser HMS *Audacious* in 1914, was the first to join the White Star fleet in September 1921 and renamed *Arabic* (the third in the fleet's history), while another NDL liner, the unfinished 35,000 ton *Columbus*, joined the fleet in February 1922 as *Homeric*. Saving the best till last, the massive 56,000 ton HAPAG liner *Bismarck*, then completing at the Blohm & Voss shipyard at Hamburg, finally made her maiden voyage in White Star colours in May 1922, seven years after being launched.

By the mid twenties, therefore, the lost *Britannic* was little more than a distant memory and her short career amidst wartime secrecy meant that the public knew little of the ship. The name would once more appear as part of the White Star fleet in 1930. The third and final vessel to bear the name, would remain in service until the end of 1960, by which time the once mighty White Star Line had become a pale

*Above: Colonel Henry Anderson, photographed while serving as commanding officer of the Citadel Military Hospital, Cairo. This photograph was taken in the grounds of the hospital in 1918, after having been invested with the CMG by the Duke of Connaught.*

*Courtesy Dr. Llewellyn Lloyd*

shadow of its former self, forced by the economic realities of the Depression to amalgamate with the Cunard Line in 1935.

§§§

If nowhere else, the story of the last of the Olympic class liners did at least live on in the memories of those who served aboard her. So what became of them?

Lieutenant Colonel Henry Stewart Anderson would enjoy a particularly long life following the loss of *Britannic*. In 1917 he was posted to the Citadel Military Hospital in Cairo, where he would serve from 1918 to 1921 as commanding officer. In 1918 he was awarded the CMG (Companion of St. Michael & St. George) before being placed on the reserve list in 1927 and after a particularly long retirement he finally died on 24th May 1961.

Captain Charles Alfred Bartlett, *Britannic's* commander, would return to his shore-based position as White Star's marine superintendent. *Britannic* was to be his last command, but he would remain with the White Star Line until his retirement. Between 1919 and 1921 he also served as aide-de-camp to King George V to advise on maritime affairs. In 1920 he was awarded the CBE for his services during the war and the following year was appointed to the advisory committee of the Royal Naval Reserve where he was promoted to the rank of commodore on the retired list. In 1931 he was made Mariner Warden of the Honourable Company of Master Mariners before retiring from the White Star Line on 31st December of that year. Bartlett still remained active even in the later years of his life, taking several trips to Australia (the first, aboard *Ceramic* in January 1932), and moved to Norfolk; first to Horning Ferry where he would spend much of his time boating and occasionally fishing, and then to Gorleston-on-Sea, the town where his wife Edith had spent her early years. Following the outbreak of the Second World War they returned to Liverpool and it was here that Charles Bartlett would spend the

*Left: Captain Charles Bartlett pictured with his wife, Edith, outside Buckingham Palace in 1921, on the occasion of his being invested with the CBE. As he was being presented with his medal, the King was moved to comment that it was not often that he gave the CBE to a man who had actually lost his ship!*

*Courtesy Alasdair Fairbairn*

last few years of his life. He died from kidney failure on Thursday 15th February 1945 at the Parkhouse Nursing Home in Waterloo, Liverpool, and two days later his body was cremated at Anfield Crematorium.

Nurse Vera Brittain would go on to become perhaps the most significant British feminist and pacifist female writer of the twentieth century. Already reeling from the death of her fiancé in December 1915, Vera would be no stranger to adversity as the war continued. In April 1917 another friend would also be killed, while the blinding of another close companion at Arras and his eventual death in June 1917 brought even more pain. The final blow came in June 1918 when her brother, Edward, was also killed in action. After the war she returned to Oxford University where she read history, rather than English as she had originally intended. As she later wrote in *Testament of Youth*, her bitter experiences of the years 1914 to 1918 had made her determined *"to find out all about it, and try to prevent it, in so far as one person can, from happening to other people in the days to come."* Vera later became a journalist and a steadfast pacifist to such an extent that during the Second World War she often

*Rev. Fleming in the garden of his manse in Inverness-shire, Scotland.*

Courtesy John Fleming

found herself being attacked by the British and American press over the numerous articles she wrote for peace groups. In 1944 she even ran foul of none other than George Orwell, who openly attacked her for her denouncement of the Allied strategic bombing campaign of German cities, although ironically, this did not prevent her name from being included in the Nazis list of well-known English citizens to be arrested had Great Britain surrendered after the fall of France in 1940. Today Vera Brittain is best remembered for four autobiographical books, although her first, *Testament of Youth*, is generally regarded as her finest work. She died on 29th March 1970.

After returning to Scotland, Rev. John Fleming wrote the only contemporary published account of the sinking of *Britannic,* for the Christian press. In 1917 he served with 47th D.A.C. of the British Expeditionary Force at Camiers in France before being transferred to the Mediterranean theatre as a part of General Allenby's eastern campaign against the Turks. With hostilities concluded Fleming took a ten-day tour of the Holy Land, writing with evident pride that the entire

*Harold Goodman in retirement at Sidmouth, Devon, just prior to the Second World War.*

Courtesy Ronald Goodman

*Patrol Leader Edward Ireland: One of the seventeen sea scouts on board the ship on 21st November 1916. Ireland finally escaped from the ship by sliding down a rope and swimming to safety.*

The Scout Association

trip had cost him less than £8, before returning to Scotland. In 1920 he married Dorothy Ballantyne and became the United Free Church minister to Ogilvie Church in Dundee. Two years later he moved to Doune in Perthshire, where he would remain for another ten years before transferring to the parish of Abernethy in Inverness-shire, remaining there until 1942. Fleming spent his final years preaching at Strathtay, near Aberfeldy, and died at Stracathro hospital on 4th May 1953.

Dr. Harold Goodman's remaining military service after leaving *Britannic* was not quite as relaxed, as his diary would later recall. In April 1916 he was transferred to France where he was assigned to the 76th Field Ambulance, working at several front line forward dressing stations. During his service in France Dr. Goodman was mentioned in despatches on two occasions and in July 1918 he was awarded L'ordre du Service de Santé (equivalent to the bronze Croix de Guerre) for his work at the hospital at Dormans. Following his demobilisation in August 1919 he reopened his surgery in Hemsworth, and after marrying Eileen Brereton in October 1923 he seems to have retired from medical practice altogether at the comparatively early age of forty-seven. He and his wife went on to have six children but, although the two girls subsequently became nurses, the four boys later pursued entirely different careers. The family moved to Somerset in 1934 and after the children had left home they moved to Ottery St. Mary in Devon, where, on 13th February 1955, he died at the grand old age of eighty.

In contrast, scout Edward Ireland's was a life cut tragically short. The heroism he displayed at the sinking had resulted in his being only the second scout to be awarded the Cornwell Scout Badge. This award was named after former scout John Travers Cornwell who, as a sixteen-year-old boy, had remained alone at his post aboard the light cruiser HMS *Chester* during the Battle of Jutland while badly wounded. Cornwell was later awarded a posthumous Victoria Cross and in recognition of his valour the Scout Association named their own highest award after one of their favourite sons. By the time he was old enough to join up, Ireland enlisted with the fledgling Royal Army Flying Corps, but in

*Violet Jessop (back row, extreme right) poses for a group shot while serving aboard the Royal Mail steamer Andes. This vessel was to be Violet's last, and she would finally retire from the sea in December 1950 at the end of a career spanning forty-two years.*

*Courtesy Margaret & Mary Meehan*

spite of seeing out the war, his star had run its brief course. On 31st July 1919 Second Lieutenant Edward Ireland, barely nineteen years old, was killed in a plane crash whilst serving with the Royal Air Force Airship Training Wing at Cranwell.

The injuries sustained by Violet Jessop during the sinking proved to be far more serious than originally thought. Unable to return to sea for the foreseeable future, Violet secured a job in London with the Banco Español del Rio de la Plata of Buenos Aires, where she was assigned to the credit department. Her cranial injuries, however, seemed to have affected her in more ways than had at first been realised. A dental X-ray later revealed that she had unknowingly cracked her skull and in the meantime she had to contend with the fact that even basic mathematics, in spite it being her favourite subject at school, was now beyond her. Fortunately her knowledge of Spanish meant that she was able to keep her job and she was transferred to the bank's information department instead.

In June 1920 she finally returned to sea, rejoining *Olympic* when the ship returned to peacetime service and in February 1923 she transferred to the new *Majestic* before leaving the White Star Line in October 1925. Even now Violet's career at sea was not over. Aside from occasional extended periods ashore she would spend the next ten years of her life working as a stewardess for the Red Star Line, mostly on the S.S. *Belgenland*, on which she undertook no less than five world cruises. In 1935 she returned to the Royal Mail Line, the company with which she had started in 1908, and although she would spend the period of the 1939-45 war ashore working in the censor's office where her knowledge of Spanish would prove invaluable, she would remain at sea until 1950.

At the age of sixty-three Violet finally came ashore for good, retiring to a small cottage in Suffolk where she would concentrate on her gardening and keeping chickens. Even in retirement her memories of the *Titanic* disaster resurfaced, particularly in 1958 when film producer William MacQuitty asked her to visit the film set at Pinewood Studios during the production of *A Night to Remember*. Unfortunately she never accepted his invitations and it was a decision she later came to regret. She always believed that the film company had done an excellent job in recreating the disaster, although the first-class female passengers' hats and the scenes of the third-class passengers being kept below were a few of the points which she felt needed to be corrected. Unfortunately she never got the chance. Her memoirs lay forgotten and unpublished until 1997, while Violet herself, after a long retirement, had died at Bury St. Edmunds hospital in May 1971.

One of the best-known *Britannic* survivors was nurse Sheila Macbeth, who, during the summer of 1976, visited the ship for one last time. Her return to the Kea Channel was as the guest of underwater explorer Jacques Cousteau, who, during the summer of 1976, was exploring the wreck of the *Britannic*. In spite of her eighty-six years Sheila was still able to get into the *Calypso*'s small yellow submarine, known as the *Soucoupe*, to take her first look at the ship in sixty years. Nor had those sixty-years been uneventful. In 1920 Sheila married John Mitchell, and went on to have three children. John's career with the Civil Service took them to India for many years and following his retirement they settled in Edinburgh, where they continued to work on behalf of the Scottish Genealogy Society. As part of this work they both personally recorded all of the pre-1855 inscriptions in every burial ground in eight Scottish counties, and recognition for this work finally came in 1980 when Sheila was awarded the MBE (Member of the Order of the British Empire) for her contribution to genealogical studies.

Following her return to *Britannic* Sheila became something of a celebrity.

*Sheila Macbeth Mitchell, photographed during Jacques Cousteau's 1976 expedition to explore the wreck of the Britannic. Sheila returned to the Kea Channel sixty years after Britannic's loss and at her third attempt was even able to make a dive to the wreck in Calypso's submarine, Soucoupe.*

Bill Tantum/THS collection

In addition to numerous radio interviews she received correspondence from other *Britannic* veterans or from their families, and in February 1977 she joined Cousteau in London for a reunion dinner with several other survivors. Towards the end of her life Sheila moved to Bath in Somerset so that she would be nearer to her daughter, and it was here, at the amazing age of 103, that she died on 15th February 1994.

Major Harold Priestley, alas, did not survive so long. After *Britannic* went down there seems to be something of a gap in his service record until 1922, although the RAMC records do note that he was mentioned in despatches in September 1918 and January 1919. In 1923 he was posted to Singapore for three years and in 1930 he was transferred to India. The tropical climate, however, was clearly not to his liking and he was soon invalided home. He died at the comparatively young age of sixty-three on 16th March 1941.

Of our remaining British cast little more is known. We know that Private Percy Tyler survived the war and it is recorded that on 5th January 1920 he was at Woking to be presented with his medals (the Victory Medal, the British Medal and the 1915 Star), but with many of the RAMC records destroyed in a bombing raid during the Second World War the research trail often goes cold. In other cases it is even more frustrating. The Guildhall Library records contain no further reference after 1916 to Captain Harry Dyke, *Britannic's* assistant commander, although a brief reference to nurse Ada Garland at the Imperial War Museum does record that in later life she worked in an unknown capacity for both Anne Todd and T.S. Elliott before dying on 24th April 1959 in Devon.

And what of the German players? With the Treaty of Versailles forbidding the reduced post-war Reichsmarine to operate any submarines you would have thought that the officers of the *U73* would have been among the first to go. Surprisingly this was not to be the case:

Kapitänleutnant Gustav Siess would remain based in the Mediterranean for the remaining two years of the war, and would go on to acquire a reputation as one of Germany's greatest submarine aces. In spite of the improved Allied anti-submarine measures, by the time he left *U73* in April 1917 he had over 154,000 tons of Allied shipping to his credit. Seiss then assumed command of *U33* and went on to become one of the most successful U-boat skippers in the Mediterranean. In the space of only two hours on March 20th 1918 he added four more vessels to the list, bringing his personal tally to exactly 261,399 tons, and his successes were acknowledged on 24th April 1918 when he was awarded the *Pour le Mérité* medal. At the end of the war he was in command of *U65* and following the Austrian surrender in October 1918 he led eleven U-boats back through the Straits of Gibraltar and home to Germany with the loss of only one craft.

In spite of the harsh post-war conditions in Germany, on 22nd February 1920 Siess was promoted to the rank of Korvettenkapitän as he settled into his new job in the now reduced German navy. Although the Reichsmarine was not permitted any submarines, or even to build them, Germany managed to get around this technicality by establishing companies in Holland where they could not only market their expertise in the manufacture of U-boats, but could also keep their technology up to date. A man of Siess' experience was simply too valuable to throw away and for the next ten years he remained in Hamburg, rising to the position of head of the marine department where his invaluable input would result in the development of the next generation of diesel engines. He died in Hamburg at the age of eighty-six on 14th October 1970.

Of all our characters, however, it is *U73*'s navigating officer who would have the most remarkable future. Following a posting to the German Admiralty and a further spell as navigating officer in *U39*, he was awarded the Iron Cross, first class, after which he continued in the same rank with *U151*. In June 1918 Martin Niemöller was given command of *UC67* and in September of that year he claimed his first three kills off Marseilles. Following the Austrian capitulation he successfully navigated his submarine from the Mediterranean back to Kiel via the north coast of Scotland. To a patriot such as Niemöller the state of anarchy that he found on returning home would ultimately force him to reconsider his future when, in January 1919, he even refused point-blank to tow two submarines to England. Leaving the Inspector-General in no doubt as to his feelings on the matter, he answered:

> "I have neither sought nor concluded this Armistice. As far as I am concerned, the people who promised our submarines to England can take them over. I will not do it."

Niemöller was ultimately excused the duty, but clearly the post-war Reichsmarine held no future for him and on 27th March 1919 he tendered his resignation.

Runaway inflation in post-war Germany and a meagre pension made any thought of his being able to afford a farm virtually negligible. Instead he enrolled as a theology student at the University of Münster, paying for his studies by working as a railway plate layer and selling the gold lace of his uniform to a jeweller. On 29th June 1924 Niemöller was ordained at the church of the Redeemer in Münster, and in spite of his Christian faith still remained very much a nationalist. Observing the political and economic turmoil of the Weimar Republic he came to the conclusion that Adolf Hitler seemed to offer the perfect solution to the country's ills and his joy knew no bounds when Hitler was elected German chancellor in January 1933. Within six months of the Nazis coming to power, however, he would begin to have serious reservations.

With hindsight it's not difficult to see why the Nazis would appear so attractive to a man like Martin Niemöller. Article 24 of the Nazi party programme called for freedom for all religious denominations and *"positive Christianity"*. The patently nationalistic line espoused by the Nazi Party also appealed to his sense of patriotism, but while Niemöller's idea of nationalism was to encourage the German race, the Nazis took the policy a sinister step further by actively encouraging the denigration of others. To a man of Niemöller's moral standing the idea of inferior peoples was anathema, but at this early stage few could foresee what was to come.

In no time at all Niemöller found himself in the strange position of being a supporter of National Socialism but wholly opposed to any state interference in the Church, and when Nazi-backed theologians actually proposed the revision of the New Testament with the teaching of Jesus corresponding entirely with the demands of National Socialism, he found himself inexorably drawn into the struggle. A collision course became inevitable in September 1933, when the Prussian Synod passed a resolution stating that all non-Aryan pastors or church officials who had married non-Aryans should be dismissed. Unable to acquiesce to such a doctrine Niemöller became a leading figure of the Pastors' Emergency League, which, by January 1934, had over 7,000 members. Matters finally came to a head on 7th January 1934 when the Lutheran ministers formally denounced Nazi domination of the church. In an attempt to diffuse the situation Adolf Hitler agreed to a personal meeting between the opposing groups at the Reich Chancellery on 25th January. But when Hermann Göring read out the transcript of a bugged telephone conversation that Niemöller had had with a colleague earlier that morning, during which he had discussed the League's memorandum to go over Hitler's head to the German president, Paul von Hindenburg, Hitler was furious. All attempts to reassure him that the Pastors' Emergency League was not intended to undermine his authority and only concerned with the authentic faith of the church for the sake of the Reich were to no avail. Hitler's position was quite clear – the clergy should leave the care of the Third Reich to him and concern themselves with looking after the church and getting people to heaven. As they shook hands at the end of the meeting Niemöller took the opportunity to remind Hitler that as Christians and men of the church they too had an obligation to look after the German people, and that neither he nor anybody else could take that away from them.

Retribution was not long in coming. That night Niemöller's house was raided by the Gestapo and only days later a bomb was mysteriously detonated inside. Niemöller was now a marked man. The Organisation of Free Synods and the Confessing Church within the German Protestant church now represented the only real opposition to Nazi religious policy and, as his reputation abroad continued to grow, so his position at home became more precarious. The hammer finally fell on the morning of 1st July 1937. Following his arrest and interrogation Niemöller was taken to Moabit prison to await trial, yet even behind bars he was by no means forgotten, with over 3,000 letters and cards arriving at the prison on the occasion of his forty-sixth birthday.

The trial began in secret on 7th February 1938, but far from being an outstanding success for the Nazi authorities it rapidly degenerated into a farce as, one by one, the charges simply collapsed. By the end of the day only two issues remained, each relating to what a pastor was or was not permitted to preach from the pulpit, and by publicly reading out the names of those in prison Niemöller was clearly in breach of a law passed by the Nazis. The result was never in doubt, but his sentence of six months confinement in a fortress and a 2,000 Mark fine was rather less than Hitler had expected. To make matters worse, Niemöller had already served eight months in detention and the fine was reduced to 1,500 marks. Upon hearing the news Hitler's fury knew no bounds. At a cabinet meeting that same day he declared *"This man is my personal prisoner,"* and within hours Niemöller was on his way to the Sachsenhausen concentration camp.

The Führer's personal prisoner would remain caged for the next seven-and-a-half years, yet even the outbreak of war in 1939 still found enough patriotic fervour remaining within him to offer his services to the *Kriegsmarine*. Not surprisingly the

*Pastor Martin Niemöller. Following his release at the end of the Second World War he went on to become a prominent figure in the World Peace Movement as well as the Campaign for Nuclear Disarmament.*

offer was declined and in July 1941 Niemöller was transferred to Dachau concentration camp. As the war progressed his continuing plight made him a symbol of resistance to Hitler and in the dying days of the war the Nazis' rush to rid themselves of their greatest problems before their inevitable defeat saw Niemöller and some 150 other special prisoners removed from Dachau in April 1945 and driven over the border to Italy. The intention had been to kill them all, but luck intervened when the party came across a German divisional HQ where a number of the imprisoned German officers happened to have friends. The following day their SS guards were sent packing and within three days the special prisoners were safely in American hands.

Following the war Niemöller's reputation ensured his quick return to prominence in the German church, while his election as one of the German delegates to the World Council of Churches confirmed his propaganda value. Unfortunately he continued to make enemies. His decision to speak out and acknowledge both his own guilt and that of Germany did not endear him to many of his fellow countrymen, while the Allies were not keen to listen to a former symbol of resistance to Nazism as he attempted to ease the conditions of German prisoners of war. His actions particularly irritated the British authorities, some of whom argued that his posturing was a ruse to organise sympathy for Germany.

As he worked to restore Germany's standing in the world, Niemöller became aware of the World Peace Movement in 1948. His criticism of Konrad Adenauer's German rearmament policy in the 1950s moved the German chancellor to state that Niemöller's actions were *"little short of treason,"* while his own supporters in the church were becoming more than a little concerned that he was now dabbling in politics. But it was the development of the atomic bomb that caused Niemöller more apprehension than any other factor. In 1952 he was invited to serve on the council of the World Peace Committee and in April 1958 he took part in the famous march from London to the atomic weapons research establishment at Aldermarston. Niemöller's anti-nuclear activities, once again did little to endear him to the authorities, especially in Germany, and he again found himself banned from making political speeches from the pulpit. Not for the first time Niemöller's preaching where his conscience led him was causing those in authority more than a little discomfort.

Martin Niemöller remained an active pacifist for the rest of his life, which ended in Wiesbaden on 5th March 1984, yet even today the concluding words of many of his public addresses are still famous the world over:

> *In Germany they first came for the Communists,*
> *and I didn't speak up because I wasn't a Communist.*
> *Then they came for the Jews,*
> *and I didn't speak up because I wasn't a Jew.*
> *Then they came for the trade unionists,*
> *and I didn't speak up because I wasn't a trade unionist.*
> *Then they came for the Catholics,*
> *and I didn't speak up because I was a Protestant.*
> *Then they came for me,*
> *and by that time no one was left to speak up.*

That a First World War German U-boat officer with such strong nationalist views would ultimately become one of the twentieth century's best-known pacifists is, perhaps, surprising; but with the benefit of hindsight and today's certain knowledge of the extremes of Germany's Third Reich as well as the horrors of the Great War, for a man like Niemöller with passionate beliefs in truth and justice, it is less so.

We end this chapter with fifteen-year-old boy scout George Perman, who would remain the longest known surviving member of *Britannic*'s crew. After returning to England George would retain his links with the sea by taking a job as an electrical apprentice at the Thorneycroft shipyard in Southampton, where he remained for five years before joining the Royal Mail Steam Packet Company as a junior electrician. Even at the age of twenty-one George was considered experienced enough to be promoted to second electrician after only one voyage. The following years would bring with them frequent passages through the Panama Canal to the Pacific Ocean, where he would later become familiar with all of the major North American Pacific ports; Vancouver would always remain a particular favourite. By the age of twenty-four he was serving as chief electrician, but after seven years at sea George finally 'swallowed the anchor' in order to pursue his true vocation in the Church of England.

After completing the three-year course in only two years, George was ordained by the Bishop of Manchester before going on to serve as a curate in Tunbridge Wells and then in Rainchurch. His first post as a vicar was at the Smithfield Martyr's Memorial Church in Clerkenwell, London, where he served for twelve years, during which time his church and vicarage were both heavily damaged in a bombing raid during the Second World War. After the war he became vicar at St. Mary's Church, Ealing, where he would remain for a further twelve years before retiring.

Following his retirement George and his wife Gertrude lived in London and Felixstowe, before moving to Worthing in Sussex. They never had any children and following Gertrude's death George moved to the *Koinonia* Christian Rest Home in Worthing. He died there, aged ninety-nine, on 24th May 2000.

Today, of the 1,062 officers, medical staff and crew aboard *Britannic* on the morning of Tuesday 21st November 1916 there are now no longer any known survivors. With their passing the human story of the *Britannic* seems to have run its course. While the people who lived and served aboard during its eleven months at sea slip into the shadows of history, the barnacle encrusted wreck of *Titanic's* *"forgotten sister"* is now attracting the interest of engineers, divers and historians as they wrestle with the one unanswered question - what was the real cause of the tragedy on the day the good ship went down?

*Left:* **The Reverend George Perman, pictured in retirement in Worthing in 1999. George Perman died on 24th May 2000, and was the last known Britannic survivor.**

CHAPTER FIFTEEN

# THE MODERN GREEK MYTH

In spite of its turbulent past, the history of the island of Kea, lying just off Cape Sounion on the southern coast of Attica, has much to recommend it. According to ancient legend, in the 16th century BC Kea was home to Aristeus, the son of the god Apollo and the nymph Kyrene, and he is said to have established the tradition of apiculture, olive pressing and cattle raising which survives to this day. Four hundred years later the island was the home of the Greek hero Keos, yet another son of Apollo, from whom the island derived its name. In later years the poets Simonides and Vacchylides were both born there, as was the philosopher Prodikus who become the tutor of such luminaries as Socrates, Euripides, Isokrates, Thucydides and Xenophon. But it was not only in the arts that Kea contributed to the ancient Greek civilisation; the politician Thiramenes, the doctor Erasistratos and the lawgiver Aristides also began their careers there as well. Perhaps the most interesting idea to be exported from the shores of Kea was the ancient tradition of the "Kean Law," which obliged those who lived to the age of seventy to commit suicide by drinking hemlock.

As the Roman Empire contracted so Kea's fortunes waned, and the years that followed brought less heroic times. As part of the Venetian Empire (when the island was better known as Tsia) Kea was an important pirate base before falling to the Turks in 1537, although the island's strategic position was still of vital importance. During the Russian Turkish War the activities of the Russian-backed Greek pirate Lambros Katsonis, who used St. Nikolo for his base, were legendary. One story tells of Katsonis being blockaded in port by the Turks only for him to escape by having his crew carry their ships over a narrow piece of land at Kokka, now known as the Pass of Lambros Katsonis. Kea was finally liberated along with the rest of Greece following the War of Independence in 1830.

In spite of this rich heritage, or maybe because of it, until recently *Britannic* has hardly even rated a footnote in the island's history. For sixty years the hull of the sleeping giant lay barely three miles from the harbour entrance of Port St, Nikolo, disturbed by little more than the occasional fishing net, while even the rediscovery of the wreck by Jacques Cousteau in December 1975 and its subsequent exploration the following summer brought only a fleeting return to the public spotlight. Within a year *Britannic* had once again quietly slipped into the forgotten pages of history.

Unfortunately, the high profile of Cousteau's expedition raised more questions than it actually answered and it was not long before many of the allegations that had

*Left: Although Jacques Cousteau visited the Britannic in 1976, it was not until nearly twenty years later that the technology existed to conduct a more scientifically exact exploration of the wreck.*

done so much to tarnish the reputation of the ship's memory in 1916 began to resurface. In the intervening years another Greek myth would be created, as the history of the *Britannic* was gradually rewritten to fit in with the presumed evidence gleaned from the wreck itself.

On the face of it, the findings of the Cousteau expedition presented a very plausible case. The fact that a number of the metal hull plates on the port side of the wreck were bent outward seemed particularly tantalising, and bearing in mind the fact that the scale of the damage was also far greater than what might be expected from a single German mine it wasn't long before historians were speculating that hidden within *Britannic's* shattered hull was evidence of an illicit cargo of munitions. Indeed, there was a great deal of circumstantial evidence to suggest that they might have had a point. The blown-out hull plates seemed to indicate that an explosion had occurred within the ship's hull. This, coupled with the position of the wreck on the official Admiralty chart inaccurately shown to be 8.75 miles away from its true location, looked equally suspicious. Even the known facts began to be distorted, and sixty years on German wartime allegations that *Britannic* was being used to illegally convey troops was now being widened to suggest the transportation of an illicit arms cache as well.

*Jacques Cousteau's involvement in the story of the Britannic came about more by accident than design. When the Titanic Historical Society of America learned that he was operating in the Aegean, they approached the Cousteau Society with the idea of locating the Titanic's lost sister ship.*

*Bill Tantum/THS Collection*

Cousteau, to his credit, did not give much credence to the munitions theory. Finding *Britannic's* cargo holds to be empty he chose instead to concentrate on the large deposits of coal spread out over the damaged area as well as on the seabed. From the available evidence, he came to the conclusion that the scale of the damage had in fact been caused by an internal coal-dust explosion, and by the time *Calypso* came to leave the Kea Channel Cousteau was quite confident that he knew everything there was to know about the wreck.

But did he? For some time the Cousteau expedition represented the only detailed exploration of the wreck and it would be almost twenty years before another explorer would pick up where he had left off. At the end of August 1995, Dr. Robert Ballard, the man who ten years earlier had been co-leader of the team that located and photographed the wreck of the *Titanic*, arrived in the Kea Channel with an array of technical equipment that could hardly fail to provide a wealth of new information, and by the time he left the first steps towards a more considered explanation of the cause of *Britannic's* demise had been well and truly taken.

Ballard had two important advantages over Cousteau. Whilst his ROVs were not as versatile as a manned diver they could stay below the surface indefinitely. So, instead of having to constantly worry about air supplies and decompression schedules, *Phantom* and *Voyager* were able to move over the wreck unhindered by any such human frailties. Another valuable addition to the expedition was the 146 ft nuclear research submarine *NR1*, equipped with some of the most sophisticated sonar equipment available together with SIT (Silicon Intensified Target) cameras. The images from this highly specialised equipment would provide the first truly detailed overview of the wreck to date. The findings of this expedition would ultimately prove to be far more revealing and, combined with a deluge of additional information gleaned from further manned explorations in 1997, 1998 and 1999, has been instrumental in dispelling most of the myths and rumours once and for all. Slowly but surely a combination of archival research and underwater exploration has shown beyond all reasonable doubt that the allegations which had been made about *Britannic's* role during the 1914-18 war have really been little more than idle speculation.

The foundations to the charge that the Admiralty had deliberately misplaced the wreck on the charts now look very tenuous to say the least. Although much publicity has been given to Cousteau's weeks of fruitless searching for the wreck using Dr. Harold Edgerton's new side-scan sonar, the fact is that if the available historic documentation had been studied in more detail then the wreck would have been located far more quickly. *Britannic's* position on the chart was certainly incorrect but the information at the British Hydrographic Office, on which the chart was based originated from a survey of the area carried out in 1947. A closer look at more contemporary documents, such as *Britannic's* log and the Board of Trade Shipping Casualties Register, would have shown that the wreck's true location was reported to be some distance from the charted position. The ship's log has never been classified as secret for military reasons, and had the scientists placed a little more faith in Captain Bartlett's navigation then they would, in all probability, have saved themselves a great deal of effort. To hold Cousteau responsible for other people's misconceptions would perhaps be unjust, but the fact remains that the revelations regarding the ship's questionable location have provided the ammunition for many – if not all – of the conspiracy theories that would subsequently be put forward.

One of Cousteau's more intriguing discoveries, subsequently confirmed by Robert Ballard in 1995, was that the wreck actually lies on a heading of 253º. This is curious in itself as the ship would appear to be headed back in the approximate direction from which it was travelling prior to the explosion. Bearing in mind that Captain Bartlett ordered a southerly course following the explosion this seems doubly odd. Nonetheless, *Britannic's* heading could have been affected by a number of factors as

she was sinking. A passage from the report of *Britannic*'s senior medical officer, Lieutenant Colonel Henry Stewart Anderson, provides an interesting point of information:

> "The wake showed that the ship was moving in a wide circle to the right."

*Above: **The MV Calypso tied up along the harbour wall on Kea. A converted mine sweeper, Calypso is quite possibly the best known marine research vessel of all time.***

*Bill Tantum/THS Collection*

If *Britannic* was making for land then why was the ship moving in a wide circle to the right? One likely explanation is that the navigation of the ship was being considerably hampered by the list to starboard. This also might explain why the rudder of the wreck is turned to port by at least 10º. It is quite possible that Captain

Bartlett was trying to compensate for the drift to starboard. The prevailing current in the Kea Channel would have been another factor. The strength of this current was convincingly demonstrated to the divers of the 1997 IANTD expedition when during one in-water decompression period (which lasted approximately three hours) the divers' platform drifted some seven miles from its exclusion zone confirming that the prevailing north easterly currents in the Kea Channel can be particularly strong and would almost certainly have had a considerable effect on the navigation of the ship at the time.

And what of the causes? When Jacques Cousteau interviewed seven *Britannic* survivors for his 1977 documentary *Calypso's Search for the Britannic*, all but one remained convinced that the ship had been deliberately torpedoed. In the face of such overwhelming evidence, therefore, it would seem that there can be little question as to the cause of *Britannic*'s loss. But it is not quite that straightforward and a closer look at the facts reveals a far more uncertain picture.

To begin with, not one of Cousteau's survivors actually saw the torpedo that was supposed to have sunk the ship. Their conclusions were primarily based on the rumours and speculation that abounded after the event, and with the British press so determined to point the finger of guilt at Germany, the torpedo theory was by far the most convenient. Of the relevant survivors' testimony only three individuals gave what might be considered to be useful evidence. However, with two alleged sightings of torpedoes on different sides of the ship, and not forgetting the vague but historically tantalising references by lookout J. Conclly to the two *"suspicious objects"* now thought to be mines, it is not so surprising that Captain Heard and Commander Staer remained unconvinced about the presence of a U-boat.

*Below: Cousteau and the Calypso divers prepare to dive the wreck of the Britannic, the first time that the wreck would have been seen in almost sixty years.*

*Bill Tantum/THS Collection*

The first real indication that Heard and Staer were right came in August 1918, when a captured German sailor from *UB109* stated while under interrogation that he had been a member of *U73*'s crew in 1916, and that the submarine had laid mines in the Kea Channel. Even Kapitänleutnant Gustav Siess in a post-war interview was a little more forthcoming on his role in the loss of the ship:

"Another of the mines laid by the *U73* off the coast of Greece sank one of England's greatest ships, the 48,000-ton liner *Britannic*, the largest vessel of any kind that went down during the war. Unfortunately, she was a hospital ship, plainly marked and all that –

but mines do not choose. It was a part of the fortunes of war that we, the submarine commanders, sometimes had infamy thrust upon us for the work done by mines."

The final reference to *U73*'s minefield in the Kea Channel comes from the memoirs of Martin Niemöller. With three men telling such similar stories at such a distance, the evidence relating to a torpedo becomes more tenuous still.

The question, of course, is can any of this be proved? Only an extensive and systematic sonar search of the Kea Channel is likely to provide the evidence of the sinker which would have tethered the mine to the seabed, but the available information regarding the position of the mine field is by no means conclusive. A plan of the minefield was logged by Kapitänleutnant Siess in October 1916, but when one stops to consider that *U73* was submerged and navigating by dead reckoning at the time the mines were laid, it would be unrealistic to expect his recorded position to be absolutely accurate. A limited sonar search of the area by the *NR1* in September 1995 seems to bear this out; nothing of specific interest was located save for a mass of promising contacts, which, on closer examination, turned out to be nothing more than rocks and assorted debris thoughtlessly dumped over the sides by generations of passing ships. There are other possibilities. In the intervening years a number of these mine anchors may well have been dragged by fishing nets, but it is equally likely that some, if not most, are still there. Nevertheless, if the initial blast point of the mine's detonation can be located on future expeditions then the debate of mine versus torpedo will be concluded once and for all.

The mine probably responsible for the initial explosion that sank *Britannic* would have been one of the twelve standard type A mines laid by *U73* on the morning of 28th October 1916. These mines, which contained an explosive charge of 150 kg, were anchored to the seabed and had an operating depth of up to 150 metres. They were deployed to a set depth by a preset control that worked by measuring the water pressure and, assuming they were intended for vessels with a deeper draft, would usually have been set to a depth of approximately seven metres.

As a rule explosive forces are far more destructive beneath the surface than above. A particularly dramatic demonstration of the principle comes in the form of the famous bouncing bomb which was designed by Sir Barnes Wallis. Wallis, who recognised that the effect of an explosive charge is considerably magnified as the shock wave travelled through the water, used this technique to destroy the Eder and

*A sonar scan taken by the US Navy's miniature nuclear powered submarine NR1 in 1995.*

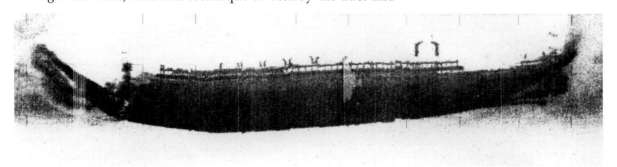

The chapel at Kea was, and still is, a prominent landmark for passing ships.

The SSV *Carolyn Chouest* at Souda Bay, Crete, in August 1995.

The nuclear powered submarine *NR1* at Souda bay, Crete, in August 1995.

Less than three miles from the Kea shoreline, the floats marking the position of the wreck on the 1998 manned expedition show just how close *Britannic* was to safety.

The point on the Kea shoreline where Captain Bartlett attempted to beach *Britannic* before she sank.

Today, *Britannic*'s foc'sle is even now virtually intact, with the anchor chains still in their gullies.

*Britannic*'s bow seems to have hardly disturbed the seabed, indicating that the ship sank more gently than Titanic which dropped 2½ miles.

After a little more than twenty minutes on the wreck, the mixed gas divers have to endure over three hours at shallower depths where they must dissolve the excess nitrogen in their system before they can safely return to the surface.

The aft port gantry davits, locked in position since 21st November 1916.

Part of the lattice metal framework which supported lifeboats 16A to 16F.

By comparing the diver in the foreground, this wider angle view shows just how large the gantry davits really were.

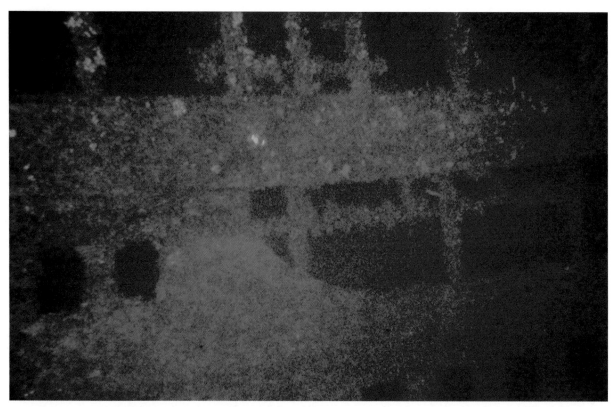

Towards the aft end of the bridge deck, just astern of the intended à la carte restaurant.

This view clearly shows how heavily encrusted the wreck has become after eighty-four years on the seabed, with sea growths of every description.

Nearly all of the windows of the enclosed forward port promenades on A and B decks appear to have imploded as the ship sank.

The docking bridge, minus all of its machinery, but still firmly attached to the poop.

The now open interior of the deck house that once contained the ship's officers' quarters.

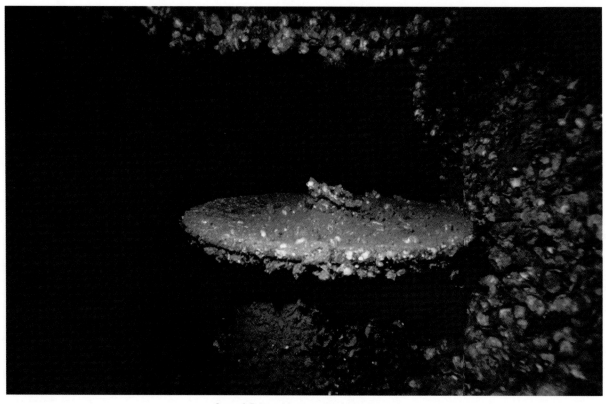

One of *Britannic*'s encrusted capstans.

The fallen telemotor pedestal on the ship's bridge.

The port running light is now almost totally covered with marine growths, but still recognisable.

A deck light, still firmly attached to the deck house.

What remains of the ship's officers' bathroom. Note the four taps, for hot and cold running fresh and salt water.

A bench end protrudes from the encrusted boat deck.

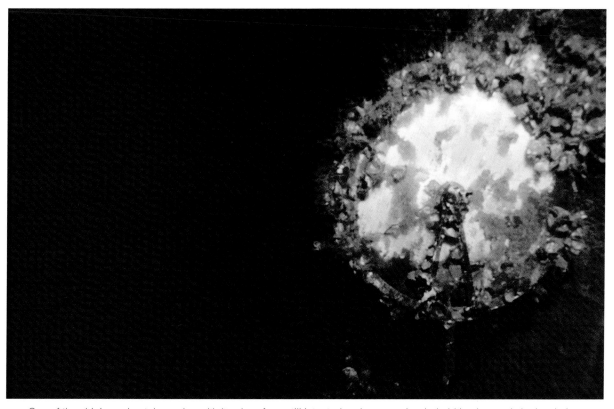

One of the ship's engine telegraphs, with its glass face still intact, dangles precariously, held in place only by its chains.

A fallen window near to the bridge, which broke away as the ship sank.

One of the many open portholes on the wreck. Contrary to regulations they were often left open to air the wards and this was a critical factor which contributed to the loss of the ship.

A shattered window in the now open superstructure.

An illustration of Britannic created by Ken Marschall who was involved with Ballard's exploration in 1995. Marschall is well known for his attention to fine detail and authenticity which he gained from the copious data provided by the exploration team.

Möhne dams in May 1943, and if the solidly built Ruhr dams were to prove so susceptible to these forces then it stands to reason that a ship would be equally vulnerable, if not more so.

Aside from the force of the explosion, location is also an important factor. As the shock waves travel through water they are dissipated in equal directions – either into the hull, away from the ship or into the column of water – but for the captain of any ship the worst possible scenario is an under-bottom explosion, where half of the mine's explosive force is directed into the hull. From the available contemporary evidence it is clear that the explosion certainly occurred very low down, with the fireman's passage at the level of the tank top being so severely damaged in the initial blast that Captain Bartlett's own report stated: *"probably the whole of the fore part of the ship's bottom being destroyed"*. This might also account for Captain Heard's observation that no one remembered seeing a column of water thrown up by the explosion. However, while the explorers were prepared to find extensive damage to the area beneath *Britannic's* forward well deck, no one had anticipated what would actually be revealed. The scale of damage was so great that surely no single weapon could account for it. There had to be something else.

And so the seeds of the theory were sown that there was a secondary internal explosion. On the face of it this is not such an implausible idea, for was it not *Lusitania* which supposedly suffered a similar fate? In *Britannic's* case, however, a variety of factors may have been responsible for an internal blast and while the supposition that the ship might have been carrying a munitions cargo, in clear violation of the Geneva Convention, should be considered, other factors such as medical supplies of nitrous oxide, gasoline or ether vapour also need to be taken into account. Nor should we overlook Cousteau's original exploding coal dust theory.

To begin with, what grounds are there for any suspicions that there may have been an internal explosion? The answer is none. Captain Heard's report was very quick to conclude that there had been only one explosion. However, the observation of the vapours that had followed the explosion made by Thomas Walters should perhaps be addressed in greater detail. Walters, a principal proponent of the torpedo allegation, was standing forward on the starboard promenade deck at the time of the explosion, and his testimony is particularly intriguing:

> "On the instant I gripped the rail and leaned inboard to await the explosion
> which seemed to occur immediately I then looked down at the water but
> had to hold my nostrils on account of the fumes which were stifling."

What could have accounted for these fumes? One could very quickly jump to the conclusion that an unspecified cargo had either exploded or caught fire to create these effects, but the facts are actually a little more prosaic. It is true that the fumes given off by an exploding mine might be considerably enhanced by the rapid burning of material surrounding the charge, but it is also true that anything from paint to metal will give off an astonishing cocktail of fumes when burnt. When one also considers that a considerable amount of available oxygen would have been absorbed in the blast and that large volumes of carbon monoxide and carbon

dioxide gas (amongst others) would be generated, there are clearly numerous possibilities to explain Walters' description.

Even so, it is still possible to offer up a convincing hypothesis. The Shipping Casualty report clearly states that *Britannic* was carrying no cargo of any description, and if any medical stores were contained within the holds it is unlikely that they would have been present in sufficient quantity to

*The interior of the once highly classified NR-1 submarine. With a nuclear power source it could remain submerged indefinitely, enabling NASA to utilise the submarine to its maximum capability during the operation to recover the wreckage of the Challenger space shuttle.*

account for the damage. The fact that no trace of any cargo has been located in any of the holds or the debris field during five separate explorations of the wreck would also seem to conclusively exonerate the British from the charge that there was an internal explosion caused by munitions. After all, Captain Cousteau had declared the holds to be empty as far back as 1976. In spite of this somehow the rumours simply refused to die. Even as late as 1995 these were enough to threaten the permit for the 1995 Ballard expedition. Fortunately wiser heads prevailed and it went ahead with the result that four explorations later, after extensive examination of the ship's holds and the associated debris field no one has been able to report any evidence whatsoever of illicit weapons. Once again the conspiracy theorists have been thwarted.

All of which brings us neatly back to Cousteau's coal dust theory; and even here opinion is divided. Not only does the coal dust need to be suspended in air in order to obtain combustion, but a required volume of air needs to be present. In that *Britannic's* reserve bunker would not have been in use at the time it therefore seems unlikely that any dust at all would have been airborne, and even more unlikely that the necessary volume of air would have been present. This, of course, is only speculation, but perhaps the greatest evidence to argue against the exploding coal dust theory is the condition of the bunker hatch itself. An analysis of the 1999 video shows that the hatch to hold no. 3 (the bunker hold) in the forward well deck seems to be substantially intact and in its correct position. Based on the fact that the force of an explosion follows the least line of resistance; had there indeed been an explosion in the reserve coal bunker it seems likely that force would have vented upwards, destroying the hatch cover. In that none of the officers on watch at the time of the sinking reported any such occurrence, combined with current observations that the hatch cover and bunker itself still seem to be intact; this is a powerful argument against the exploding coal dust theory.

In one key respect an investigation of the combustibility of *Britannic's* coal is now academic. To date only one sample has received anything like competent forensic analysis, and as the flammable methane content would have long since evaporated, it is not possible to state with any certainty just how combustible the sample might have originally been. All that can really be said with any certainty is that the sample probably originated in South Wales, could have been classed as bituminous (a soft coal which burns with a yellow flame) and probably had a volatile matter content ranging between 12 and 17.5%. So, while a coal dust explosion in the reserve bunker cannot be ruled out altogether, the fact that the dust particles would not have been in suspension and that the sealed reserve bunker probably lacked the required volume of air required to create the necessary conditions, adds to the argument against this theory.

The answer to the riddle of why the visible damage is so extensive almost certainly lies in the manner in which *Britannic* sank. Many of the survivors said that, in spite of the starboard list, during the last moments of her life *Britannic's* stern rose high into the air and almost to the point where it was perpendicular with the water. This conjures up visions of a *Titanic*-style departure from the surface, with the ship diving perpendicularly into the depths as related by Rev. John Fleming in his book. The simple fact is that the ship could not possibly have sunk in that manner. *Britannic's* overall length was a little short of 883 feet, which would have made it impossible for the ship to plunge straight down into water which is barely four-hundred feet deep. Unlike *Titanic*, *Britannic's* bow touched the seabed some time before the stern disappeared from view and as a result the stresses which tore *Titanic* apart before she sank were concentrated at an entirely different point on *Britannic*. Once *Britannic's* bow had touched the seabed it would have been impossible for it to pivot with the bulk of the hull itself, which still remained above water, and with the entire weight of the vessel now concentrated in the bow, not to mention the fact that it had already been severely weakened by the effects of both the explosion and the high-speed dash for the shoreline, the stresses exerted in this area would have been massive. More importantly these stresses would have been exerted in such a way that the steel plates would fracture and buckle in an entirely random manner. In the world of marine forensics this is known as "chaotic fracture," and this phenomenon alone can quite easily explain the crucial fact that a number of the hull plates are bent outwards.

In spite of this heavy damage the hull still remains in one piece, even if it is only by virtue of a number of deck plates at the level of the well deck. As on *Titanic* the two 50 cwt Stothert and Pitt cargo cranes remain comfortably *in situ*, which might even suggest that the overall structural integrity of the surviving deck in this area is a good deal stronger than might be supposed. Moreover, with *Britannic* lying on her starboard side, while *Titanic* remains upright, it is all the more remarkable that these cranes are still attached.

Because the effect of the damage on the starboard side remains hidden it is presently only possible to speculate that the initial explosion and subsequent violent vibration of the ship may have caused a failure of *Britannic's* riveted seams. If a number of external riveted seams in the location of boiler room no. 6 had indeed been damaged then the subsequent flooding of a number of compartments within the starboard double skin might help to account for the initial list to starboard. In fact, such occurrences were not uncommon. There is ample documented evidence of similar rivet failures on warships, the most prominent cases including the British battle cruiser HMS *Hood* and the battleship HMS *Prince of Wales*. In more recent years the discovery in 1998 of the wreck of the American aircraft carrier USS *Yorktown* provided more visible evidence of the effect. There is, interestingly, evidence of a failure of riveted seams on *Britannic's* port side, just forward of the blast damage, although an analysis of the now corrugated steel plates would seem to suggest that this probably resulted more from the stresses exerted on the area during the sinking process.

Nor is this a case of being wise after the event. The weaknesses of riveted seams were all too apparent to the sea captains of the late nineteenth century. On 14th February 1872, Captain Digby Murray of the *S.S. Republic* reported that while docking his ship at New York, the severity of the frost had been such that the iron had become so brittle that the seams of two bow plates had been damaged after a minor collision with the pier. The recollections of Kapitän zur See von Egidy, who commanded the German battle cruiser SMS *Seydlitz* at the Battle of Jutland, were also very precise on the matter when analysing the damage sustained to his ship:

> "The torpedo bulkhead held, but it was seriously strained, as were parts of the armoured deck. Where the rivets had gone completely, the holes could be stopped with wooden pegs. Where they only leaked, which they did in great numbers – more than enough for our needs – they became a distinct menace because there was no way to plug them effectively."

So clearly, even the great battleships of the era were susceptible to the weaknesses of riveted seams, and the fact that the British dreadnought HMS *Audacious* and the armoured cruiser HMS *Hampshire* were both sunk following single explosions is ample proof of even their vulnerability. Bearing in mind that both of these vessels had better protected hulls and increased internal subdivision, not to mention considerably better trained damage control parties, this also helps to put the loss of

THIS PLAQUE IS PLACED
IN THE MEMORY OF
THOSE WHO PERISHED
IN THE SINKING OF
H.M.H.S. *BRITANNIC*
NOVEMBER 21, 1916
AND DEDICATED TO ALL THOSE
WHO LOST THEIR LIVES
IN THE WAR OF 1914-1918
NOT IN BATTLE, BUT STILL IN SERVICE
TO THEIR COUNTRY
Presented by
The Titanic Historical Society, Inc.,
Indian Orchard, Massachusetts and Dr. Robert D. Ballard

*Dr. Robert D. Ballard who is best known for his discovery of the wrecks of the Titanic and Bismarck, was in the Aegean exactly ten years after finding the Titanic, exploring the wreck of her even larger sister.*

*Britannic* into a proper perspective. This secondary evidence therefore supports the theory that *Britannic* probably sustained damage of a similar nature. Because *Britannic* lies on her starboard side it is unlikely that this will ever be known for sure, but the fact remains that once the list to starboard was initiated it was only a matter of time before the open portholes of E and F decks were submerged. Had these portholes been closed then *Britannic* may well have survived long enough to join *Olympic* in the White Star Line's post-war fleet.

Although not immediately apparent, the manner of *Britannic*'s sinking bears a number of interesting similarities to that of her elder sibling. The damage inflicted on *Titanic* by the iceberg extended over a length of six watertight compartments while *Britannic*'s external damage, although more localised, was equally extensive. With the fireman's passage broken and two of the forward watertight doors failing

197

to close properly, within two minutes of the explosion the forward six compartments, including boiler rooms 5 and 6, were flooding uncontrollably. On paper *Britannic* should have been capable of surviving even this scale of damage, but as the ship continued to heel to starboard so water began to enter the ship through the portholes which had been opened that morning to ventilate the lower wards. By the time the news arrived on the bridge that the water had risen as far as D deck, Captain Bartlett knew that his ship was doomed as, one by one, the safety features conceived in the drawing office at Harland and Wolff were overwhelmed.

While *Titanic* and *Britannic* both sank by the bow, once the process had begun the similarities become less marked. *Titanic* took over two-and-a-half hours to go down and over this period of time the stresses which gradually built up in the hull slowly broke the ship apart. As the stresses on the forward expansion joint increased the funnel stays of the forward smokestack came under increasing pressure until they could no longer take the strain. At that point one by one the individual stays gave way as the smokestack toppled forward, smashing the port bridge wing in the process. Minutes later the stresses throughout *Titanic* were great enough to tear the ship apart as the hull finally broke in two in the area of the aft first-class staircase. As *Titanic* disappeared beneath the surface she was probably still in one piece (barely), but shortly afterward the forward and aft sections seem to have separated as they continued their two-and-a-half mile journey to the bottom of the Atlantic. By the time they touched the bottom the two sections were almost two thousand feet apart.

By comparison *Britannic*'s final moments were less drawn out. Sinking in only fifty-five minutes, barely one-third of the time it took for *Titanic* to go down. The stresses which tore *Titanic* apart simply didn't have time to build up in *Britannic*'s aft hull. This might not have been the case had the ship sunk on a more even keel, but in the end the list to starboard probably helped to dissipate the forces throughout the hull in a completely different manner. Consequently the video analysis of *Britannic*'s expansion joints shows no indication whatsoever of their having been opened up during the sinking and the hull is virtually intact. Nevertheless, *Britannic*'s funnels did detach as they touched the water, but instead of imitating *Titanic*'s near perpendicular dive, once *Britannic*'s bow had touched the seabed the stern could rise no further. Moments later the hull completed its roll to starboard, the stern settled back and quickly sank beneath the surface.

After careful analysis of the available historical, video and forensic evidence, one by one the myths and innuendos which have accumulated around *Britannic* can be stripped away. Instead of unsubstantiated conspiracy theories we now have more solid evidence to determine how and why the ship went down. Perhaps future expeditions will reveal more detailed forensic analysis of the site, but in the meantime it is now possible to interpret *Britannic*'s last hour afloat with reasonable accuracy:

> The initial explosion occurred on the starboard side in the area of the forward well deck at 8.12 a.m., resulting in extensive damage in the areas of hold numbers 2 and 3. The immediate hull whipping response referred to by many survivors throughout the ship as a "shudder," probably further added

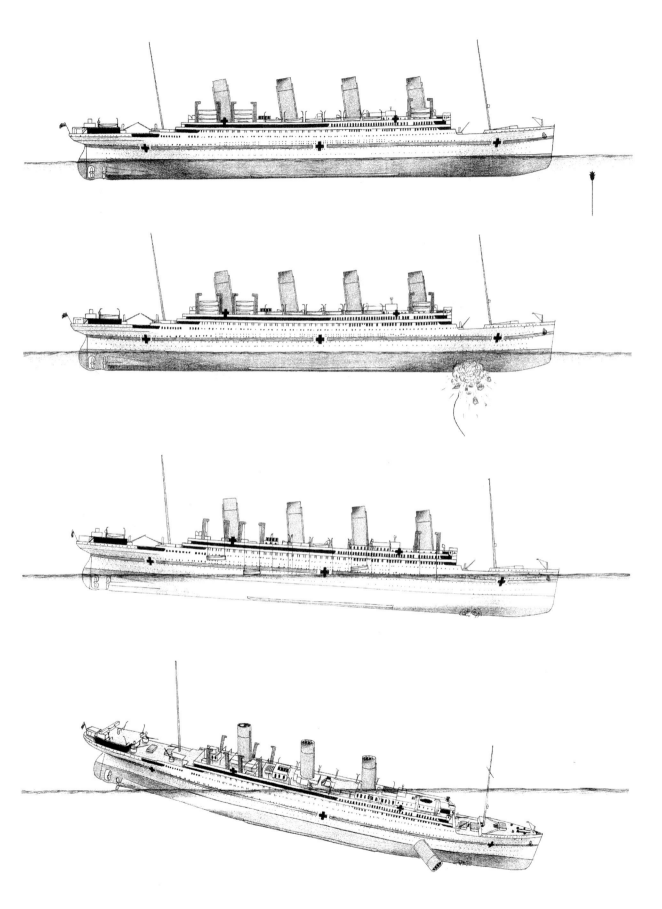

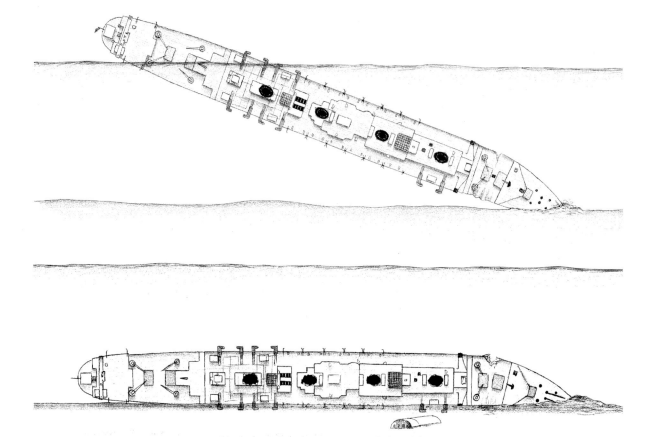

*Neil Egginton 2001 ©*

to the scale of the damage.

Following the explosion Captain Bartlett attempted to steer the ship at the fastest available speed towards the nearby island of Kea in order to beach the ship in shallow water before it foundered. An analysis of the official report into the sinking indicates that during this dash the forward holds began to fill more rapidly, suggesting that further damage was inflicted to the already weakened bulkheads.

8.35 a.m.: Captain Bartlett ordered the engines to be stopped and the lifeboats to be sent away. *Britannic* continued to heel to starboard, with the result that within minutes it was no longer possible to lower any more boats on the higher port side.

8:45 a.m.: As the ship seemed to be settling more slowly Captain Bartlett ordered the engines to be restarted, but as the ship moved forward she once again began to settle more quickly.

As *Britannic* continued to founder the ship's bow eventually came into contact with the seabed. From this moment on any further forward movement became impossible, and the angle of trim of the ship's sinking hull would have probably reached its zenith. At this point the combination of the ship's forward momentum, combined with a strong north easterly current, served to swing it around to its final 253º heading. Bearing in mind the stresses which would have been concentrated in the area of the bow at this time, it is not surprising that the already weakened structure beneath the well deck would suffer further damage as the bow was forced deeper into the seabed.

9.07 a.m.: *Britannic* rolls over onto her starboard side and founders in the Kea Channel, approximately two-and-a-half miles north west of Port St. Nikolo.

Once it had fully settled on the bottom the main body of the hull would have rested on the seabed and the area of the foc'sle would have remained unsupported. Whether or not the subsequent collapse was immediate or occurred at a later date is not clear, but video analysis of the affected area seems to suggest that the stresses exerted upon the hull by the weight of the bow eventually caused it to crack, causing the foc'sle to settle forward onto the seabed. This would have had the effect of further prising open the hull (a bit like cracking open an egg), causing additional areas of the structure to collapse in a random and unidentifiable manner.

§§§

Considering that *Britannic* has lain on the seabed for nearly ninety years the overall condition of the wreck is remarkable. Unlike *Titanic*, lying 27,000 feet down in the icy dark waters of the North Atlantic, *Britannic* lies in only 400 feet of crystal-clear Mediterranean water, and during the day visibility can be as much as thirty metres; on a particularly good day it has been estimated as high as forty metres.

The two wrecks are, in fact, total contradictions. One would have thought that *Titanic*'s cold, dark environment would have better preserved the wreck, while *Britannic*, lying in shallower, warmer and more oxygenated waters, would be more prone to the ravages of time. Yet the reverse seems to be the case. While the rusticles that adorn *Titanic*'s shattered hull continue to slowly eat away at the ship, *Britannic*'s hull, sheathed in barnacles, corals and sea growths of every description, tells a very different story. Far from destroying the wreck the growths have actually helped to protect it. Aside from the blast damage the external appearance of the hull is generally in excellent condition except that none of the smokestacks remain in position. This should come as no great surprise as they were reported to have broken away as the ship sank. When Jacques Cousteau first visited the wreck in 1976 he could only locate one of the stacks, but the sonar technology provided by the *NR1* in 1995 provided the means for a more extensive search of the area, which quickly located the other three. The missing stacks lie approximately five to six hundred feet to the north of the wreck and at least two of them appear to be in particularly good condition, retaining much of their original oval shape.

All of the deckhouses with the exception of the wooden captain's bridge and the aft mortuary remain *in situ* and show little sign of collapsing even now, although isolated patches of deterioration, particularly on the portside children's playroom, are visible. Even on the bridge there are identifiable remains of what once existed. At least three of the engine telegraphs (manufactured by J.W. Ray Ltd. of Liverpool) still hang there, though they have all fallen from their mountings, while the wheelhouse telemotor (built by Brown Bros. & Co. Ltd., Edinburgh) remains upright. The bridge wheel pedestal is still in position, although it too has fallen from its mounting and hangs at the angle of the deck.

Further aft nearly all of the davits and associated deck machinery remain attached and in their original positions. The only noticeable signs of corrosion in this area seem to be in parts of the solid bulkhead which runs along the entire length of the boat deck, although the thicker steel plates of the hull show no detectable sign of deterioration. The only openings within the hull itself come in the form of the occasional porthole, although the pattern is somewhat random.

The interior of the wreck has also provided some particularly pleasant surprises, especially within the foc'sle, which revealed a number of well-preserved linoleum floors and bathing areas. Subsequent dives have also shown that whilst the four smokestacks may have become detached during the sinking, any attempt to enter the stokeholds through the funnel casings is all but impossible as the tops of the funnel uptakes have been found to be completely intact, indicating that the blast-damage from the boiler explosions which were reported by some survivors were effectively contained within the hull. A few ladders tantalisingly point the way to further discoveries in the bowels of the ship, but to a properly equipped diver the available space is just too limited.

To date, internal penetration of the wreck has been generally controlled and confined to the area of the superstructure or higher levels of the first-class forward entrance. But while the cavernous interior is largely intact, there seems to be no evidence of what was once the grand staircase. Sadly, the ornamental glass dome is also broken, although parts of the iron framework with elements of the original red and white glass are still very recognisable. Nevertheless, current evidence would seem to indicate that any future exploration deeper within the hull might indeed reveal far better preserved areas than hitherto seen.

EPILOGUE

# THE FUTURE

Over the last few years *Britannic* has been steadily giving up her secrets. One by one the questions which may uncover the mystery surrounding the ship are being answered, and as the process of further investigation continues it is likely that the few remaining uncertainties will eventually be resolved. In the last two years alone at least one known survivor of the incident has been located in Britain at a time when it would have seemed incredible that any would still endure. Perhaps the final chapter is not yet written.

But what does the future hold? Currently the British-based company, Governcheck Limited, holds the UK rights to *Britannic,* and it is sympathetic to the importance of the area as a national heritage site. Nevertheless, there are a number of external and no less important factors that have to be taken into consideration. The British Ministry of Defence is becoming increasingly sensitive to underwater operations carried out on any wreck classified as a war grave and the British Government also retains what is referred to as "Sovereign Immunity" regarding its sunken warships. More importantly, because *Britannic* lies within Greek territorial waters it is only possible to carry out any activities at the site with the express agreement of the relevant departments of the Government of Greece, and bearing in mind their own rich cultural heritage the Greek authorities currently exercise what are probably the most restrictive regulations on sports divers anywhere in the world. Fortunately this policy has been instrumental in protecting the ship till now and it will, hopefully, continue to guard the wreck from the activities of souvenir hunters, who, if caught, would face particularly severe penalties.

As attitudes to underwater cultural heritage swing increasingly away from the damaging practices of the past, it is hoped that *Britannic*'s future will become more secure. Today the outlook is reasonably encouraging but without a crystal ball it is impossible to foretell her ultimate fate. As long as expeditions are properly monitored and controlled, there is every chance that her remains will stay intact and we will continue to be able broaden our knowledge of this period of British military history. Indeed, during the last five years alone there has been an enormous increase in the volume of information retrieved.

It should now, therefore, be possible to lay to rest the rather demeaning sobriquet attached to *Britannic* as *Titanic's forgotten sister*. *Britannic* has a special place in history and it is hoped that this book will help to restore the esteem in which she was held by all those associated with her during her short life. *Britannic* was, after all, the largest British ship in service at the time of her premature departure, and played a major role in the successful evacuation of sick and injured troops from the Dardenelles during the 1914-18 war. Men are honoured for their deeds but no less should their creations be celebrated for achievement. For the era in which *Britannic* was built she was a masterpiece of marine technology, but never designed for the stage that sealed her fate. Perhaps now is the time to bestow a tribute to her untimely passing and secure her proper place in our collective memory.

Britannic's complement of lifeboats included two 34ft motor lifeboats, built by the Thornycroft Company of Southampton. Each boat was equipped with its own short range wireless installation for communicating with the ship when in port, or when conducting searches.

PLAN AND SIDE ELEVATION OF THE MOTOR LIFEBOATS
DESIGNED AND CONSTRUCTED BY MESSRS. SIR JOHN THORNYCROFT AND CO LTD.

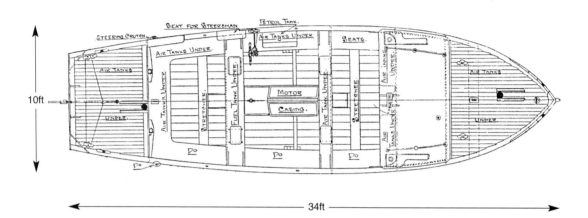

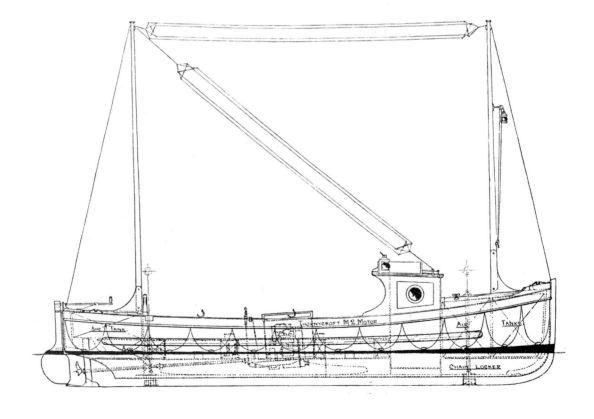

The following reports (appendices II; III; IV.) have been reproduced exactly as they were transcribed in 1916. No attempt has been made to correct any of the punctuation or spelling errors, in order to remain faithful to the context of the original documents.

*Report into the loss of HMHS Britannic by Captain Hugh Heard and Commander George Staer (PRO File No: ADM137/2171):*

H.M.S. Duncan,
24th November 1916.

Sir,

Having enquired into the circumstances attending the loss of the Hospital Ship "Britannic," we have the honour to make the following report. It must be premised that the enquiry was necessarily incomplete owing to the shortness of time at our disposal and the difficulty of finding witnesses scattered over the whole fleet.

2. The following is a brief description of structure of "Britannic" in the region of the explosion. Rough sketches are attached. Forward of Bridge were situated the Fore Peak and Nos 1, 2 & 3 holds, No 3 hold being a reserve coal Bunker, Water tight bulkheads separating these compartments. No 6 Boiler Room was immediately under Fore Bridge & No 5 Boiler Room being immediately abaft No 6. A W.T. tunnel ran from forward bulkhead of No 6 and under Nos 3 & 2 holds to No 1 hold, compartments over which were situated Firemans quarters.

Unless therefore the W.T doors in this tunnel were closed the boiler rooms were in free communication with Nos 1, 2 & 3 holds in the event of Tunnel being damaged.

The Watertight doors were automatic in action and could also be closed by means of handles abaft doors or from deck plates on E deck.

3. There was one explosion only. This took place on Starboard side low down and in the vicinity of the bulkhead between 2 and 3 holds, breaking this bulkhead and thus filling Nos. 2 & 3 holds. Whether the bulkhead between Nos 1 & 2 holds was broken is not certain, but it is probable. Anyway No. 1 hold also filled either in this way or through the tunnel.

4. It appears that the bulkhead between No. 3 hold & No. 6 Stokehold was not broken, but water from the holds gained free access through the W.T. door between stokehold and tunnel which was not closed, the tunnel having been broken.

5. Water also had free access to No. 5 Stokehold through the W.T. door between 5 and 6. It is clear that this door was not wholly, although there is evidence to show that it may have been partly, closed.

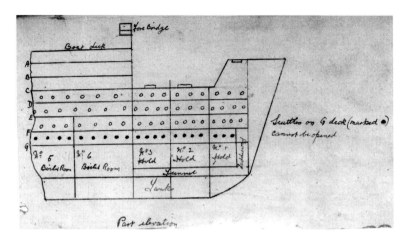

Compared to the apparent limitless expenses of
Lord Mersey's Titanic enquiry in 1912, and the
thousands of words set down in the most minute
detail by the Court recorders, the investigation
into the loss of the Britannic is quite scant by
comparison. Two days of investigation and the
written testimony of only four witnesses were all
it took for Captain Hugh Heard and Commander
Staer to complete the 726-word report.

Vice Admiral Cecil Thursby's presumption that a
more thorough investigation would take place
back in England proved to be misplaced, with the
result that the brief report prepared at Salamis
along with these three rough sketches, provide the
only official reference to the calamitous events of
that morning.

Crown copyright - Public Records Office

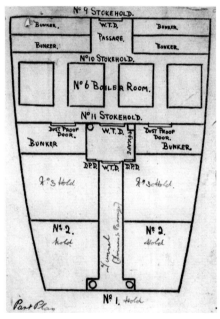

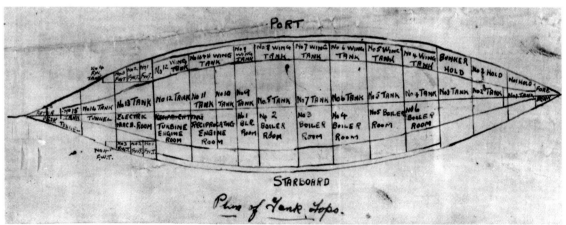

6. There seems to have been a period of 1 to 2 minutes from the time of the explosion until the water in the stokeholds was too deep for work to be performed, when these doors might have been closed. This would have secured the two boiler rooms, measuring about 35' x 90' in area, from incursion by water. This might have saved the ship, but without plans of the whole structure it is impossible to offer an opinion.

7. We are confident that no water penetrated abaft No. 5 stokehold in the lower part of the ship.

8. A further means for the admission of water was by side scuttles. The W.T doors before the stokehold seem to have been closed except in the tunnel. The scuttles on F deck should not have been open as it was contrary to orders at that time, but there is evidence that these orders were occasionally disobeyed. Many of the scuttles on E deck were open.

   The ship taking a list of about 25 degrees to starboard and getting down by the bows would quickly bring these under water. Direct evidence shows that about 15 minutes after the explosion, the scuttles on E Deck (normally 25' out of water) on a line between the foremost funnels were awash, and water was coming along this deck from forward.

9. Question of mine or torpedo. The water was deep, probably over 100 fathoms and there is a current through the Zea Channel. This against the mine theory.

   Three persons gave good evidence of having seen

a) periscope

b) The wake of a torpedo immediately before the explosion and in its direction. This man F. Walters, Deck Steward having been an Officers Steward in the Navy had seen torpedo practice. He did <u>not</u> pretend to have seen the torpedo.

c) The wake of a torpedo on port side apparently missing aft. It is to be noted that the sea was glassy smooth.

   On other hand there is no evidence of a column of water having been thrown up outside the ship.

   The effects of the explosion might have been due to either a mine or a torpedo. The probability seems to be a mine.

   We have the honour to be,

   Sir,

   Your Obedient Servants,
   H. H. Heard.
   Captain.

   G. H. Starr.[†]
   Engineer Commander.

[†] *Due to a typographical error, Commander Staer's name was incorrectly recorded at the bottom of the page.*

**Report into the loss of HMHS Britannic by Captain Charles Alfred Bartlett (PRO File No: ADM137/1229):**

H.M.T. ROYAL GEORGE

AT SEA.

November 30th 1916.

To the Director of Transports, Admiralty

Sir

It is with great regret that I have to report the sinking of H.M. Hospital Ship Britannic No. G608[†] by an enemy mine or torpedo, on the morning of the 21st. November at a position in Zea Channel, near the Gulf of Athens, Port St. Nikolo Lighthouse bore S. 48 E (Mag) distance 3 miles at the time of the explosion.

The ship at the time was steaming 20 knots, weather fine and the sea smooth, bound to Mudros to embark sick and wounded and was painted and carrying all the signals, in strict accordance with the Geneva convention.

We had on board a crew numbering 673 all told and in addition carried a Medical Staff comprising 22 Surgeons, 3 Chaplains, 77 Nurses and 290 Orderlies of the R.A.M.C.

No passengers were carried whatever.

We left Naples on the evening of the 19th. inst. and proceeded on the direct route for the Port bound to. At 7.52 A.M. on the 21st we passed Angarlestro Point on the Island of Makio Nisi, distant 4 miles and set a course N. 48" E (mag) to pass through Zea Channel.

At 8.12 A.M. when in the position above mentioned a tremendous but muffled explosion occurred, the ship trembling and vibrating most violently fore and aft, continuing for some time; the ship fell off about 3 points from her course. Emergency Quarters were sounded on all Alarms throughout the ship, the engines stopped, and orders rung below to close water tight doors, at the same time sending out the S.O.S. signal by wireless.

My first impression was that we had struck a mine and would probably be safe. I gave orders to clear away all boats and have all possible ready to be sent away. After an interval, steering gear appeared to have failed, I turned the ship around to port to head for land by the engines, but the forward holds filled rapidly and water was reported in Nos. 5 & 6 boiler rooms, so I stopped the engines and ordered all boats possible to be sent away, but to stand by near the ship.

The ship seemed to stop settling a little and I passed word to stop lowering boats and again attempted to work ship toward the land, but she again started to settle rapidly and water being reported on "D" deck, I gave the order for all to leave the ship, passing word to the engine room and blowing on the whistle for the last alarm.

The ship was sinking very quickly then, going by the head and listing to starboard and soon the water came to the bridge and Assistant Commander Dyke having reported to me that all had left, I told him to go and shortly after followed myself, walking into the water by the forward boat gantry on Starboard side, the third funnel falling a few minutes later. I was picked up about 30 minutes later by the motor boat.

Whilst in the water I saw the ship sink, having listed well to Starboard and when finally disappearing her stern was almost perpendicular, the time being given by those in the boats as 9.7 A.M.

When rescued by the motor boat I was informed that some boats had fouled the propeller on Port side and a number of men had been thrown into the water and injured, the two motor boats picking them up, so after a thorough examination of the vicinity I ordered both motor boats to proceed to Port St. Nikolo with the injured, passing word for all the other boats to follow. Whilst on the way we could see the H.M.S. Heroic and the Destroyer "Scourge" making for the scene, they did splendid work in picking up the boats and then proceeded to Piraeus with the rescued.

Having landed with most of the injured at Port St. Nikolo, where we were well received and the injured men taken to shelter, the arrangements being superintended by the French Consul, I sent a telegram through him to the French Legation at Athens, also one to S.N.O. Mudros.

In all about 160 persons landed at St. Nikolo and later the Destroyer "Foxhound" arriving we were all embarked and reached Piraeus about 5.30 P.M. when every care and attention was given us by the Rear Admiral, his Officers and men on the "Duncan" also by the French warships in port.

After a careful roll call it was found that in all 1 Officer and 28 men were missing, the Officer and 7 men being of the R.A.M.C. the remainder being crew.[††]

This loss I deplore as in my opinion it was caused by the wrecking of the boats as I feel confident all hands left the ship.

I have nothing but praise for the cool and orderly way all Officers, men and boys behaved throughout, there not being any sign of excitement or panic at any time. Lt. Col. Anderson R.A.M.C. the S.M.O. and his staff did splendidly not only at the sinking of the ship but afterwards in their great care of the injured, Surgeons using the Kapok from life jackets for dressings.

A number of Nursing Sisters pluckily came from boat to boat to aid the injured, finally landing with them at Port St. Nikolo to care for them.

Twenty eight Life Boats were lowered and two Motor Boats, the latter doing excellent service in quickly searching the scene and picking up many from the water especially those injured.

<u>TORPEDO or MINE</u>

The explosion occurred whilst "Britannic" was in about 65 Fathoms of water, and a mine might have been the cause, but there is good evidence that the tracks of two Torpedoes were seen, one of which struck the ship starboard side forward, the other missing the ship from the port side aft. Also two men declare they saw an object which they took to be a Submarine twenty minutes after the explosion just off the starboard side.

The damage was most extensive, probably the whole of the fore part of the ship's bottom being destroyed and in my opinion penetrating to No. 6 boiler room. Water was seen to be thrown up to "E" or "D" deck forward at the time of the explosion, and a cloud of black smoke was seen, the fumes for some time being suffocating.

In conclusion I am anxious to express my grateful thanks to Vice Admiral Sir Cecil Thursby K.C.M.G., Rear Admiral Hayes Sadler C.S.I. and the French Admiral for their promptness in sending rescue ships to us, also for the great comfort and care given to one and all, and for gifts of clothing which we received from the Officers and men of both fleets.

I would add that the Captain and Officers of H.M.T. Ermine and H.M.T. Royal George deserve thanks for their care of us whilst on their ships proceeding home.

I have the honour to be, Sir

Your obedient Servant

Charles A. Bartlett
MASTER

*† Britannic's official number was actually G618.*

*†† For some reason the name of 40213 Pte. Leonard T. Smith was not listed along with the other casualties in Britannic's log, though his name does appear on the British war memorial at Mikra on the southern outskirts of Thessaloníki. This being the case, the final total of those killed at the sinking of the Britannic comes to 21 crew, one officer and eight men of the RAMC.*

*Report into the loss of HMHS Britannic by Lieutenant Colonel Henry Stewart Anderson, Senior Medical Officer (Author's Collection & Imperial War Museum document no. 90/37/1):*

From:- Lieut. Col. H.S. Anderson.

Late Commanding Troops, H.S. Britannic.

To:-   D.M.S.
          Malta.

Hamrun Hospital,

5th December, 1916.

Sir,

I regret to report that an explosion occurred at 8.12 a.m. on the 21st November, 1916. The "Alarm" was sounded within two minutes. Fortunately the morning was warm and sunny, the sea calm, and apparently No. 59594 Pte. J.W. Cuthbertson was the only man in the forward barrack room on "G" Deck and extricated himself uninjured although the stair-case had been blown away and the room quickly flooded.

Captain J.L. Rentoul was responsible for the Nursing Sisters, paraded them on the Compass Deck with life-jackets and blankets, and saw them all lowered safely on the Starboard Side.

Mrs. E.A. Dowse, R.R.C., Matron, entered one of these boats as soon as the last of the Sisters and Stewardesses had taken their seats. Miss B. Mattison, V.A.D., stood up in her boat and controlled the rowing.

Lieut. R.A. Sheckleton had charge of the only patients on board (men of the R.A.M.C. personnel) and at once assembled them with their life-jackets on the Boat Deck.

Major H.E. Priestly, C.M.G., Company Officer, having seen the Detachment parading with their life-jackets on the after part of "A" Deck, went below, searched the three barrack rooms on "F" and "G" Decks and then proceeded to the Boat Deck where he supervised jettisoning rafts and satisfied himself that all the R.A.M.C., except eight men with him had left. He remained until called to the last boat by Mr. C. Lancaster (Purser) about 9 a.m. and entered it after the men, i.e.:-

| No. 102182 | Pte. | Bateson, N. | No. 46907 | Pte. | Brelsford, H. |
|---|---|---|---|---|---|
| 5601 | " | Busson, W.H. | 106860 | " | Jacklin, H. |
| 48657 | " | McDowell, W. | 46121 | " | Netherway, W.H. |
| 54671 | " | Radcliff, J. | 84080 | " | Ward, A. |

Privates Busson and Netherway carried out their police duties in an exemplary manner.

Q.M. & Lieut. J. Starkie who left the deck to procure as much bread as possible, found on returning that the bridge was submerged and had only swum about 100 yards, using the "crawl stroke", when the ship disappeared at 9-8 a.m.

Captain H. Slater, Orderly Officer, No. 14503 Sergt-Major G. Pottinger and No. 56795 A/Q.M. Sgt. F.H. Nichols left in the last boat but one, about 8-55 a.m. having seen the boats filled with the correct numbers.

No. 41002 Sgt. S.S. Halliday and No. 5154 Cpl. S. Ogden saved the pay-books and some of the Office Records.

The Pay-books were taken to Mudros by the R. N. and it was stated that they would be forwarded to the N.T.O., Southampton.

Captain E.G. Fenton, who had been shipwrecked at the beginning of last month, knowing that he would occupy the space of two men, deliberately left the Boat Deck and descended by rope and drop although unskilled in climbing and swimming.

At least three of the boats lowered on the port side failed to get out from the ship; two of them were smashed to splinters by the propeller blades which stopped for a few minutes just before a third boat came into contact with them. Captain T. Fearnhead states that he and two others remained in it and he was able to push against the blade to move the boat away from it. Each boat should have contained more than eighty persons and from the three over two hundred must have been dashed or taken to the water.

The wake showed that the ship was moving in a wide circle to the right.

Lowering from the port side was abandoned about 8-45 a.m. when the engines started again. The port side launch was lowered at this time. I went down in it and found the survivors and wreckage already far away, with the Starboard Launch and a few boats close to them.

The middle propeller was then working above the surface. When the water reached the Bridge Captain C.A. Bartlett, C.B., the Master, swam out, ordered the Starboard Launch to make for St. Nikola (Zea Island), and remained standing on a raft until my launch reached him about 10-30 a.m. and was ordered to proceed to Port St. Nikola. H.M.S. SCOURGE and S.S. HEROIC were then approaching.

Miss Dowse was the first of the Staff to reach the injured and passed from one boat to another rendering aid and distributing her sisters where they were most needed. She sent six to St. Nikola, six to the HEROIC and finally embarked on the H.M.S. SCOURGE.

No. 33642 Pte. A.W. Binks was dead when picked up; his body was conveyed to Piraeus on board the HEROIC and buried on the 22nd November, 1916 with military honours at Paramo Cemetery.

No. 12423 Sgt. W. Sharpe died about noon on the 21st. November, 1916 at St. Nikola from his injuries and the French Vice-Consul promised to arrange the funeral.

This gentleman and the inhabitants of St. Nikola showed much practical sympathy and freely opened their homes to us. Francesco Psialas took out his boat and picked up three or four survivors. These and others were entertained in his house. The local doctor came promptly to assist with the injured of whom there were about ten serious cases.

A Dressing Box and Hypodermic Syringe from the O.C., H.M.S. SCOURGE proved very useful.

Before two p.m. the staff surgeon of H.M.S. FORESIGHT arrived with stretcher parties and skilfully transferred the injured to the H.M.S. FOXHOUND which departed about 3 p.m. with 171 survivors on board, the greater number of these being Ship's Officers and Crew.

I deeply regret that Lt. J. Cropper and Privates 81292 G.J. Bostock, 52640 H. Freebury, 84010 T. Jones, 41692 G. King, 40213 L.T. Smith, and 35188 W. Stone are missing, and the following injured:-

14 Seriously:- Captain W. Payne, Privates, 25027 H. Ash, 32174 R. Adams, 53787 J. Fisher, 47118 J. Gleave, 1535 T. Kelly, 102006 T.C. Love, 69059 A. Morris, 37957 W.S. Bull, 33578 G.N. Smith, 4313 J.W. Sugden, 35397 W.K. Thompson, 103908 B. Talbot, and 84153 A. Worrall.

6 Slightly:- 1970 Sgt. W.J. Brunt, 4808 Sgt. W. Foggin, 7590 L/cpl E. Gregory, 350 Pte. H.A. Hogbon, 23998 Cpl. O.H. Mugg, and 84016 Pte. E.H. Rowbotham.

I understand that twenty-one of the crew are missing, but have not been able to hear if this is the final estimate.

Long before reaching Piraeus each survivor had realised that the Royal Navy is still the best of hosts, and the open-hearted kindness of the French and British fleets during our stay surpassed all expectation. They fed the hungry, clad the naked, and made everything as easy and pleasant as possible for us.

Of the forty-one cases requiring admission to Hospital twenty were N.C.O.s and men of the R.A.M.C. and of these nine were taken to the Russian Hospital and eleven on board H.M.S. DUNCAN. Several of the patients for the shore were gently cared for on the FOXHOUND until the early hours of next morning owing to paucity of Ambulance Motors.

Fleet Surgeon J. Roche, R.N. gave most valuable aid not only in taking so many patients on the DUNCAN, but in attending cases on other ships and on shore.

He took complete charge of transporting all the patients for embarkation on the 27th. November, 1916, and although many were seriously injured they were moved without mishap. Surgeons Mann & Paxton also earned our gratitude by their kind and constant attention to patients.

Lieutenant W. H. Rogers, R.N.R. did many acts of spontaneous kindness and always found time to smooth the difficulties encountered promptly and decisively.

Similarly Major Huntingford, Royal Marines, gave opportune assistance.

The cheerful hospitality of Rear Admiral Hayes-Sadler, C.B. was inspiring and left no detail unprovided for. The survivors numbered more than a thousand, and their wants were many and urgent, and the sailors were tireless in ministering to them promptly, and most successfully for the next seven days.

Major Priestly and the other Officers were accommodated in the Phalére Hotel, Miss Dowse and the Nursing Sisters in the Aktaion Hotel at Phaleron.

The hard pressed Surgeons and ladies of the Russian Hospital spared no pains in attending the patients, and very kindly allowed Miss Dowse to assist them with Nursing Sisters and four Orderlies. Mr. and Mrs. Anastasiali, the Serbian Relief Committee, and a few residents were indefatigable in their kind attentions.

Rear Admiral Hayes Sadler reported the casualties from Piraeus as soon as they had been estimated, and I have to thank him, his staff, Captain H. Heard, and the Commanders of the DUNCAN, FOXHOUND, SCOURGE, and HEROIC for their exceeding kindness.

In conclusion I attribute the admirable self-control of the Nursing Sisters to the cool and accurate judgement of Miss Dowse and to the fact that she had already won the complete confidence and devotion of all.

As her boat touched the water she saw the destruction of the first port-side boat to be broken, yet remained silent lest any might become unnerved and unfit for the duties that lay before them.

The highest praise is due to Major Priestly for his quiet and determined courage. After his gallant conduct on board, he took a prominent part in tending the injured at St. Nikola and later remained alert until the last patient had been admitted to Hospital about 1 a.m. on the 22nd November, 1916. He remarked that it was a mere picnic compared with a day in a prisoners camp.

At his request I have pleasure in stating that Pte. Busson, already mentioned, was throughout conspicuous for his steadiness without showing a trace of emotion.

Henry S. Anderson.

# BIBLIOGRAPHY

Anderson, Roy. *White Star*. T. Stephenson & Sons, 1964.

Archbold, Rick: *Ken Marschall's Art of Titanic*. Madison Press, 1998.

Ballard, Robert D. & Archbold, Rick. *Lost Liners*. Hodder & Stoughton, 1997.

Ballard, Robert D. & Archbold, Rick. *Ghost Liners*. Madison Press, 1998.

Beaumont, J.C.H. *The British Mercantile Marine During the War*. Gay & Hancock, 1919.

Beaumont, J.C.H. *Ships and People*. Geoffrey Bles, 1926.

Bentley, James. *Martin Niemöller*. Oxford University Press, 1984.

Brittain, Vera. *Testament of Youth*. Virago Press, 1997.

Brittain, Vera. *Chronicle of Youth: The War Diaries of Vera Brittain 1913-1917*. Victor Gollancz, 1981.

Eaton, John P. & Haas, Charles A. *Falling Star*. Patrick Stephens, 1989.

Fleming, Rev. John A. *The Last Voyage of His Majesty's Hospital Ship Britannic*. Wordsmith Publications, 1998.

Fremantle, Admiral Sydney R. *My Naval Career*. Hutchinson, (n.d.)

Garzke, William H. Jr., Mills, Simon A., Dulin, Robert O., Brown, David K., Ridder, Dale R., Foecke, Dr. Timothy & Bemis, F. Gregg. *The Saga of HMHS Britannic*. ASNE/SNAME Symposium Paper, September 1998.

Haws, Duncan. *Merchant Fleets: White Star Line* (Vol. 19). TCL Publications, 1990.

Hayes, Bertram Fox. *Hull Down*. Cassell & Co., 1925.

Jessop, Violet. *Titanic Survivor*. Sheridan House Inc. (New York), 1997.

Louden-Brown, Paul. *The White Star Line: An Illustrated History 1870 - 1934*. The *Titanic* Historical Society, Inc., 2001.

Macbeth, Sheila. *Pages From a Nursing Sister's Diary*. (Unpublished diary, 1916)

Maxtone-Graham, John. *The Only Way to Cross*. Patrick Stephens, 1972.

Mills, Simon. *HMHS Britannic: The Last Titan* (Second Edition). Shipping Books Press, 1996.

Mills, Simon. *Preliminary Findings of Explorations to the Wreck of HMHS Britannic, Kea Channel, Northern Aegean*. Marine Forensics Panel, 17th January 2000.

Moss, Michael & Hume, John R. *Shipbuilders to the World: 125 Years of Harland and Wolff, Belfast 1861-1986*. The Blackstaff Press, 1986.

Mullins, Cliff. *Coal Analysis of Sample 137490*. Report for Marine Forensics Panel by Minton, Treharne & Davies Limited, 28th July 2000.

Niemöller, Martin. *Vom U-boat zur Kanzel*. Martin Warneck Verlag, Berlin, 1934.

Oldham, Wilton J. *The Ismay Line*. The Journal of Commerce and Shipping Telegraph, Liverpool, 1961.

Plumridge, John H. *Hospital Ships and Ambulance Trains*. Seeley, Service & Co., 1975.

Rostron, Arthur. *Home From the Sea*. Cassell & Co. Ltd., 1931.

Schmidt, Dietmar. *Pastor Niemöller*. Odhams, 1959.

Shaum, John H. & Flayhart, William H. *Majesty at Sea: The Four Stackers*. Patrick Stephens, 1981.

Thomas, Lowell. *Raiders of the Deep*. Heineman, 1929.

Tyler, Percy D. *The Story of the Sinking of HMHS Britannic*. (Unpublished journal, 1916)

Williams, David L. & de Kerbrech, Richard P. *Damned by Destiny*. Teredo Books Ltd, 1982.

*The Titanic Commutator* (Quarterly magazine of the *Titanic* Historical Society, Inc.,
  Post Office Box 51053, Indian Orchard, Massachusetts 01151-0053, USA.)

**TV and Video:**

*Calypso's Search For the Britannic* (Warner Home Video, © The Cousteau Society, 1977)

*The Titanic's Lost Sister* (Nova/WGBH, 1996)

*The Doomed Sisters of the Titanic* (MPH/History Channel, 1999)

*Titanic's Sister: HMHS Britannic* (Periscope Publications Ltd., 2001)

*Inside The Britannic* (Brentwood Communications, International Inc., 2002)

# ACKNOWLEDGEMENTS

The task of assembling the information contained within this book over the last ten years has been monumental and it would be ungracious to emphasise any one person's generosity in particular. The only way to offer credits in a fair-minded way is to list those concerned alphabetically. In the event that I have missed anyone then I can only apologise unreservedly and promise to have their names included in any future editions. In the meantime, I would like to thank the following:

Liz Alp and Christopher McCullogh for their information on Private C. McCullogh, Dr. Robert D. Ballard for including me in his 1995 expedition to the wreck and for being gracious enough to furnish this book with a splendid foreword, Mrs. Jennifer A. Clarke for the information and photograph of Private Henry Freebury, Neil Egginton for his technical drawings, Alasdair Fairbairn for access to the Bartlett family archives, John Fleming Jr. for access to his father's extensive photographic collection, Bill Garzke of the Washington based Marine Forensics Panel SD-7 for their assistance in *Britannic*'s damage analysis, Ronald S. Goodman for permission to use photographs and extracts from his father's diary, Frank Gutmann for his invaluable help in obtaining vital information from the various German archives, John Harvey for permission to use illustrations from the Cropper family papers, Ian Hughes for providing the information and photograph of Master-at Arms J. A. Milne, David Hutchings for clarifying the finer points of Metacentric Height, Ed & Karen Kamuda for access to Bill Tantum's 1978 Cousteau photographs, Dr. Llewellyn Lloyd OBE JP for making available his research into the life of Colonel Henry Anderson, Paul Louden-Brown for being kind enough to fill in any blanks – both factual and visual, Ken Marschall and Madison Press for permission to reproduce some of his brilliant illustrations, Innes McCartney for knowing everything there is to know about U-boats, Margaret & Mary Meehan for trusting me with her priceless photographs of Violet Jessop, Angus Mitchell for allowing access to Sheila Macbeth's famous scrapbook and for arranging for it to be copied, Cathy Offinger for being the consummate organiser, *Britannic* survivor Reverend George Perman for allowing me to record his memories on two occasions, Harold Roberts for providing the photographs of Captain Harry Dyke, Bill & Eric Sauder for supplying their copy of *Britannic*'s Specification book, Tim & Marion Sargeant for their reminiscences of George Perman and Anthony Walsh for furnishing me with a copy of Private Percy Tyler's original manuscript.

Nor should we forget the divers whose efforts have done so much to help in the study of the condition of the wreck today. Kevin Gurr's IANTD team led the way in 1997, followed by Nick Hope and the members of the *Starfish Enterprise* dive group in 1998. The final expedition to date was led by GUE's Jarrod Jablonski in 1999 and, although it is impossible to name every individual member of each team, particular thanks are due to Leigh Bishop, Dan Burton, Jamie Powell and Robert Royle who provided the underwater photographs that are reproduced in the colour section, and to Geraint Ffoulkes-Jones for passing on invaluable contact details via the *Britannic* 98 website. Neither should we forget the Greek assistance, and I am also indebted to Captain Ioannis M. Fournarakis HCG (Maritime Attaché at the Embassy of Greece in London), Kostas Thoctarides and Rena Giatropoulou.

Finally, I would like to acknowledge the debt I owe to all the museums and organisations without which there would be no logical starting place. The British Library, The Guildhall Library, The Hydrographic Office (Sharon Nichol), The Imperial War Museum, McMaster University, Hamilton, Ontario, Canada (Renu Barrett), Merseyside Maritime Museum, National Newspaper Library at Colindale, the Public Record Office at Kew, the RAMC Museum at Keogh Barracks in Aldershot (Captain Peter Starling), the Science and Reference Library, the Scout Association (Caroline Bignell), Slough Central Library, Southampton Maritime Museum, The *Titanic* Historical Society, Inc. and the Ulster Folk & Transport Museum.

I would also like to thank Lorraine Cunningham and Deborah Lindsay at Harland and Wolff, for granting permission to reproduce the shipyard's plans and drawings. Lorraine has asked me to point out that copies of these plans and drawings, along with those of the many other vessels built at Queen's Island, can be obtained from: Harland and Wolff Technical Services Ltd, Queen's Island, Belfast BT3 9DU, Northern Ireland.

**Simon Mills**
*August 2002*

# INDEX

# COLOUR PLATES

*† We would like to thank Ken Marschall for allowing this illustration to be published.*

**Illustration by Ken Marschall © 1997 from LOST LINERS, a Hyperion/Madison Press Book.**